CREATIVE ACTS FOR CURIOUS PEOPLE

How to Think, Create, and Lead in Unconventional Ways

Sarah Stein Greenberg

Foreword by David M. Kelley

Illustrations by Michael Hirshon

TEN SPEED PRESS
California | New York

d.
HASSO PLATTNER
Institute of Design at Stanford

Contents

Foreword

Throughout my thirty-plus years at Stanford, there's always been something special about working with the students at the d.school. They arrive thinking that we're going to fill them with ideas, but what really happens is they get a glimpse of their own ingenuity and resilience. We get to be there at the moment when they realize their own potential, and I feel lucky to be a part of it.

Yet these kinds of realizations don't come from just understanding an idea—they come through the experience of trying, and failing, and trying again. One of my big regrets is that it's hard to deliver these moments to people who aren't able to take our classes and workshops in person. But this book does the trick. It is chock-full of recipes for these special moments. We call them creative acts, and like any good recipe, the real magic is not in the instructions on the page but rather in putting those instructions into action.

I tell my students that when it comes to creative work, exactly what their creative practice looks like is less important than the fact that they have one to begin with. Back in the day, we used to call this being "mindful of process." Yes, the product is important, but how to get there deserves at least as much attention, if not more. Creative Acts for Curious People is all about how to get there.

Creative work involves making things seem tangible and real, but what you really take with you to the next challenge or job is not what gets made, but the way to make it, and the understanding of how to do it again. Like the d.school itself, this book contains as many how-tos as there are people who contributed their knowledge to its pages. There's a lot of wisdom here, from d.school stalwarts to a new generation of teachers and designers of whom I couldn't be more proud.

And I can't think of a better guide to lead you through these exercises. Sarah has gathered some of the most fascinating, unique, and useful assignments from the transformative classes of the d.school's first decade and a half. In our world, she's famous for giving students that special—and sometimes difficult—nudge that pushes them to discover the creative confidence and potential they have inside but have yet to discover. She has a wonderful knack for seeing deep into things to pull out the kernel that gives them meaning and makes them sing. Each of these many assignments and the six essays sprinkled throughout are framed with a bit of Sarah's magic, and I am excited to see what creative acts emerge—not just for the curious, but for everybody.

David M. Kelley
Stanford, California
February 10, 2021

Introduction

As a child I was obsessed with Peter Pan. I reread my treasured clothbound volume until the cover frayed. And despite the cold Philadelphia winters, I often kept the window cracked open at night; if Peter chose to alight on my sill, he'd have no trouble getting in. To me, Peter represented all that was fearless and brilliant about kids. He sang out a flight plan to a place in my imagination ("second star to the right and straight on 'til morning") that celebrated imagination itself and blurred the line between pretend and reality. Along with Wendy, Peter's band of Lost Boys imagined their own version of society into existence simply by acting it out—an idea that has never left me.

Another important teacher of mine was Fred Rogers, with whom I visited every day via public television. A full-fledged adult (though his trademark sneakers slyly suggested otherwise), he knew that kids needed a safe place in their minds to explore their feelings or talk out the difference between right and wrong. No part of *Mister Rogers' Neighborhood* was fast-paced, but I found it thrilling when Trolley clanged and it was time to follow it down the tracks to the Neighborhood of Make-Believe.

Now, many decades later, every time I arrive at work I walk into a place that feels to many people like it exists in one of these imaginary worlds.

At the Stanford d.school, we've created an environment where normal rules are suspended and we constantly use our imaginations. Our purpose is to help everyone unlock their creative abilities. We cook up special ways for people to interact with each other. We make a lot of time for feelings, and we act like that's no different than doing any other kind of work. We speak a language of encouragement. We're hard on work but soft on people, and we don't confuse kindness with weakness. We try things out before we know exactly what will happen, and then we spend time thinking and talking about what, exactly, just happened. Our furniture rolls around.

Our way of being and working contains a standing invitation to everyone to join us. Almost without exception, we can convince you to come up with a secret handshake at a moment's notice. We know how to engage a room of adults in a fierce game of Rock Paper Scissors played at top volume. We can give you a bin filled with art supplies and teach you to make something world-changing with them. We can show you how to stop self-censoring your most interesting ideas.

With these methods, we help thousands of people each year expand their creative abilities and apply them to the world. And then those thousands of people help thousands of others do the same. What is this shared, waking daydream? It's our belief that more creative, meaningful work emerges when we help each other undo the mindsets that limit us and instead hold each other up as creative individuals. At the d.school we make the choice to approach our work this way every day. You can, too.

Although the d.school's methods are full of joy, I constructed a significant portion of this book during a sad and sobering year. At times the gap between my source material and the world around me felt wide. Our approach to creative work is amplified by collaboration; how does that evolve when people cannot physically come together? Design doesn't yet have a wide repertoire of tools to acknowledge and fight systemic racism; but if we claim to be human-centered, it must. Since our mission is to democratize access to design, how do we navigate a fracturing, polarized world? When the land is on fire, can nurturing more creative humans bring water?

Design offers methods not for a changed world, but an ever-changing one. In the face of current challenges—those here today and those yet to come—we all need ways to prepare to act even when we are uncertain. We'll always need to find our way to our reservoir of creative abilities, and figure out how to apply those abilities to each situation.

This book contains a wide range of activities developed and taught at the d.school, plus a few that were created elsewhere by members of the extended d.school family. Many terrific design toolkits and templates are widely available these days; the goal of this guide is to offer you a taste of the kinds of experiential journeys we take at the d.school across a variety of subjects. It gives you the opportunity to experience what it feels like and looks like to learn at the d.school, which you can apply to many different contexts. The skills you will develop are fundamental for stretching your creative abilities: things like becoming aware of your inner critic, bonding quickly with new creative collaborators, and engaging people intentionally to learn more about their lives and spark new ideas.

These experiences, called "assignments," form the main part of this book. They follow an arc similar to what you'd experience in a course at the d.school, though there are many more here than you could ever fit into one class. Some assignments will take twenty minutes or an hour, and others could take weeks, depending on how deep you want to go. Among the assignments you'll also find a few essays that share insights we've gained by designing these kinds of learning experiences. Knowing more about how they work will help you to get even more out of them and to adapt them to your context.

Throughout the book I refer to the concept of *design,* a word that means different things to different people. The d.school is part of a global shift: from a world where designers have a very specific, narrow mandate predicated on the idea of design being mainly about aesthetic finishing to a world where design plays a broader role in society. One aspect of this shift in design has to do with inclusiveness: we fundamentally believe that everyone is creative and everyone can use design to improve the world around them. This aspirational way of thinking about design was described by the Hungarian painter László Moholy-Nagy in the 1940s: "Designing is not a profession but an attitude . . . [it should be] transformed from the notion of a specialist function into a generally valid attitude of resourcefulness and inventiveness." The first section in this book is an illustrated story of what this broad definition of design can look like. It follows a real group of our students through the ups and downs of using design tools and mindsets to address a challenge at a hospital in India.

Another important implication of the expanding role of design is the responsibility that comes with taking that attitude of inventiveness and creating products, experiences, and systems that change the world around you. When you design, you shape the world for others, whether you're redesigning the evening routine for your family or an entire public health system. Many of the assignments in this book are about cultivating deeper awareness of how you work so you can be a thoughtful citizen creator.

The d.school approach prepares you to take on any challenge in life or work without knowing exactly how to do it before you do it. The world is changing too quickly to learn everything you need to know about life while you're in school. Knowing how to learn is the fundamental ability you need to cultivate in order to thrive in the twenty-first century. Thinking and learning like a designer is tremendously powerful, and the assignments here will keep you learning indefinitely.

Many of these assignments may seem fantastical, but they are actually both practical and useful. Keep this in mind when you encounter *The Banana Challenge* (page 152), the zombie apocalypse prep in *Favorite Warm-Up Sequence* (page 54), and more. These exercises embody playful yet rigorous ideas, and they'll help you begin to act your way into a new creative reality. It's no wonder that some of our ideas sound strange when encountered outside of the d.school, since it is an alternate universe compared to many organizations and environments. When people grow up and stop believing, many end up creating schools and jobs and social norms that constrain creative thinking and action.

We are fortunate to have carved out this special place where we can set the conditions for creativity to emerge right in the heart of a world-class research university. It's both a gift and a challenge: our methods build on deep knowledge and the spirit of scientific and technological discovery that pervades Stanford's campus. We also challenge the norms and orthodoxies of an institution with 125 years of history, 16,000 driven students, and 2,200 staggeringly accomplished faculty.

The d.school's success is a great argument for welcoming a little oddness into your midst from time to time, a provocation to explore alternative ways of producing new ideas. Our approach to design brings productive, creative tensions: an emphasis on humanness in a time of technological prowess; an embrace of naive, unprejudiced questions in a sector that specializes in expert answers; and a jostling of hierarchy and status to break down barriers across fields and amplify collaboration between unexpected allies.

When we use, teach, and share our ways of learning and working, extraordinary ideas appear. When we practice certain intentional behaviors, they quickly become more natural. As you make your way through these assignments, I hope you also feel the sheer joy that comes from working in this more human, more connected, and, yes, sometimes more childlike way.

Being childlike has helped d.schoolers pursue wide-ranging endeavors. They've designed treatments and resources to help children born with clubfoot avert a lifetime of stigma and disability, launched flourishing creative hubs in the heart of countries undergoing political repression, found new ways to unite journalists and technologists, started businesses that created jobs and economic value, and brought humanity and efficiency to the heart of government bureaucracy. They've tackled the esoteric (redesigning how lawyers conduct research), the environmental (solar lighting to give more than a hundred million people around the world an affordable alternative to carbon-polluting kerosene lamps), and the economic (storytelling and media services that help locally owned businesses thrive across the United States).

These outcomes are impressive, as are the innovations that propelled them. Even more amazing: the people behind these solutions all started as beginners, with little or no familiarity with design or creative collaboration. By trying and learning these methods, they found truly novel ways to look at an opportunity. That is the d.school's special contribution: we help open the door to people who have not previously seen themselves as working in a creative field.

But success is never about a single moment of insight. These examples are good ones because the d.school's founders spent time in an environment that encouraged their natural creative abilities to emerge and because they didn't stop practicing those learned behaviors after they graduated. They began to believe in and act their way toward a different future.

For some of us this space is physical, and we call it the d.school. But everyone can open a d.school in their own mind.

I hope this book helps you do just that. By trying one new assignment that lets you notice an old pattern in your behavior. By challenging a habit of thought that's getting in your way. By helping you find a new practice that fuels your imagination. By supporting you as you celebrate and lift up the inventiveness and resourcefulness of the people you lead, teach, or work among. This book isn't just for people on the path toward becoming a professional designer; it will help anyone bring design principles and practices into any profession or endeavor.

Like our students, you might be working on sprawling, complex topics and aspire to push your skills to the same places they do. You might be tackling focused projects much closer to home that matter to you, your family, or your community. Whatever the context, our goal is to help you come out of each assignment you try knowing that you can do a little bit more, a little bit better than you did before.

And you're in charge of how you do that: none of these assignments has to be used exactly as written. Each is meant to be tinkered with, adapted, and remixed. Skip around the book, try something new, let it rest, and then take it off the shelf for a browse when you need some fresh inspiration.

The experience of doing these assignments is the value you will take away. The emphasis is not on mastering tools or technique, although you'll encounter a few. A tool or a practice by itself is just a way to start: it can eventually be overused, misused, or forgotten. But the mindset or approach you learn and the self-awareness you cultivate are both flexible and durable. These assignments are just a bit of new input for you to react to. With a little creative prompting and structure, you can summon new perspectives from within that might not have emerged otherwise.

I hope to meet you in your d.school sometime soon. It's not too hard to imagine.

Getting
Started

Think about the last time you tried to change, fix, design, or solve a problem in your life and you really didn't know what the outcome would be. Maybe it was a challenge you took on following a promotion at work, the search for an apartment in a new city, or an effort to organize your neighbors to deal with a block-wide problem. You might have felt a mix of things—excitement, commitment, and nervousness—all at the same time. You might have been secure in your skills and prepared a creative approach, yet still felt like a beginner. This is really common: when faced with an open-ended challenge that doesn't have one fixed, right solution, we can all feel like beginners. And it's true—we are inexpert in that particular problem. However, if we have practiced how to tackle an open-ended situation and learned how to handle all of the complicated feelings that arise while doing so, we can improvise our way through any challenge.

This is a story about a group of beginners facing a large, messy, creative challenge and bringing all they had to it. It's a story about a big opportunity hiding in plain sight and about finding a signal within a noisy, complex system by listening to the clarion call of human suffering and fear.

It's about resilience, inventiveness, improvisation, humility, and many leaps of faith.

It's also a story about Edith Elliot, Katy Ashe, Shahed Alam, and Jessie Liu, four graduate students pursuing degrees in international policy, civil and environmental engineering, and medicine. Their lives took an unexpected turn when they met during a d.school class called *Design for Extreme Affordability*. As part of the class, they began to work with the Narayana Health Hospital chain of cardiac care centers founded by a charismatic surgeon, Dr. Devi Prasad Shetty, based in Bangalore, India. The team was asked to travel to India, find opportunities, and design solutions to improve the patient flow in order to help the hospital get closer to its mission to deliver high-quality, low-cost care on a wide scale.

When they started, the team had a lot of support and a willing partner, and they had already experienced a few of the assignments included in this book, specifically *The Monsoon Challenge* (page 89); *I Like, I Wish* (page 212); and *Stanford Service Corps* (page 264). But their biggest advantage was that they went into the situation without being fixed on the exact problem they would tackle. What the students thought might be the need and what they actually found turned out to be two very different things. No matter your skill level or the scope of the challenges you take on, approaching the unknown with the spirit and tools of inquiry will help you uncover bigger and better opportunities than you could imagine beforehand.

That's just how design works. It can take you on a journey to learn not just how to solve a problem, but also how to identify what problem might be so worth solving that you reorganize your life around the endeavor.

That's where we hope this story ends, anyway, but that's not where it begins. Like so many great tales, this story starts with a miscommunication.

HMMM. I'M NOT SURE WHAT YOU SHOULD DO, BUT DON'T WASTE YOUR TIME. JUST STAY OUT OF THE OPERATING ROOM!

TEN MINUTES IN AND THINGS ARE NOT GOING TO PLAN . . .

EDITH, LOOK AT HOW MANY PEOPLE ARE WAITING IN THE HALLWAY. LET'S FIND OUT WHY.

AND THAT'S WHEN THE TEAM MET ANAND, A NURSE.

LET ME INTRODUCE YOU TO SOME OF MY PATIENTS.

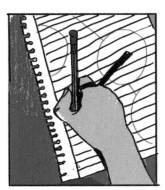

EDITH AND KATY REUNITE WITH JESSIE AND SHAHED AT THE D.SCHOOL, AND THE TEAM BEGINS TO UNPACK AND SYNTHESIZE WHAT THEY'VE LEARNED.

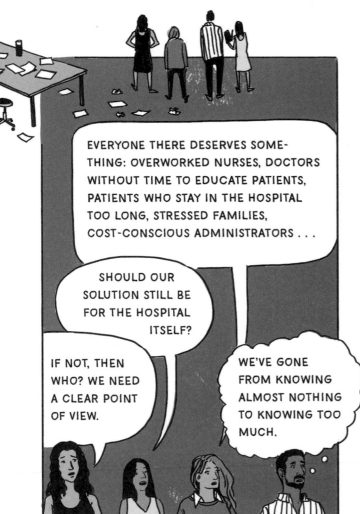

EVERYONE THERE DESERVES SOMETHING: OVERWORKED NURSES, DOCTORS WITHOUT TIME TO EDUCATE PATIENTS, PATIENTS WHO STAY IN THE HOSPITAL TOO LONG, STRESSED FAMILIES, COST-CONSCIOUS ADMINISTRATORS . . .

SHOULD OUR SOLUTION STILL BE FOR THE HOSPITAL ITSELF?

IF NOT, THEN WHO? WE NEED A CLEAR POINT OF VIEW.

WE'VE GONE FROM KNOWING ALMOST NOTHING TO KNOWING TOO MUCH.

WE GOTTA PICK UP OUR PACE.

WHAT ABOUT THESE COMPETING NEEDS? WHAT WOULD HAVE THE MOST IMPACT?

DON'T FORGET WE NEED TO DESIGN SOMETHING THE HOSPITAL COULD IMPLEMENT!

GUYS. TENSION. LET'S PAUSE. IS OUR TEAM OK RIGHT NOW? I WISH—

FEARFUL, ANXIOUS FAMILY MEMBERS NEED A WAY TO ADVOCATE FOR AND CONTRIBUTE TO PATIENTS' HEALTH.

IF THE FAMILY KNOWS WHAT'S HAPPENING, THAT COULD BE A NEW ROLE BETWEEN THE DOCTORS AND THE PATIENTS . . .

WE'VE GOT IT. IT'S ABOUT THE FAMILY. LET'S MAKE SOMETHING TO IMPROVE THEIR EXPERIENCE.

YOU KNOW, EVERYONE HERE IS TRYING TO HOLD ON TO TIME IN THE HOSPITAL. THE PATIENTS TRY TO STAY. EVEN THE DOCTORS ARE RELUCTANT TO SEND THEM HOME.

IT'S TERRIFYING WHEN YOU DON'T KNOW WHAT'S HAPPENING. SO MUCH UNNECESSARY PAIN COULD BE RELIEVED WITH A LITTLE INFORMATION.

IS IT JUST ME . . . OR ARE WE GETTING SOMEPLACE USEFUL?

THE TEAM EXPERIMENTS WITH AN IDEA ABOUT TEACHING FAMILY MEMBERS TO HELP CARE FOR SICK LOVED ONES AT THE HOSPITAL. THE PLAN IS TO SEND THIS PROTOTYPE TO THEIR PARTNERS TO GATHER FEEDBACK FROM PATIENTS AND THEIR FAMILIES, BUT . . .

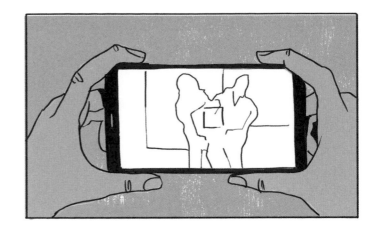

GUYS—TRY IT AGAIN. YOU KEEP CRACKING UP! WE'RE TRYING TO CONVEY REAL MEDICAL CONTENT.

I'M ACTUALLY MORTIFIED.

OUR VIDEOS ARE STILL SUPER CORNY . . .

HOW ELSE ARE WE GOING TO KNOW WHETHER WE'RE ON THE RIGHT TRACK?

C'MON, ANAND WON'T JUDGE US. AND IF THEY'RE ROUGH, HE'LL GET MORE CANDID FEEDBACK FROM PEOPLE.

OKAY . . . LET'S RUN IT AGAIN AND THEN SEND IT.

AFTER A WEEK OF WAITING, SHAHED RUNS UP TO THE TEAM WITH NEWS

HEY! I JUST HEARD FROM ANAND . . .

THE FAMILIES LIKED THE VIDEOS! THEY STARTED TO PRACTICE THE SKILLS RIGHT AWAY . . . AND ASKED FOR MORE!

SERIOUSLY!?

HMMM . . . MAYBE THE INFORMATION LANDS *BECAUSE* THEY'RE FUNNY AND DRAMATIC?

I JUST GOT GOOD NEWS TOO! WE GOT SOME FUNDING, SO SHAHED AND I CAN PILOT THE IDEA IN INDIA THIS SUMMER.

LET'S PACK!

SHAHED AND JESSIE ARE NOW IN INDIA AT THE HOSPITAL. THEY'VE CONVERTED A WAITING ROOM INTO A CLASSROOM, AND ARE DEMONSTRATING THE TECHNIQUE OF TAKING A PULSE, WHILE FAMILY MEMBERS FOLLOW THEIR LEAD. A LONG LINE OF PEOPLE WAITING TO GET IN IS SNAKING THROUGH THE HALLWAYS OF THE HOSPITAL.

YOU WON'T BELIEVE IT, BUT THERE'S A LINE AROUND THE CORNER.

WHOA. I DON'T THINK THIS IS JUST A CLASS PROJECT ANYMORE.

AFTER A WILDLY SUCCESSFUL PILOT, THE TEAM REGROUPS IN CALIFORNIA.
THE FOUR TEAM MEMBERS ARE STANDING TOGETHER CONFERRING. THEY ARE STRESSED ABOUT THE OPPORTUNITIES PULLING THEM IN DIFFERENT DIRECTIONS.

THE PILOT SHOWED WE HIT ON A REALLY BIG NEED.

JUST OUR INCREDIBLY ROUGH PROTOTYPES PROVIDED SURPRISING VALUE TO MANY PEOPLE.

YES! WE DID IT, TEAM!

WELL . . . DOES THIS THING REALLY HELP? LOOK—WE ALL HAVE SCIENCE BACK-GROUNDS. THE FUZZY FEEL-GOOD STORIES AREN'T GOING TO BE ENOUGH TO KEEP THIS GOING. SO LET'S GET SOME HARD DATA AND SEE IF IT'S ACTUALLY WORKING.

TIME OUT. I WORKED CRAZY HARD TO GET INTO MED SCHOOL.

SAME. I'M SUPPOSED TO FOCUS ON THAT NOW.

YEAH, KATY AND I BOTH HAVE GREAT JOB OFFERS. I FEEL THE PULL. BUT . . . LET'S GET SOME MORE DATA AND THEN SEE HOW WE FEEL.

WHILE RUNNING A NEW PILOT AT A HOSPITAL IN MYSORE, INDIA, THE TEAM STUDIED THEIR INTERVENTION WITH THE HELP OF RESEARCHERS FROM STANFORD MEDICAL SCHOOL USING RIGOROUS TESTING METHODS. THE STUDY FOUND THAT WHAT FAMILY MEMBERS LEARNED FROM THE TRAINING LOWERED THE RATES OF POST-SURGICAL COMPLICATIONS (71%) AND PREVENTABLE HOSPITAL READMISSIONS (24%). AND, IT SIGNIFICANTLY DECREASED FAMILY ANXIETY.

THESE STUDY RESULTS ARE AMAZING!

PEOPLE ARE NOW CHOOSING THIS HOSPITAL BECAUSE OF OUR FAMILY TRAINING PROGRAM. THEN THEY GO HOME TO THEIR VILLAGES AND RETURN WITH OTHERS . . . SOMETIMES ONLY FOR THE TRAINING . . . I CAN'T GET OVER IT.

ME TOO! I CAN'T BELIEVE THE STRONG EFFECT WE'RE SEEING WITH SUCH A LOW-COST PROGRAM. I KNOW I SAID I WAS DONE. BUT I'M STARTING TO WONDER . . . COULD THIS TRANSFORM HOW HEALTH CARE IS DELIVERED?

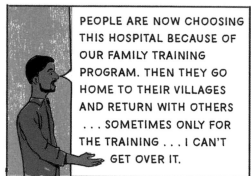

LET'S KEEP GOING. WE'VE GOT TONS OF NEW IDEAS AND INSIGHTS FROM THE PILOTS.

HEY GUYS—HAVE YOU LOOKED AT YOUR INBOXES LATELY . . . ?

HOSPITAL A WANTS TO PILOT!

HOSPITAL B WANTS IT ACROSS THEIR WHOLE CHAIN.

WOW . . . HOSPITAL C SAYS THE TRAINING IS INCREASING OVERALL PATIENT SATISFACTION AND THEY'RE NOW USING IT AS A KEY PERFORMANCE INDICATOR.

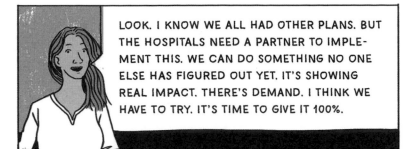

Edith, Katy, Shahed, and Jessie became the cofounders of Noora Health, whose mission is to train patients and their families with high-impact health skills to improve outcomes and save lives.

The service became a streamlined version of their very early prototypes. Existing staff (usually nurses) are trained using interactive videos and printed materials. Those nurses run sessions with family members to train them on helping to care for their loved one's condition. It happens in the ward, before or after visiting hours, making it as easy as possible for people to access. The family members learn tangible skills through activities and exercises, and it's making a difference.

By the end of 2020, the organization had trained more than 5,000 nurses and more than 1 million family members in 160 hospitals across India and Bangladesh.

In addition to cardiac surgery recovery, Noora Health now offers training in other therapeutic areas like maternal and newborn care, general medical, and surgical care.

Demand for their service grew so quickly during the pilot phase that one team member fondly called it "mayhem." The founders decided to alter their educational and career plans and step fully into the unknown. They recognized that they had designed something worth implementing, and they jumped in. The four relocated to India and built Noora Health from the ground up.

Jessie and Shahed both delayed medical school for several years before returning to complete their degrees, and Shahed returned to Noora afterward, becoming co-CEO. Katy served as Noora's founding Chief Design Officer, and Edith as CEO. Anubhav Arora, an engineer from Delhi who provided in-country design and logistical support starting in 2013, became employee number one: Director of Operations. And Anand Kumar, the enthusiastic and committed nurse the team met on their very first research trip in 2012, became Director of Training.

When you read about how far Jessie, Shahed, Katy, and Edith took Noora Health, it's easy to forget that they started at the very beginning not knowing where they would end up. But there were many moments along the way when it was not clear that they would be successful—moments of feeling stuck and uncertain, moments of tension as the team tried to craft a clear direction for themselves, and moments when other firm commitments seemed like the safer route than betting on a very new idea.

They gained clarity by seeing the pattern that emerged from their discussions with patients' families at the hospital: for the families, being there was expensive, emotional, and frightening. The team listened to those voices and wound up creating something people really needed. It turned out to be a major moment of learning.

Reflecting on this time, Edith says, "If we had gone in with the problem statement 'reduce readmissions to the hospital,' we wouldn't have gotten to the same solution. Our problem statement was very emotional. It was about reducing fear and suffering. That's what we were hearing from family members over and over. We weren't hearing from people, 'I'm afraid of the thirty-day post-surgical complication rates!' But by focusing on the human problem, we're now addressing the medical one."

In tackling this challenge, the Noora Health team went on a journey of learning and experimenting in order to build conviction in a particular creative direction. Obviously, that's not simple. You can explore one way to think more deeply about this—and how design and learning are closely intertwined—in *The Journey from Not Knowing to Knowing* (page 73).

The Noora journey, like most design and most learning experiences, has emotion running right through it. It's the electrical current that charged the insights, powered the supportive (but not conflict-free) team dynamic, and sparked the hope lit by the initial positive feedback to the early ideas. Emotion shaped the team's direction and, woven together with concrete evidence that their solution worked, fostered the team's decision to take a leap of faith and launch the concept into reality.

You may choose to channel your creative energies in many different ways, but one thing will be true no matter your context: feelings count. Learning to observe and register feelings in others is crucial to *Widening Your Lens* (page 119), because it helps you connect to how the world might appear through others' eyes and kindles your imagination for what you could create. Learning to appreciate the feelings of teammates with conflicting viewpoints and to collaborate in an open and vulnerable way is the key to creative teamwork. And registering your own emotion is central to cultivating intuition about how to direct your creative energies. Recognizing and grappling with *The Feeling of Learning* (page 161) and *Productive Struggle* (page 207) will prepare you to handle this challenging—and joyful—aspect of working creatively.

When you are ready to apply your creative abilities to more complex projects, the strategies in *Putting It All Together* (page 251) will help you think about how to frame and scope your work. Leaving the right amount of openness in your approach will allow you to discover needs and opportunities that are meaningful, important, or novel.

Design is a wonderful, scary, tremendous roller coaster, just about every time.

Let's go!

The Assignments: Find Your Path

Developing your design abilities is personal, and the way in which you use this book will be too. If you happen to read it from front to back, you'll find that the assignments are loosely organized according to how we might introduce them to new students. However, no design project precisely resembles another, and no designer works exactly like the next one. If you are hoping to develop a specific skill, you might want to navigate these assignments in a very particular way. The following index will help you find that path or perhaps lead you to discover a new one.

See things in a new way

train your attention, make the hidden visible, and move beyond the obvious

Work well with others
build trust, courage, energy, and joy

Make sense of your insights
tune up your critical brain, uncover connections, interpret information, and form hypotheses

Come up with ideas
generate new directions and unleash your imagination

Build something

make fuzzy ideas concrete and think with things

Tell a compelling story

find the essence of an idea and communicate it to others

Put your work out there

cultivate judgment and solicit feedback to make your work better

Take control of your own learning

notice and reflect on the changes in your thinking, abilities, and work

Locate your own voice

find inspiration, passion, and perspective

Get out and discover

stretch your senses and escape old routines

Pick up the pace

rapidly free up your thinking and try
things before you feel ready

Slow down and focus

cultivate patience and spaciousness so
you can do your best work

Have fun

experience hilarity and encourage play

Work toward equity

build consciousness and develop humility,
challenge bias, and put effort into ethics

Peer into the future

dream about the big picture, question assumptions,
and envision the implications of your work

Tackle a whole project

gain fluency and graduate to a greater level
of skill and ability

1 Blind Contour Bookend

Featuring the work of Charlotte Burgess-Auburn, Scott Doorley, Grace Hawthorne, and art teachers everywhere

I've learned a lot about dealing with a very picky "person" who seems to share my brain with me: my inner critic. She cares too much about whether I'm completely original, entirely comprehensive, and indisputably rigorous. She'll whisper (in my head) that I shouldn't share my idea if I can't immediately describe a random-ized controlled trial that backs it up, or if anyone has ever talked about a similar concept before in the history of the world. We struggle together, and over time I've learned how to listen to the grain of truth she offers without getting completely stalled and unable to make progress in my own creative endeavors.

It's helpful to develop a range of personal practices for dealing with your inner critic, and this assignment is a great one.

Producing creative work—actually getting it out of your head and onto the page or into the world—requires you to deliberately suspend your evaluative brain at specific moments. You want to temporarily defer judgment on what might work in order to explore a new concept without prematurely dismissing it as impractical or unfeasible. To develop your creative abilities, you need to learn how to turn off your internal self-judgment so it can't act like a censor.

This doesn't mean every idea you have is a great one, but it gives you the discipline to separate the moments you're generating from the times you're evaluating.

Blind contour drawing is a common practice used by artists to shortcut the distance between the eye and the hand. With practice, when the eye follows a curve, then the hand draws the same curve on the page without thinking about it. The process skips the judging brain.

This assignment adapts the practice for a different purpose: to help you locate and wrestle with your critical functions (your ability to judge and to critique). It helps you experience what it feels like to not judge your work and to let your creativity flow.

This activity is useful anytime you're feeling deflated about the quality of your work or you've just caught yourself doubt-ing your own potential.

Grab a pen and paper.

Identify someone you can see from where you are sitting. You could be on a train, at a park, in a really boring meeting, or sitting across from someone else doing the same assignment.

Now, take just one to two minutes to draw this person while looking at them the entire time. Most importantly: *draw the other person without looking at the paper and without lifting your pen from the paper.* (If you do lift your hand, you will not be able to find your way back, and the temptation to look will be overwhelming.)

You are making a translation of what you see with your eyes into a line with your hand—without any visual feedback.

When time is up, then you can look at your drawing.

Think about what you felt as you were sketching and how you feel about your drawing now.

Reflect on the following questions:

Did you make a great drawing? (Unlikely.)
What did that feel like?

Did you laugh along the way?
If so, what was that laughter about?

What did the voice in your head say?

What did it try to make you do?

What's at the base of those feelings?
Where's that coming from?
When is it important to judge a piece of work, and when might it be important to not judge?

This exercise helps you get into the habit of separating the process of making and creating from the process of critiquing or judging.

The first step toward doing this is to know where your judgment lives and recognize what it feels like and sounds like. If you're like most people, the first time you do this assignment, a voice inside your head will strongly urge you to look at your paper to judge whether your marks are in the right place. *Does my drawing look like my subject? Did I put her mouth in the correct spot?*

Judgment is incredibly important: you need it to survive and to course-correct your way through life. But the ability to put your critique on hold is what allows you to sometimes pursue a wild idea. Think of it as a set of sliders or knobs that you can dial up and down. When you need to judge and make decisions, dial it up to eleven and say, "I have chosen this because of that and that." But sometimes dial it down and say, "I'm not judging, I'm just producing right now. I'm just making stuff, and I'm going to worry about judging it later." That's a skill that everyone needs to practice.

I love to use this activity as both the first and last assignment in my classes, as it can reveal to students their own progress. By the last day, they have stopped wrestling with their inner critic and have started noticing their own capacity for enjoying the act of just producing—all the worry about judging is suspended until after the work is made.

—*Charlotte Burgess-Auburn*

How to Talk to Strangers

Featuring the work of Erica Estrada-Liou and Meenu Singh, with inspiration from Kio Stark

In an era when so much interaction takes place online, approaching a stranger in person seems to be getting harder. Many of us were raised to be cautious of strangers, but it seems that today, more than ever, we hesitate to do what used to be second nature or even required in a close community: chat while in line at the supermarket or ask a stranger for directions. You might feel uneasy around a stranger because you don't have context for who they are. Uneasiness might be amplified by your own bias or shyness. But design work requires you to break through this barrier. Without engaging new people and ideas, you can't get over your preconceived notions.

The word *stranger* even implies the idea of strangeness. In everyday life you might avoid strangeness. But creative work requires you to become more open to things you find strange or unusual. Without strangeness, you are left only with sameness.

This assignment helps you confront the stranger barrier. Eventually you will find "strangeness" appealing because you know it is essential to your work.

You're going on a series of missions that must be done outside of your home, classroom, or office.

You can do this as a solo challenge or, if you feel uncomfortable by yourself, with a partner.

Start small. Choose a path in a safe place where you will encounter other people walking. Perhaps you're going to walk from home to the library. Now, say hello to every single person you see on the path. Do this for one minute.

How many people did you say hello to?
How did people react?
How did your behavior change from start to finish?

Your second mission is about triangulation. There's you, a stranger, and an object that you both can see. Comment on that object in order to strike up a conversation with the stranger. You can find something to say about anything; don't be clever, just be obvious. "Oh wow . . . you can get those apples from this grocery store? I didn't know they carried them here. Are they good?"

Then converse.

When it's over, think about the following (or discuss with your partner):

What was the object you chose?
How did the person react?
Compare this mission to the first mission.

Your third mission is harder.

Pretend you're lost and ask a stranger for directions to a specific destination nearby.

If you get the person to give you directions, then ask them to draw you a map.

If they agree to draw you a map, then ask them for their phone number so you can call them if you need more help and get lost along the way.

If they agree to give you their phone number, then call them to see if they answer.

If they answer, thank them for their help and let them know you found your destination.

Now reflect (or discuss with your partner):

Who did you ask for directions?
How did you choose them?
How far did you get?
What was the barrier to each next step?
This mission asked you to tell a small lie. How did you feel?

Many people think no one will say yes to having an interaction with a stranger. Getting over this fear is liberating and valuable on its own. And it's a broader reminder to challenge your own assumptions about how people behave. People who do this assignment often get really excited when they go further than they thought they'd be able to go. If you want to go even deeper, check out Kio Stark's wonderful book *When Strangers Meet,* which directly inspired this assignment.

The third mission is deliberately provocative, because of the pretense. Some people decide immediately that they won't do it, and they choose a destination whose location they genuinely don't know, so there is no falsehood. Despite the low stakes of the assignment, it gives you a lot of rich emotions and experience to reflect on. It's a very good lead-in to a broader consideration of the ethics of interviewing to gain empathy and insight.

You have to make a conscious decision to be transparent and authentic, and this experience shows how easy it is to slip into a less-than-transparent interaction. It's a good preparation for being upfront about telling people what you're really working on and why.

—Erica Estrada-Liou

3 The Dérive

Featuring the work of Carissa Carter, with inspiration from Guy Debord and William S. Burroughs

The best designs feel so simple. You look at them and think, *Why didn't I come up with that?* Great designers can take what everyone has been looking at and perceiving in the same way and see something else. They see a slightly different world even when they are looking at the regular world.

It's a skill that's hard to acquire. This is an assignment for cultivating that capacity.

You can do this on your own or with others. Distributed teams or groups of friends could even do it simultaneously, as there's no need to explore the same territory. It's especially interesting to compare notes and debrief with other people afterward.

———

Bring a notebook and a pen, and depart on foot from your office, classroom, home, or whatever place is your starting point. Don't plan where you're going to go. You're not taking a journey; the journey is taking you.

Let it.

Choose a specific quality to follow. A great starting point is your senses. You might select a color, a sound, a smell, or a texture. You might follow some weird line that you see on a building. And that brings your eye to something else with that same quality.

Set a timer for an hour. When it goes off, you're done.

Allow yourself to totally get lost, slow down, and not pay attention to where you are. (*Dérive* means "drift," but, obviously, stay safe and watch out for uncovered manholes.) If you forget what you're doing, just return to directing your attention in a deliberate way.

Capture what you're noticing however you want: through doodles, sketches, a list. Your goal is to wander and record how you did so, but not to make the most detailed map along the way.

When you're done, take a little bit of time to clean up your notes, and then share your *dérive* with someone.

———

You get used to a certain environment, and then you make assumptions about what it's like all the time. This assignment breaks you out of your normal way of taking in data and gives your brain and your senses a new protocol. It helps you to make completely different observations.

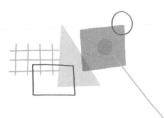

When I teach this, it usually goes down as people's favorite activity. Everyone comes back transformed—without fail. I think it's because people don't realize they can see their environment in this way. One time a guy followed "acceleration." Someone else looked at things that were yellow. The smellers usually come back with a radically different understanding of what's happening around them.

If you think of the world around you as your data set, you are always looking at it the same way. But if you take a dérive, you'll realize that you've been looking at your data in just one way, and now you can perceive a totally different thread in that data.

I love to prescribe this when people are blocked, stuck, or don't know where to begin. Sometimes in your work you have so much data to process that you don't know what slice of it to take. Those are really good moments for a dérive.

—Carissa Carter

4 Handle with Care

Featuring the work of Leticia Britos Cavagnaro, Maureen Carroll, Frederik G. Pferdt, and Erica Estrada-Liou

It's a tremendous honor to be invited into someone's inner life.

If your aim is to design for others, you need to understand their real feelings and perspectives. At the heart of this work is the practice of engaging directly with the people your design work will serve or affect. If you develop the skills to meaningfully engage with people, you get to listen to their stories and motivations, their needs and hardships, their dreams and concerns. Beneath the surface is where you'll find deep insights that help you imagine not just what could be better, but also how to make it so.

As you develop and refine your own approach to this type of work, you'll discover that you have a certain power when you do this. In the best cases, there's a real connection—even if it's temporary. People say things like, "I haven't gotten to talk about myself like this before; thank you for being such a good listener." Or "I'm telling you things I don't even talk about with my close friends."

However, you never want someone to walk away from an interaction feeling like you just extracted their stories and ideas.

Taking advantage of a person's time or personal stories solely to benefit your own work is not an ethical way to deploy your design skills.

This assignment is one small way to prepare for engaging with people. It helps you walk in the shoes of someone you're interviewing even before you meet them. It's not about the mechanics of the interview; rather, it's about building up your consciousness of how the other person will experience meeting with you. This can help engender humility and consideration in any setting in which some people are listening to other people's personal stories, like in health care or some parts of law.

This preparation will help you keep that mindset front and center while you're engaging others throughout your design work. All you need is your phone and at least one other person.

————

It's generally better to interview people in pairs in order to interpret what you learn through multiple perspectives. This assignment involves connecting with a partner while preparing to launch your design work. You can also do this with a large group—say three to fifty people.

Decide together how long the assignment will last. Five minutes is a good minimum. Set a timer.

Each person unlocks their smartphone and hands it to the other person. If you are doing this exercise with more than two people, stand in a circle and instruct everyone to pass their phone to the right (you too!).

Do what you want with the phone you've been given. People will exhibit different behaviors in this situation. Some will hold the phone at arm's length as if it's fragile—or radioactive. Others will start swiping right away. Do not stop until the timer goes off. It may feel long and uncomfortable. Let it.

Once the alarm rings, debrief with your partner or the whole group using these prompts:

How did it feel to have someone else going through your personal information?
How did you behave as the explorer?

What subconscious principles, if any, guided your actions?

There are no right or wrong answers to these questions. Your goal is to expose feelings and unearth realizations about the value of our own information and stories and to take that learning into how you want to behave when you are exploring the personal lives of others.

If you are working alone, you can still do this with a friend or family member. Unlock and exchange phones and see what each of you does and how that feels. Just as with the group version, set a timer and hold yourself to it.

————

This assignment was developed to help students deeply question their level of responsibility when conducting interviews during design work. The experience doesn't give you a moral checklist. But it does give you a visceral feeling of the power you have as an interviewer and what it's like to expose yourself to someone else's scrutiny.

Immersion for Insight

Featuring the work of Lena Selzer, Michael Brennan, and the Civilla team, with commentary from Adam Selzer

It is very hard for people to relate to a complex system in a personal way. However, doing so is important for anyone who is trying to use creative approaches to fix or remake many of the systems that shape daily life; for instance, health care, government, education, and beyond. Designing a system is such an abstract idea that you need ways to provoke a deep inner understanding of that system. You need to stretch yourself to relate to it emotionally and intuitively. With better context and empathy, you will ask better questions, embrace more humility, and make better decisions about your design work.

This assignment is one way to start understanding a system using your senses and emotions, as well as your intellect. It's based on the practice of immersion, in which you follow the exact steps of someone who might need to engage in the system. Does that sound uncomfortable? You're already on to something. Depending on the system, going through those steps is likely pretty intimidating to others as well, and you need to be able to relate to that emotion even if you're experiencing only a fraction of it yourself.

Many of today's vital institutions and organizations are getting bigger and bigger,

and decisions about how they run are made farther away from the places where people are actually using the services. Your exploration of any system may reveal hints of this. For example, you might find an unintentionally messy or confusing design, the kind that happens when no one thinks through a whole process from end to end and different layers build up and conflict with each other over time.

In other cases you find examples of design choices that actively cause harm—steps in a process that are meant to keep people waiting, to force them to repeatedly prove themselves worthy of a service, or to minimize the chances of the institution having to provide a benefit—think, for example, about private health insurance claims in the United States or places where voter ID policies make it harder or more complicated for out-of-state college students to vote.

One vivid example worth redesigning is the unbelievably complex public benefits system in many states. This assignment involves an immersion to understand that specific system, but you can adapt it for many other contexts you want to design for or understand better, like health care, education, veteran's affairs, and so on.

Regardless of where you apply your creative skills, this assignment will help you see how powerful it is to practice immersion to increase your insight. This kind of tool will be very useful as you explore some of the final, most advanced assignments toward the end of this book.

Your goal is to go through the process of applying for public benefits online, although you will stop short of filing the application. Many states now offer a way for people to apply online for public benefits like food assistance, but the process is still far from simple. Give yourself a strict time limit of twenty-five minutes. »

Regardless of your actual resources, act as though you don't have a computer at home; instead, use a library computer or your phone. This adds to the difficulty and better reflects what people without computer access will experience. Read everything carefully. Try not to make any mistakes.

Very important: Do *not* submit the application. Do not call and distract workers in a public benefits office, asking them to help you instead of helping someone else. In other words, learn everything you can about this system without creating any extra burden on it.

That's it.

After your time is up, reflect on what you've learned. This assignment isn't easy; odds are you won't complete the task within the allotted time.

Your goal is to identify surprises and opportunities and how they felt along the way. What are the gaps between how the system is supposed to work for the applicants and what you observed? Did you persist to the end? What questions did you come away with? What additional hurdles would someone without access to technology face?

——————

This assignment is most helpful if you are a financially secure individual who wouldn't normally depend on public benefits or, regardless of financial status, are unfamiliar with a system you want to understand. Going through this exercise should give you a personal connection to the work that you're about to engage in.

We designed this assignment for new team members or state leaders who work with us on this topic. Inevitably it reminds us that for most people who engage this system, the experience isn't designed to help them succeed.

There are so many small moments that lead to big insights. The participant has to know what to search to find an application online. Often, they aren't able to set up an account, or they discover that it's not easy to fill out on their phones. Health and Human Services sites aren't usually optimized for mobile, so people spend a lot of time trying to navigate the application and avoid errors. Some people have an emotional reaction when the application asks if they are homeless; for many people, this is a routine question. Even if you know this intellectually, it lands emotionally—and has a lasting effect—from this immersion.

When we started this work, the public benefits application in Michigan was really long. It typically took more than forty-five minutes to complete. Applicants were asked to enter the same information multiple times, including questions as personal as "What was the date of conception of your child?" Participants often described that it felt like the application was designed intentionally to make them fail. Lawyers said, "I can read it, but I don't understand what it means." Having challenges with literacy or disabilities such as visual impairments doesn't make it any easier. There are so many barriers that become visible only if you go through the experience yourself.

Most people who try this assignment fail to finish the application. They don't get the satisfaction of checking all the boxes. It's humbling. And that's part of the point.

Now, just because you dabbled in this system for a few hours doesn't mean you completely understand it. We might have deepened our commitment and insight, but we still don't fully understand the complexity. This assignment always reminds us that for most people who engage this system, it isn't primarily a learning experience. It's not something that they can turn off and on again.

—Lena Selzer and Adam Selzer

6 Shadowing

Featuring the work of Ariel Raz, Devon Young, Jennifer Walcott Goldstein, Peter Worth, and Susie Wise

Two deadly phrases that always condemn promising ideas to the rubbish heap: "That would never work here," and "We tried that before and it didn't work." They are often uttered by weary veterans of an organization or system—people who have been trying to make things better for years or those for whom change is threatening. These reactions—and others like them—remind us that it's hard to address a challenge creatively without getting stuck on worn-out ideas about fixed constraints. We are frequently asked for help with this at the d.school.

When you're trying to bring fresh thinking to an old problem, you need a way to inoculate yourself against those deadly phrases. One way to do so is to put on a pair of "fresh eyes." We'd love to just send you to the eye doctor and get a prescription for these, but until that's possible, try the practice of shadowing.

Shadowing helps you observe a context and the behaviors within that context without the constraint of preconceived ideas. It helps you adopt a deliberate, temporary naïveté in order to see things differently and come up with potential improvements.

This assignment is a crash course in empathy and understanding. We often assign it to help school leaders or teachers see school through a student's eyes, but you can apply these ideas and the practice of "shadowing" to any organization or situation.

It's great when you're feeling cynical about the possibility for change, or just a little stuck. The trick is to think about how to get inspiration by shadowing a nontraditional expert. It could be the maintenance person in your office building, who knows the hidden rhythms and needs of the community better than anyone. It could be someone who just started a job with your

group and has a totally fresh perspective on what your culture is like. Could a parent do this with a kid? Or vice versa? Absolutely. You'll learn the most if you choose someone whose experience is unlike your own. For example, if you're a high school teacher with a knack for math, pick a student who is struggling with algebra. If you are a quiet, introverted person, choose an outgoing type. If you're a White female, consider selecting a male of color who navigates a whole different set of challenges from the ones you face. Choose who you're going to shadow, and then use these instructions to get the most out of the assignment.

At a basic level, shadowing is a simple practice: you pick someone whose experience you want to understand, then spend a day following them around and doing everything they do. Prepare to shadow by writing down your learning goals for your Shadow Day, choosing a person you will shadow, and questioning your assumptions. Ask yourself:

What do I hope to learn about the person I am shadowing?

What do I hope to learn about the broader context and system?

What do I hope to learn about myself through this challenge?

Get ready. Spending a day shadowing is different from the way you normally show up! Think through what to wear and what to bring with you. Give some thought to how you will break the ice with your shadowee. If shadowing is a new practice in your organization, you'll have to spend some time beforehand explaining your goals and getting permission from the person you're hoping to shadow.

Spend an entire day shadowing, capturing your observations along the way. The purpose of your Shadow Day is not to simply observe, but to immerse yourself in your shadowee's experience. Work, eat, and walk along with them. When teachers do this, they spend the entire day—from waiting at the bus stop to long after the final bell—walking in the shoes of their student.

At the end of the day, take some time to reflect on your observations, then question them, and find opportunities for positive change and action. Preserving time to do this will help you make sense of what you saw, heard, and felt.

What was the most memorable experience from your Shadow Day? Why?

What surprised you? What delighted you?

How did your experience differ from your expectations?

What did you discover that is related to your design goals?

What did you learn that was totally unexpected?

Get ready to act. Based on your Shadow Day findings, think about how to make the most use of them. Is there a story you want people to hear? Conclusions you want to circulate? Design a small experiment for making changes, using the following prompts to stimulate your thinking:

What is the most pressing need that should be addressed?
What's something you can try next week to learn more about your new insights?
What makes you most excited to take action? Most nervous?

Shadowing can be used in many environments; one place we've used this assignment a lot is with educators. In the K–12 school context, shadowing is a positively disruptive experience. Educators' search for meaning and root causes can lead to valuable insights and a different relationship with the things they do and see every day. Ultimately, this can change how they behave or even how the entire school functions.

Some walk away with smaller observations—like how physically exhausting it is for children to sit all day, or that the students don't get enough relaxed, unrushed time to eat and be nourished—or bigger ones, like how students experience the school's culture.

One teacher who shadowed a student noticed that the middle school students did not engage with adults other than when they were called on. And the school did not reflect the middle schoolers' presence in any public way. She immediately wanted to do a big student-work gallery walk to show the kids that the school cares about them and their work. As a small experiment, she just tried it with her own class. She posted a ton of different student work in the hallway outside of her classroom.

It was influential immediately and started to lead to broader change. Her colleagues noticed her display and asked why she had mounted it. The principal of the school got very excited. Students saw their work being shown off and expressed pride. Other teachers started to do it. It was a small, easy hack, and it led to more widespread and systematic ways of showing students that their work is appreciated.

You can adapt the practice of shadowing to suit any organization or context. Sometimes just the act of public empathizing can start to shift a culture.

—*Ariel Raz and Devon Young*

7 Fundamentals

Featuring the work of Aleta Hayes

In any creative practice, there are just a handful of important ideas. They show up differently across contexts but are always there. If you pay attention to those principles, you can respond to any situation. As a dancer and choreographer, Aleta Hayes uses her fluency in the fundamentals of movement to help her students—many of whom have never taken a formal dance class—to express emotion regardless of their technical background.

What fundamentals matter most to how you express yourself? Think about projects or work you have produced of which you are particularly proud.

What are some fundamental principles or skills present in these projects that you have mastered?

How could you use this mastery in other spaces and places?

I love fundamental principles.

That's what I like about classical ballet. How you raise your arms, how you place your weight: it's very codified. I enjoy researching and unearthing that code in its many forms. Think of the innumerable African dances: there are as many ways to sense the ground—and understanding the ground gives me access to the space all around me.

As a little kid I had a dream that I could speak in all languages. Now I have the possibility of doing so; I realized through dance that I can. Because the way people use space, and the way people use gravity, and the way people relate to one another is speaking this language.

—Aleta Hayes

8 A Seeing Exercise

Featuring the work of Rachelle Doorley and Scott Doorley, with inspiration from Abigail Housen and Philip Yenawine

There is something around you that is hiding in plain sight.

At this very moment, you are processing an incredible amount of information: the sound of that fly buzzing at the window; the way the shadows are spilling across the room; the fact that, yes, you did turn the oven off after you cooked dinner last night (good for you!). But how much of this information are you consciously noticing? Just a tiny fraction. Your brain is constantly protecting you from total information overload by filtering what you register.

Learning how to control your filter—so you can pay close attention to what's right in front of you—will help you see what others miss. And the effects are powerful: the research of educators Abigail Housen and Philip Yenawine, whose work inspired this assignment, showed that this control supports the overall growth of your creative and critical thinking skills, which transfer to many areas of your life and work.

This assignment helps you slow down the connection between your eye and your brain so you can make discoveries about what you know, but don't know you know. Lurking in this huge category of

unconscious observation are thousands of opportunities for design and creative work.

Sometimes you'll notice either literal or figurative "duct tape," a temporary fix someone has placed on a problem that really deserves a more considered solution. You might see the equivalent of what architects call a "desire line," a path that people are walking because it's easier or more intuitive than the official paved one. When you get really good, you'll see the omissions. What's missing?

———

Find a photograph. A documentary photograph drawn from real life is absolutely perfect. Look for a shot by a photographer interested in the everyday. Journalistic photos are sometimes too dramatic but work in a pinch. Street scenes are great; you want a lot of detail, multiple people in the frame, and some ambiguity about what's happening. You can practice with the image on this page.

Now, ask yourself the following questions:

What's going on in this picture?
What do you see that makes you say that?
What else do you see?
What do you see that makes you say that?

Repeat. And again. And again.

Consider keeping a journal or log and doing this exercise once a day. At the beginning, fill up a few pages per photo. Once you practice a few times, you'll never run out of observations to record.

———————

This assignment helps you understand how much detail is part of your daily life. Background detail is what makes the world feel vivid and real, a quality that you want to imbue all of your creative work. Noticing detail is the first step toward being able to design it into your work.

In normal life, I find that people look at an image for less than fifteen seconds. When I run this assignment, I have to pull people away after fifteen minutes. Afterward, when I walk home, I see everything totally differently. A stain on someone's backpack. White shoes. I start to notice all the details, which as a designer is really important.

—Scott Doorley

9

Talkers & Listeners

Featuring the work of Leticia Britos Cavagnaro and Melissa Pelochino, with inspiration from Maren Aukerman and Mano Singham

In any group you're a part of, there's natural variation in how people process information and share their ideas. Some people generally talk out loud to figure out what they mean; others sit back, observe, and contemplate. But these traits are situational, not fixed, which means that the context you're in may determine just how much each person voices their ideas.

Sometimes the issue is power dynamics: a boss gets more air time or a doctor's perspective is valued more than a nurse's.

(That same nurse might be the most vocal extrovert in another group.) Or it's about socialization, which can be the case when men speak more than women or nonbinary people or some group members participate in their second or third language. All of these dynamics inhibit a culture in which everyone can benefit from the ideas and contributions of diverse thinkers and doers.

But you don't have to accept that the norms of the rest of the world will determine how your group functions—whether it's your book club or your team at work. You can design your own norms. You just need a way to call attention to this challenge, without casting blame or silencing anyone.

This assignment is about surfacing the unspoken assumptions between people who talk more and people who talk less— whatever the reasons. It assumes good intent on the part of every participant, and it helps create self-awareness and other-awareness. We need this ability to look inward and also around us to unlock real learning or build trust within a creative culture.

Do this assignment with five to fifty people. You will be rewarded with a group of individuals who have greater empathy and understanding for how the other members contribute best, leading to a more collaborative environment.

———

Invite all participants to define themselves as either a talker or a listener. For the duration of this assignment, all must select one or the other. Since how you act can depend on the situation, select the group that best fits how you are showing up right at this moment.

With your fellow talkers (or listeners), go to a corner of the room that is separate from the other group.

Take about fifteen minutes to identify some of the similarities and differences among your group members in terms of how you participate, as well as the similarities and differences you've observed in how people in the other group participate when everyone is together. You should

notice some interesting variation even within your own group. Come up with at least three questions that you want to ask the other group.

Bring the groups back together and, if possible, arrange the two groups in two lines so you're each standing opposite a person from the other group, like a face-off. This might feel a little strange, but the arrangement is a reminder that even though the groups have differences, you're hoping to see eye-to-eye in a new way.

The first group poses their questions to the second group, and then vice versa. It's that simple.

Once you start noticing and reflecting on these essential behaviors, the discussion can easily go on for an hour. Often someone has to end the activity before people have had enough, because you have run out of time.

This assignment is powerful because it reveals the assumptions people have about what motivates others. It helps you understand how people interact on a level that is usually known but unspoken. And this understanding profoundly influences the group's performance.

For instance, a common question from the listeners to the talkers is, "Why do you feel that you have to start talking right away and leave no space in a conversation?" A talker might respond, "Well, I can't speak for everyone, but in my case, I feel that if I am the first to speak, it breaks the ice and encourages others to engage."

You can actually see the assumptions form in the air between the groups. And then, poof! they disappear in the middle. You could do this to help bridge many organizational divides where there's a gap in understanding.

If you're leading a group or teaching a class or running a household, you aim to create a world in which your people can do their best, but the responsibility isn't all on you. This experience creates more ownership for everyone. In order to participate and contribute, everyone needs a way to actively engage.

—Leticia Britos Cavagnaro

10 The Wordless Conversation

Featuring the work of Glenn Fajardo

Emerging research indicates that building relationships with people from cultural backgrounds different from your own may actually spark your creativity and reinforce your ability to be innovative. (These can be professional, friendly, or even romantic relationships!) But there's a catch: the relationships must be more than superficial. There's a link between the depth of these relationships and the degree of creativity you can derive from their cultural diversity.

Some people have the advantage of working closely with others from a range of backgrounds or living in a diverse town or city. And increasingly, we can form meaningful work and personal relationships online and in distributed professional teams, which opens up the world for many more of us.

In all teams, for effective collaboration to occur, you as an individual must have some basic needs met, like feeling respected, understood, and valued. In internationally diverse teams there are additional needs: you want to know people will be patient with you and that they'll eventually understand you. You need to feel that others won't assume you're not smart because you can't speak their language well; that despite any language or cultural difference, people will work to learn your strengths and weaknesses, your likes and dislikes;

and that you'll all be accountable and responsive to each other.

This is no small feat, so this assignment helps you build and deepen relationships across borders, especially between people who don't speak the same primary language. Use it to launch or deepen new international relationships to lead to deeper connection and greater creativity. You'll need to collaborate with a partner who is from a different cultural background than yours, however you define that difference. And if you're so inspired, you can certainly run this same assignment with folks you know who are close to home.

———

Both you and your partner will need two important communication tools: a smartphone that can take pictures and video, and a messaging app that can send those file types.

Schedule twenty minutes with each other to complete the assignment at least twenty-four hours from when you begin.

You will be sending image and video files back and forth, so be careful about eating up your data on your mobile data plan. Most people will want to use WiFi, if possible. »

Between now and your scheduled twenty minutes with your partner, over the course of one full day use your phone to shoot at least fifteen photos and/or short videos from your regular daily life. Don't worry about looking cool, and don't try to impress. The key to this assignment is to build a real relationship, so consider documenting the following:

Your thoughts, feelings, and responses throughout the day.
Scenes from your life, from morning through afternoon and evening.

Your surroundings and environment.
People and objects you interact with.
Activities you engage in.

Make sure you get photos/videos from different times in your day: five to ten photos and/or videos *each* between 6 a.m. and 10 a.m., 11 a.m. and 4 p.m., and finally between 5 p.m. and 10 p.m. Don't send your partner any of this content—yet.

The more photos or videos you take, the better; you will need a lot to choose from when you meet up with your partner at the scheduled time.

When it comes time for your meeting, you will be ready to have a no-words conversation with each other. There is no need to start a call. The conversation will take place entirely through the photos and videos that you shot.

Do not use any words, and no emojis either. (That would be too easy!)

Here's how the conversation works.

On text or chat, send your partner a photo or short video you shot.

Then within thirty seconds, your partner responds with a photo or video they shot that somehow relates to the photo or video they just received from you.

Then you respond within thirty seconds with another photo or video that relates to the previous photo or video from your partner.

Keep going back and forth, as if you were having a conversation with each other.

Try your best to "listen" and relate to each other. Although there are no words, you are trying to have a conversation. (This is not just about sending random photos and videos back and forth.)

Listening and relating can take many different forms. You might respond with something very similar (they show you their breakfast of eggs; you show them your breakfast of noodles). Or you might respond with something very different (they show you their soccer game outdoors; you show how you felt while being cooped up inside on a rainy day). Don't worry about being perfect or clever. Just give yourself no more than thirty seconds to respond each time.

After you are done with your conversation, take five minutes to write down the following two reflections.

First, how did you feel over the course of your conversation?

Second, what did you learn about the other person?

Share these reflections with your partner (you can talk now!) so you can use them as another way to connect and build your relationship.

———

This assignment is powerful in part because it completely removes any existing language barriers by focusing on a language you already share: visualization. (In a case where any of your team members are visually impaired, flip this into an audio-only assignment, in which you capture interesting sounds throughout the day to communicate the same fundamental experiences: feelings, environment, activities.)

A beautiful way to build on and preserve the output of this assignment in a larger group is for each pair of partners to make a one- to two-minute film by stringing together their photos and video clips in the same sequence in which they were originally shared. Set this tiny movie to music, and you've got a lovely, lasting document of what might have been your very first conversation with your partner. Years later, when you look back on all the creative work this relationship ushered forth, you'll be glad to have an artifact that captures these initial moments of opening up and sharing across cultures.

In addition to deepening human connection, this assignment fosters noticing and curiosity about people's everyday lives. You pick up on details in order to converse during the assignment, and I often see people ask each other about those details afterward, helping build relationships. The format also surfaces both parallels and contrasts in people's lives, nudging you to find both patterns and diversity.

—Glenn Fajardo

11

Favorite Warm-Up Sequence

Featuring the work of Sarah Stein Greenberg

I have large opinions about small talk. Its prescribed blandness confines our first interactions with new people to the safe categories of interests we're all supposed to have in common. Sometimes it breaks down along stereotypical gender lines: sports are supposedly for men, clothes for women; weather for everyone. In my mind, small talk is just about the cruelest way that people have found to bore each other while providing reassurance that we're not a threat to the social order.

Surely there's a better way to connect with our fellow humans!

There absolutely is. And it's essential if you want to shift people's interactions from "politely distant" to "creative collaborators."

Despite our social norms for engaging strangers for the first time, I've found it remarkable what people will share with each other after a relatively short period if you take care to set the conditions well. This bonding lies at the heart of launching effective and open-hearted collaboration.

Here are three creative ways to bring people together at the start of something. You can use them independently or in the sequence given here. And while these

are useful for work purposes, they've also made popular appearances at weddings and other family gatherings.

The activities are deliberately sequenced to start easy and move toward more personal disclosure by the end: small steps to big talk, if you will. You begin by pairing up with one other person (a gentle start for all the introverts). Then you and your newly acquainted partner find another partnership to join, so you already know one other person in the group. You keep these same quartets intact for the final round, which helps everyone reach toward deeper issues to conclude.

The Story of Your Name

Find someone in the room you don't know well and pair up.

Exchange the stories of your names.

You can interpret this prompt in many ways, which is why it works so well and delivers such a wide range of interesting stories. It could be how you came by your name, why you've changed your name, that funny time you were confused with another person of the same name, the meaning of your last name in the mother tongue of your grandparents, and so on.

Share a few of the interesting stories that emerge.

Zombie Apocalypse Prep

Sticking tightly with your Story of Your Name buddy, find another pair to form a quartet with. Now the four of you discuss what unique skills you bring to the entire group in the room that will aid in your mutual survival when the zombie apocalypse hits—which could be any minute.

This is disarming for any group of experts who are used to introducing themselves via their field and past achievements. Instead, this round becomes an opportunity to connect with the surprise sourdough baker, carpenter, or mixed-martial artist in the room.

You'll find that a whole range of unexpected talents emerges. Ask a few people to share with the group as a whole what surprising skills they will now be counting on from their quartet members.

Round Three

Remain in your Zombie Apocalypse Prep quartets, but return to the present and think about your public persona. Taking care that everyone in the foursome gets a turn to share, talk about how you're each seen in your field or at work or school today and how you'd *like* to be seen or known.

This prompt is also intentionally flexible. You might, for example, want to share that you've long been known as the person who gets things started, and you're trying to become known as someone who always follows through. Or you might think about a bigger arc: what's the legacy you wish to have in your community or domain over the course of your life?

Thank the members of your group and say goodbye for now.

———————

Noticing what people share—or even how they (and you) react to these kinds of encounters—is a tremendous asset for you in your creative work. It will support your ability to notice important subtext in all kinds of situations and make you a better and more thoughtful collaborator throughout your life.

I like to use this sequence when I am with a group of people who have never met each other before and will be working closely together, including in classes with students, at global conferences, and in workshops designed to stimulate collaboration for breakthrough scientific research. It works because it builds toward disclosure and intimacy, but without asking too much of total strangers.

12 Interview Essentials

Featuring the work of Michael Barry and Michelle Jia, with inspiration from Rolf Faste

At the beginning of a creative project you aim to discover new opportunities. Interviewing people in depth helps you avoid accepting by default the way a problem has been framed in the past. Developing your skills as an interviewer can help you overturn your assumptions and come up with relevant and potentially innovative ideas by putting real people's needs at the center of your work.

This assignment helps you learn to host a semi-structured conversation, meaning it has clear purpose and is not random. You'll try to learn things about the other person and how they relate to your creative challenge that you can't predict. You won't know precisely what you will discover in an open-ended interview, but you are likely to learn things of critical importance along the way.

When you start interviewing, you might think there's some kind of buried treasure you're trying to uncover. Dig deep enough, and it will suddenly present itself. But just like mining for precious metals, an "extraction" experience can leave your interviewee feeling exposed or taken advantage of and won't yield the insights that are most relevant to your endeavor. That approach is too reductive; without

employing a broad lens, you might find out what someone thinks about different television shows, but never realize they are much more interested in movies and don't think highly of people who are glued to the screen all the time. Instead, your purpose is creative research, during which new connections are made through the exchange of dialogue, and both you and the person you're in conversation with have novel realizations about the world and how you both make sense of it. As you hone this craft, you'll learn how to build a conversational bridge between the topic that you're interested in (usually the subject of your design project) and the way the other person's life experiences relate.

Before starting, take note of any power dynamics that may be involved. The difference between this type of conversation and a more spontaneous one is that you've initiated it for a particular purpose. If it goes well, you might gain a lot of insight, information, or direction for your creative work. Is that a shared purpose or yours alone? If you're a person of status, means, or privilege, what might you do to ensure that you're not taking advantage of someone who has less of these? One example, direct compensation, is below. But you also might consider whether you're the right person to conduct the interview; maybe a teammate or colleague who has greater affinity for these issues should take the lead while you play a documentation or supporting role. Becoming a good interviewer includes pausing when someone else is the right person for the job, not just honing your abilities to elicit details during a discussion. Since this assignment is about conducting a practice interview, identify someone to talk with where this won't be an issue so you can try out these techniques without concern.

This assignment helps you focus on just three important foundations: the behaviors, pacing, and interactions that help you create and hold space for your interviewee to think out loud, the ways you can move the interview along without damaging that "holding space," and finally, understanding—through experience—how the quality of your conversation changes over time.

———————

Plan ahead and find someone who is willing to give you an hour or two of their time. It should be someone you know, but maybe not too well. For me, one of my landlords would be a perfect person to ask for help with this assignment. They are a couple about a generation older than me. One comes from Japan and the other from the US. They have a daughter, a grandson, and a number of very long-term tenants because they are exceptionally kind and caring. I've known them for more than a decade, and while we've talked about many things (difficult neighbors, rent increases, local coffee shops), I've never tried to explore a topic I was working on from one of their points of view. I know I would learn an enormous amount, and I think they would be pleased to help me refine my interviewing skills. That's the kind of

person you're looking for. Once you have an interviewee in mind, follow these steps to plan and execute your interview.

Create the Space

A depth interview usually lasts for one to two hours. It takes that much time to build rapport, follow multiple story threads, embrace moments of silence, and explore all the topics of interest to you. Plan to hold the conversation in an environment where the interviewee is comfortable. You will benefit from their time, so make sure you've thought about what the exchange means to both of you, and decide how you want to honor this relationship. It might be appropriate to offer some kind of compensation, especially in a professional context. In other cases, you could bring a gift.

Because you will need to reach out in advance to set things up, identify ahead of time what you're interested in learning. If you're not working on a specific project right now, choose one of the design challenges from the final section of the book as a practice topic. The *Family Evening Experience* (page 258) is a good one because it's very open ended. Tell your interviewee whether this is pure practice, or if you are planning to use the insights you gain to start work on a real project. Note that you are interested in their life experience and perspectives, that there are no right or wrong answers, and that your plan is to listen and learn.

Envision the Arc of the Interview

It's helpful to use a mental model of the arc of your interview. Think about it as a hike you're taking alongside a fascinating partner. It starts in gentle terrain; at this

early stage, you feel out your relationship with your interviewee, establish a connection, and show your interest in their comments through your body language, verbal affirmation, and explicit appreciation for them. You can't take a shortcut through these foothills. Spend time to build rapport, or you won't get to new or substantive insights later on.

As the path climbs higher into the hills, you gain a greater sense of the landscape around you, and this context will help you better understand the significance of specific examples or opinions from your partner.  The conversation becomes more personal (as long as that feels comfortable for your hiking buddy). You hear some great stories that unfold at length as you walk along together. During this section of your hike, you keep these stories going by asking for more color or by advancing the conversation to new topics.

Nearing the summit of the mountain you're climbing, you pause together to explore some of the emotions that have come up. You look back on the ground you've already covered to see how different parts of the landscape are connected.

As the path descends the other side of the mountain, reflecting on earlier parts of the conversation helps you both make sense of the ideas, perspectives, and feelings that were shared.

As you arrive at the end of the trail, you'll share what stood out to you from the journey and the main things you're taking away. You'll ask if you got it right and what they are thinking about. You hear one or two new reflections that surprise you—a moment where your interviewee shares another idea or reaction that turns

out to be the one that stays with you all the way home.

Color, Advance, or Reflect?

In addition to creating and holding space for your partner, you can toggle between three rhetorical actions: color, advance, or reflect. In our hiking metaphor, these actions are like stopping to admire the detail of a particular scene (color), continuing the hike forward on the path (advance), or pausing to rehash the interesting moments from throughout the trip (reflect).

You already communicate using color and advance all the time with your friends and family: "She did WHAT!? Then what happened?" In an interview the only difference is that you are using these actions with intention. The third action, reflection, requires more technical skill. It's about creating a safe space and then prompting someone to reflect on their own experiences, needs, or beliefs, and it's where much of the new insight that reframes how you think about your challenge or opportunity comes from.

With your chosen topic in mind, write down a few examples of how you might keep the conversation moving.

Color
For example, if you're discussing someone's evening routine, you might get to the topic of dinner. You could hear, "So my favorite food is a baked sweet potato. Well, not like regular baked but in this special way. My mom used to make it when we lived in Texas . . . yeah, that's definitely my favorite food." As you practice, you'll notice opportunities for more color, like "this special way," "My mom used to make it," and "we lived in Texas." You could ask:

"In this special way? What made it special?"

"When would your mom make it?"

"Was this special to Texas in some way?"

Use color questions when you hear something interesting, emotional, personal, or specific and you want your interviewee to talk more about it. This is about taking someone else's lead and following their cues, which is how you fill in the blanks for common color questions, like:

"Can you help me understand what you mean by _____?"

"Can you walk me step by step through how you do _____?"

"Can you draw me a visual diagram of how _____ is laid out?"

"With whom / when / how would you do _____?"

"Interesting! Say more about _____?"

"Tell me about a time when _____?"

Advance

Advancing questions help you bring in something new that your partner hasn't been talking about. It's how you weave in your agenda. "So, we've been talking about your dinner habits, can you describe how that relates to the rest of your evening experience?" Other helpful bridging phrases are, "We haven't yet talked much about _____" or "I'm also curious about _____; how does that connect to what you're saying?"

Reflect

To more deeply explore someone's perspective, reflection questions refer back to statements the person has already made during your conversation. They are so useful—and nuanced—that you can focus just on this one skill in the assignment *Reflections & Revelations* (page 94). For quick practice now, try out a simple variant

in which you check back in on something your interviewee has already said. "Earlier, when you were talking about ____, I heard you implying that ____. I don't want to mischaracterize. How would you say this in your own words?" This reflection question is simply a way to repeat or rephrase something they have said and see if they agree.

Take Your Hike, Slowly

During your interview, don't hurry. This hike is more of a wander than a march. Try leaving a moment or two of silence after someone seems to finish a statement. It's easy to just react when someone's mouth stops moving and pile on your next question. But there's often a powerful difference between when someone stops speaking and when they are actually "done." If you always ask your next question immediately, you miss important moments of recollection or introspection. Almost always, the other person will fill in a silence by continuing their train of thought in an interesting direction. This is part of the skill you need to follow someone else's lead. Not only do you verbally respond to the content they offer, but you also nonverbally respond to their pacing and pauses by holding the space for them to speak further. This is the final goal of this assignment: to notice how the quality of your dynamic and their responses shifts over time. Once you get a feel for how intimate and personal a conversation can become through your ability to create and maintain space for someone else, you gain a fluency with creative research that allows you to act intuitively and gracefully in the moment and worry less about how you are phrasing a question.

At the very end of your conversation, open the door for something new. Ask a question or

two that allows your interviewee to surprise you or lead you to something you didn't anticipate. Two classic ones are: "Can you think of anything else I should know about your views on this topic?" and "What else should I have asked you?"

When you're done, ask your interviewee for feedback. What were the highs and lows of the experience for them? What would they suggest you do differently? What were they thinking along the way that they didn't say?

———

This practice is not easy. When you're interviewing for discovery, you have specific things you want to know relating to your project. Yet you must follow the other person's lead and energy. You'll learn over time how to balance those goals by rehearsing your approach and practicing.

Overall, if you place your focus on becoming a good listener and observer of both verbal and nonverbal cues—even more than becoming a good questioner—your conversations will soar to new heights.

It's crucial to understand the shape or the arc of an interview relative to time. As an interviewer, the stuff you're most interested in doesn't happen until late in the interview, and usually just for a short span of time. There's a period of work you just have to put in; the amount of time spent going up the hill is way different than hearing the revelation at the top. You need to build the holding space before you get to the summit. And that just takes time.

—*Michael Barry*

13 Party Park Parkway

Featuring the work of Dan Klein and Scott Doorley

Great collaboration on creative teams requires psychological safety. To feel safe, you have to build trust, which comes from knowing that the people around you have your back and are invested in your success, and you in theirs. You might all have slightly different priorities, life experiences, and ideally different things to contribute, and knowing more about each other helps you build stronger relationships. Those relationships matter a lot; they free you up to disagree at times about the specifics of the work without anyone interpreting the disagreements as existential threats to the team. This matters for groups beyond the workplace too: a pod of roommates, travel companions, or parents in a playgroup can all use this assignment to build a stronger rapport.

Since trust can't be faked or rushed, you have to create deliberate opportunities to build it. This assignment will give you a new set of tools for using space to invite trust. For example, when you go to a play, the lights are dimmed and the area on stage is designed in a specific way to help you believe in the premise and the action. In a similar way, this assignment uses space and physical dynamics to influence the way people speak with each other and help them feel closer.

You can do this assignment with one or more teams of three to six people when you want to build relationships that enhance creative trust. It requires a small amount of imagination and one person to set the scene during each round of the activity. You don't need elaborate sets or any materials, just a willingness to change your physical position during the experience.

———

Designate one person to keep track of the time. It helps if they give a one-minute warning before the end of each round.

Round 1: You Are Standing at a Party

Stand up with your group. Ask everyone to imagine you are at a pleasant cocktail party or social event, and you're all meeting for the first time.

The topic of discussion is broad: "What do you do?" or "Introduce yourself" both work well.

As a group, you've got eight minutes to talk, so each person gets a short amount of time to describe themselves or what they do to the rest of the group.

You might notice that the conversation stays pretty surface level. People say things like, "I'm a teacher." "I'm a reporter." »

"I come from Baltimore." Most people have a routine answer they use in polite social environments.

Round 2: You Are Sitting on the Ground in a Park

Now ask everyone to imagine that it's later that night. You've all hit it off at that party. In fact, they've closed down the venue! You decide to walk to a park to continue the conversation.

You sit down on the ground. Go ahead— actually sit on the "park" ground.

Use another eight minutes for the round, but shift the conversation to an unusual question: discuss how you think other people see you. Remember to sound a one-minute warning before the end to make sure everyone has had a chance to speak.

At the end of the round, you need to stretch your imagination further. It turns out that you've been sitting on someone's private lawn this whole time, and they've politely asked you to leave. Someone in your group offers to drive everyone home, but there's a catch—they've got a very small car. Nonetheless, you all pile in!

Round 3: You Are Sharing a Tight Space

For this round, rearrange yourselves so you are sitting as close together as possible (though you do not need to physically touch). The person in the room closest to the light switch should turn it off, so the lighting is similar to how it would be if you were driving around late at night. Add a little drama: maybe the car has gotten a flat tire, and while you're waiting for the tow truck, you have the final stage of your conversation huddling together inside the car because it's too cold to stand outside.

Now the conversation is about how you want to be seen . . . who you really are.

So how do you want to be seen? Set the timer for eight minutes again, and let each person in turn talk. When the timer goes off, turn the lights back on.

Often in this exercise the group will ask to have the lights turned back off. Everyone usually wants to keep going.

Finally, wrap things up with a debrief.

How did the experience go for everyone? What did you notice?

Make sure everyone has an opportunity to verbally process what they experienced.

There's something magical in the transitions that happen in this assignment: from standing to sitting to being in a small car. They offer new layers of depth for the interaction. You will see and feel a shift in the room when you say, "Sit down and talk to each other at the park." People just go into a different mode. Their body language changes. Then when you all get yanked off the lawn and thrown into the tiny car, people reach a whole other level.

Establishing lasting trust takes time, but you'll be surprised by how much trust you can begin to build through these intentional interactions.

Creating a shift in how people interact with each other, how they are arranged to interact with each other physically, supports the personal engagement you're hoping to usher forth. For any experience you design, think about how you want people to behave and feel, and then design the space to support that behavior. In this assignment, you can draw on different resources to effect the shift in dynamics that you want between rounds 2 and 3. For example, with some groups you can ask people to get under a table or sit under an archway to feel more like they are in a small car together.

Many people get stuck in routines because their space isn't designed to be flexible. But even in the most formal conference room, you can shift the dynamic and alter how people relate to each other in that space. The easiest trick? Remove all the chairs.

You can do this too on your own: redesigning your work space to shift the way you are working can be surprisingly powerful.

In all my experience playing this game, people are mostly taken aback by how quickly they get so deep. I haven't had anyone say "That was too much." And I'm thoughtful about what groups I run this with.

For instance, I wouldn't do it with a team that I was trying to convince to do new things. But I would do it with a team in any kind of organization that was already on board with the idea of trying things differently. I'd do it at the first class at the d.school, because there's an earned reputation that things are going to go differently there.

—*Dan Klein*

14 Maturity, Muscle, Variety

Featuring the work of Nicole Kahn

Design is for everyone—and also, it takes practice. To Nicole Kahn, repetition and persistence yield the hard-earned qualities that distinguish her as a skilled designer compared to someone starting out. It's not just raw talent.

What are your beliefs about the essence of creativity and design? Where does that essence come from? Is it something you're born with, something you can develop, or a combination of the two?

Think about the people in your life who you consider to be creative.

What sets them apart from others? What do they do differently?

What do maturity and muscle mean to you in the creative work you do?

How could you expose yourself to greater variety in order to build these two skills?

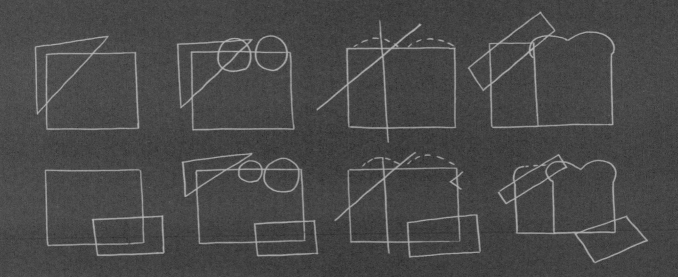

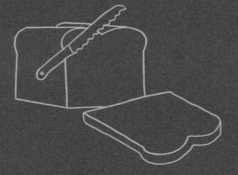

Here's the dirty little secret, friends…

There's nothing revelatory about design. It's very intuitive. There are people, they have needs, we make guesses. We build something for them, we put it back in their hands. We learn from that, and we iterate.

The only difference between me and a total beginner is maturity, muscle, and the variety I've seen.

—Nicole Kahn

15 Empathy in Motion

Featuring the work of Susie Wise

You are an expert in your own life and context—but no one else's.

Yet striving to understand what's important to others is a big part of design (as well as all the other relationships in your life). When you prioritize human needs, you often get better outcomes than by simply designing around a shiny new technology or what someone in the faraway head office thinks might be effective. Understanding others is the type of work you never finish and you never perfect, but nonetheless you always aim for. The process of working toward understanding becomes part of your toolkit if you are willing to go on a journey and learn what opportunities arise.

This work calls for humility. It's not a simple poll to see what people want, nor a patronizing exercise in superficial listening. It's a dynamic process of connection, curiosity, and collaboration, in which you change course over and over as you encounter feedback and new perspectives.

In many situations, designers have more power than those who will wind up using or living with the results of the design work. You've likely experienced this when the education level, affluence, health, or social capital you have or represent is greater than that of the community in

which you are working. Without consciousness of these dynamics, you can miss the mark in understanding the community's needs. The community may then feel it's being misrepresented or exploited, or you may implement solutions that harm rather than help.

Even when you are part of the group that will live with the impact of the design work, you still should approach the situation with humility. For example, if you are a veteran working on a project to help other vets navigate the mental health offerings at the VA, your experience may differ radically from the experience of those who need the most help. If you're a former classroom teacher who now creates curriculum for others, you may have blind spots when it comes to how teachers or students from a different race or ethnic background might experience the same piece of content.

This assignment offers one way to start actively shaping the bigger picture of the relationship between you and the ultimate owner of the creative work. It's part of designing your design work. This approach will help you get to interactions that are much more dynamic and collaborative than a creator-muse relationship. In this loosely structured activity—which you can do before an important project meeting, research session, or workshop—some people will bring design or facilitative expertise, and others will bring the expertise of belonging to that community or having experience with the challenge at hand.

———

Plan to spend time together with the people you are creating with and for in advance of the "work" phase of your relationship. Specifically, arrange to travel together to the location where you and a community stakeholder will be working together on a project.

Where feasible, choose public transportation. This assignment is most useful when there is a power differential between the two people, and in this case, it should be set up so that the person with the lesser structural power knows the path to the bus or train. This helps balance the power. It creates an opportunity for empathy in motion.

Situating this assignment during transit is deliberate: you're often side by side, instead of face to face across a table or other barrier. Instead of the heightened dynamic of one person staring, listening intently, and recording the other's words, this arrangement is unscripted. Just like talking to kids while driving in the car, it can be a disarming moment. It is about both getting to know the other person and starting to build the relationship while taking the power dynamic into consideration.

Even if you are not working on a formal project, you can use this approach to build a deeper, more two-way relationship with someone. Travel to a PTA meeting together with another parent from a different part of town. Plan to carpool to a weekend religious service. Your goal is to experience side-by-side travel in a way that highlights the contextual intelligence of the person who might be seen as less "expert" in your pairing by conventional standards. Be very sensitive to how you ask this person to join you, and get clear on your motives—to spend some time together and build a more equitable relationship—before you suggest it.

When I've used this assignment where I live in Oakland, California, the community members are the people who actually know how to navigate around the place. The more traditionally privileged design students working with them are less capable and have less relevant expertise. Lived experience offers tremendous value, and this activity reinforces that.

A big part of design is humility: you have to embrace the idea that even though you can make things, there's still a lot you don't know. We all need ways to practice that and remember what it feels like from time to time.

—Susie Wise

16 What's in Your Fridge?

Featuring the work of Lia Siebert

How do you know where to get started with a complex topic? And, if you've been working on the same issue for a long time, how do you inject some fresh perspectives through an individual, human lens?

This activity helps you see something familiar in a totally new way, through someone else's eyes.

It has a lovely side benefit, too: when you use this kind of opener among people who know each other, almost always you hear things like, "I learned more about you today than I learned from having the desk next to you for five years."

This assignment is a great twenty- to thirty-minute activity for pairs or groups.

Introduce yourself to a partner by sharing a photo of the inside of your fridge.

This may feel a bit uncomfortable at first. What might your partner see in your choices and habits that you don't often reveal to others? What do you see in theirs?

Use this assignment to practice your skills of close observation.

What do you notice about your partner's fridge? What might you infer about your partner as a result? If you need a place to get started, look at the two pictures side by side and compare their similarities and differences.

Ask "why?" a lot. You know you're doing well if you start to hear family stories, embarrassed laughter, pride, fears, hopes, or rituals. Anywhere you sense some emotion is a good place to pause and discuss further.

This activity has many possible starting points. Besides the fridge, other good candidates are pictures of your bathroom cupboard, bookshelves, car trunk—you get the idea. The trick is to select something thematically related to your work that's more personal than you would generally show a stranger, but not so private that you can't get people talking.

I was inspired to create this warm-up activity by the work of artist Mark Menjivar, who photographed different people's fridges all around the world. The images were surprisingly intimate, even if the owner of the fridge wasn't pictured. For the shift worker, for the hunter, for the family who lived down the block from a supermarket . . . they all looked remarkably different.

The original inspiration helped me launch a project with people from the health care sector focused on childhood obesity. I thought getting straight into talking about food norms and habits might be difficult. What people think they should do is often very different from what they actually do. In that gap lie important insights about beliefs, values, barriers, challenges, and motivations. Once you get people talking within this gap, you reveal many opportunities for creative solutions. This simple assignment gave the group many insights about human behavior that they took with them throughout the course of their work.

—Lia Siebert

17 Expert Eyes

Featuring the work of Susie Wise and Melissa Pelochino, with inspiration from Alexandra Horowitz

Your brain is constantly making short-cuts to help you process the immense amount of information perceived by your eyes, ears, and other senses. It ignores some things and rapidly interprets other things. It's just trying to give you the most helpful information at the right time, which makes a difference if you're hungry or scared. This helps you move through the world efficiently. But the efficiency comes at a cost: you develop habits and get stuck in ruts of thinking and noticing. Your beliefs, your previous experiences, your pace, and even your cognitive load at the moment all affect what gets through the filter and the conclusions you draw as a result.

To work more creatively, you want your brain to be able to wander down new pathways. You need to take in information that helps you get beyond your regular perception—and you want to train yourself to do this at will.

This assignment helps you adopt multiple lenses as a powerful way to open up what and how you perceive.

Walk around the block for twenty minutes or so. This could be anywhere: your neighborhood, a farm, a bowling alley, and so on.

Draw what you see in a notebook.

Repeat this exact same walk three or four more times and ask someone with a different expertise to join you each time. Being an "expert" can mean many different things; you just want to be with folks whose discipline has trained their eyes in a specific way. Try a civil engineer, an artist, a landscaper, a historian, a transit worker, a community volunteer, or a small business advocate.

Ask your expert to talk aloud and tell you what they notice. Each time, sketch what the expert sees.

Afterward, compare your original drawing, the one you drew when walking by yourself, to your subsequent drawings.

What new and varied details or insights are there? How has your perception of the area shifted?

This assignment is the ultimate way to consider how multiple stakeholders add meaning and insight to a problem space or opportunity. You might even see how assumptions about people and places get in your way of learning more about where you are.

One time I walked the block with a landscape architect. He pointed to a tree and showed me how you can tell that there's drought damage, and he pointed out all these forces that you'd never notice in a million years that shape the landscape and affect people. We both noticed a crack in the sidewalk, but I just walked by it, and he had tons of things to say about it.

—Susie Wise

The Journey
from Not Knowing
to Knowing

How often have you asked a kid in your life, "What did you learn in school today?"

It's a natural question we've all uttered hundreds of times, perhaps delighting but more likely aggravating our nieces, nephews, and neighborhood kids, or our own children. When we ask what someone has learned, we're usually referring to the knowledge—or *stuff*—they're collecting. *Stuff* is content and facts or procedures to do something concrete like make tenses agree or handle an improper fraction. Very important, although just one part of the picture. Next time you start to ask the "what" question, instead, try out *"How* did you learn in school today?" Thinking about the *how* starts to bring us into the world where we also hold up and value the process of learning.

Learning is the critical skill for our always-in-flux modern era. It's what helps you face unexpected, unpredictable challenges. But a habit of focusing on the *what* reveals how frequently we ignore learning itself as a specific skill to acquire. What gets learned is very different from how we learn something . . . and the next thing, and the next thing, and the thing after that. If the *how* is less considered, it holds us back from flexing our full abilities as learners.

The good news is that there are approaches you can draw on to help round out how you think about learning. In addition to more *how*-oriented approaches—like Carol Dweck's growth mindset and Linda Darling-Hammond's work on all types of inquiry-based learning—design offers everyone another way to learn. At its most essential level, *design is a process of learning in action.* The powerful way that design helps people to be learners may even account for the accelerating demand for people to become familiar with design in business, education, and all kinds of unexpected fields like law, science, and government.

Academics are getting a handle on how people learn, but for most of us, it's still a mystery. We just know kids do it naturally. A toddler who knocks over a bowl of cereal is performing a physics experiment to investigate gravity. And when she does it again, she's performing a complex psychological experiment to test her caretaker's reaction. And again, to examine the sociology of the family unit in response to repeated stressful stimuli. And again, possibly just for fun or to show everyone who's actually in charge.

Kids are super learners; they notice and seize opportunities for learning. They experiment to generate new data, then interpret that data and repeat their experiments to build on the initial basis of what they've learned. They perform these activities in a complex social environment rather than a sterile abstraction of one, and they engage in learning on a "need to know" or "want to know" basis. It is mind blowing.

Once learning becomes more formal, results vary. We've all been in a class that felt too fast or too slow, too big or too small, too theoretical or too applied, even if that same class was working well for the person in the next seat. From personal experience you know that one size or shape doesn't fit all. But even if you know what doesn't work for you, do you know your own shape of learning? Can you describe it? The contours, the irregularities, and the volume, not just the outline? If not, can you discover what learning looks like to you?

Matt Rothe, who teaches design to spur innovation in sustainable food systems thinks so. He uses the following short, powerful assignment to help his students find the answers to these questions. Try it out.

18 Learning How You Learn

Featuring the work of Matt Rothe

Identify several learning moments in your life—at school, at work, at home, while traveling, and so on—when you gained a deep understanding or insight. Think of moments that were really impactful, that you really enjoyed, or that, in retrospect, were turning points.

For each moment, write down five attributes of the experience, like where you were, who you were with, and what was happening.

Look across this set. What patterns or themes do you notice? Form a hypothesis for why those experiences led to these powerful moments of learning.

Finally, think about how you can use that hypothesis going forward to help you achieve your goals. Can you recreate those conditions? Can you use those insights to be more selective about the opportunities you have to advance your own learning?

Matt says this is the single most impactful assignment he gives. It becomes the foundation for transforming the experience of education from one of passive consumption to a posture of active experimentation. That's the shift from fixed knowledge to continuous learning.

This is a design mindset, one that assumes the world around us is currently imperfect and that we can be resourceful and inventive in a way that improves our own experience and that of others. Adopting this mindset gives you the agency to build up your own capacity to meet the demands of the future. And as the world continues to change around you, you'll gain strength not just from what you have learned, but also from how you are learning.

Put more urgently: right now, the world needs you to adopt this mindset and help us all get better at learning how to learn. A common refrain in the early twenty-first century is the observation of how fast the world is changing, how many new technologies and social forces are shaping our lives, and how hard it is to keep up. By definition the future is always uncertain, and it's ever easier to feel a heightened sense of unease and confusion about what your hometown, your country, or our planet will look like in the next few years, months, or even weeks. The methods of design are powerful tools for learning more when the answer is unclear.

In an era like this one, we all need the ability to adapt, to be resilient, and to be creative and generative even when we are uncertain. This is a moment when seeing ourselves as designers can help us the most. It's not enough to know how things have worked in the past; we must be open to creating a dynamic future.

Design itself has evolved over the past century to arrive in a new form at this moment, hopefully just in time. Most people think design is just about the creation of physical objects; it's also much more. The foundational tools of design are now widely applied to making new experiences, systems, and even ideas. It's a broad "just get in there and solve problems" kind of field, combining a range of tools for learning to confront new challenges without preexisting solutions.

For example, several years ago a former d.school student, Alex Lofton, hatched an idea for how to make it easier for young people to afford to buy a house. This was informed in part by the financial constraints that he and many of his peers were experiencing in their late twenties and early thirties. The initial concept was an online platform where friends and family could pool many small contributions and support the prospective home buyer in exchange for a little piece of ownership of the home—sort of a Kickstarter model for property purchases.

As Alex and his team built rough prototypes and shared the idea with other people, they uncovered many different challenges to their original concept, and they began to converge on a more targeted need and group. They became determined to find a way to make it more affordable for educators to buy a house in expensive markets where they have a hard time living on a teacher's salary in or even near the same (expensive) community where their school is located. The solution became more specific and robust, and the concept more mission-driven. In 2015 Alex and team founded Landed, a company that directly helps essential professionals like educators and health care workers afford a down payment through a shared equity arrangement and provides services to help them navigate the daunting home-buying process.

Or take the story of Gina Jiang, another d.school alum who is a doctor based in Taiwan. Despite the advantage of working in a health care system that offers both affordable and high-quality care, Gina works to address the problem that doctors do not have enough time to spend listening to individual patients in Taiwan's busy hospitals. She set up a space for creativity and collaboration—the very first local patient experience and innovation center—which "makes time" for patient care issues that might otherwise be overlooked.

Opening a physical and organizational space revealed unexpected opportunities, including an idea from one wound-care nurse with a long-term patient who, it turned out, had been making custom ostomy bags for other patients. These bags (used by people who have had an often lifesaving surgery that changes how their body eliminates waste), were comfortable, could withstand Taiwan's heat and humidity, and helped prevent ostomy hernias. But this patient had never before shared her ideas and approach. Gina and her team worked closely with the nurse, patient, and manufacturers to develop a new version that could be produced on a much larger scale and also met the goal of enhancing the dignity of patients who used them. Critical to Gina's process were some of the same tactics included in this book: creating journey maps to carefully document the highs and lows of someone's day and deliberately instilling fun and humor in the dynamic of the creative team while working on a challenging project.

You may not yet have heard of these two exceptionally creative, dedicated people, but they are using their creativity and design skills to make meaningful work happen in fields as disparate as real estate and health care. They exemplify the core design behaviors of inventiveness and resourcefulness, as well as empathy, experimentation, and being mindful of how their process affects their outcomes. In both Gina and Alex's cases, they set out on their design journey without knowing all the answers or even all the right questions. And this is the same behavior that has been described as a key to the success of some of design's biggest luminaries, like Charles Eames.

Eames; his wife, Ray; and many of the other designers at the Eameses' studio were often beginners on the topics they tackled (as in their long-term relationship with IBM during the early days of computing). However, they produced exceptional work in part because they were insatiably curious and incredible at learning about new things. They had a type of confidence that comes from knowing you can tackle a problem you haven't seen before.

Design is now being used to tackle many types of problems that no one has seen before, because the fundamentals of design help you learn quickly. The parallels between design and learning are starting to be investigated formally, but you don't need to wait for academic confirmation to know that this feels right. As you continue to develop your practice, you'll find yourself increasingly adept at taking on challenges of all kinds and sizes. You too can become known for being equipped and willing to dive into uncertain challenges whenever they come along.

Richard Saul Wurman, an architect, graphic designer, and prolific creator of ways to bring people together with new ideas, described Charles Eames in the following way, hinting at the expansion of design's relevance to all of us in a fast-changing world with many unknowns: "You sell your expertise, you have a limited repertoire. You sell your ignorance, it's an unlimited repertoire. [Eames] was selling his ignorance and his desire to learn about a subject. The journey from not knowing to knowing was his work."

The journey from not knowing to knowing is every design project in a nutshell. It's the design story of the founders of Noora Health (see page 7) and of Jill Vialet (*Unpacking Exercises,* page 126). And it can be your story every time you face a problem without already knowing the answer. Through design, you may even discover that no one has yet asked the right question. What is discovery? It's yet another word for learning.

Developing your design abilities is a new way to think about *learning,* and this approach can grow with you for the rest of your life. At this moment in history, it's vital: so many people, communities, and organizations need better, more human, more ingenious approaches to address the needs that face us and our rapidly changing contexts. The assignments in this book can help teach you how to meet those needs with creative confidence. You may not always know exactly what to do, but you'll know how to figure it out. That's how design can help, even on the occasions when your world turns upside down.

Learning *how* to learn is *the* fundamental ability you need to thrive in our dynamic century. It's at the heart of every assignment in this book: philosophies and ways to approach the world with an inquisitive, open mind; to frame opportunities to change things; to make your ideas tangible and testable in order to learn what's possible.

The philosopher Eric Hoffer said, "In a time of drastic change it is the learners who inherit the future. The learned usually find themselves equipped to live in a world that no longer exists."

Let's be learners. Let's be designers. Let's inherit the future and do everything we can to shape it for the better.

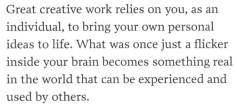 Identify, Acknowledge, Challenge

Featuring the work of Chris Rudd

Great creative work relies on you, as an individual, to bring your own personal ideas to life. What was once just a flicker inside your brain becomes something real in the world that can be experienced and used by others.

But lurking around those flickers and sparks are lots of unconscious biases that you may not mean to express or perpetuate. Social constructs affect all of us and permeate our thinking. This assignment helps make those constructs visible, so they don't accidentally influence the work you put out into the world. But it won't leave you feeling helpless; it gives you a chance to actively challenge those narratives or biases and fuel your work in new ways.

You can practice this on your own or do it as an assignment with a group of people working together.

Start by identifying the specific groups affected by your work. Name at least ten. Groups may include people of various backgrounds based on race, religion, physical ability, ethnicity, nationality, affluence, sexual identity, gender identity, and many others. For example, within the broad category of race you might name "Black people," "White people," and "Indigenous people" as three different (though still quite broad) groups. Devote space on a board or wall to each group identified.

Next, write down all of the assumptions and stereotypes you have ever heard or are aware of for each group. Some will be positive, and some will be troubling to name. They won't all be consistent with each other. Put each one on a separate sticky note. Remind yourself and others: these aren't indications of your beliefs; the goal is to surface the stereotypes floating around in the culture.

Now start to manipulate this data. Take any positive stereotypes and move them to the top of each board. Move negative stereotypes to the bottom; keep neutral comments in the middle. This visualization aspect is key. You won't get the same results if you don't externalize the data and make it observable.

Pause to reflect on how you feel—and how anyone else in the room feels. Ask some questions. How do these stereotypes (both positive and negative) show up in your context currently? How might this show up in the way you do your work? How do they show up in your solutions and designs? Next, use the insights from this reflection to create an open-ended "How might we?" question and lay the groundwork to find a path forward. For example, you may have landed on an insight that

when you're interacting with a person who uses a wheelchair, you've assumed that they automatically need your help with certain things. Though difficult to acknowledge, that very productive insight indicates a bias that would affect anything you designed that someone in a wheelchair might encounter.

Some "How might we?" questions you could develop include:

How might we learn more about the real needs of each person whom we encounter?

How might we start by understanding a person's strengths, not their perceived weakness?

How might we understand what a person in a wheelchair experiences in the environment in which we are designing?

The crux of a good "How might we?" question is that it doesn't already contain a solution, which leaves you room to come up with many and then decide which ones are worth pursuing.

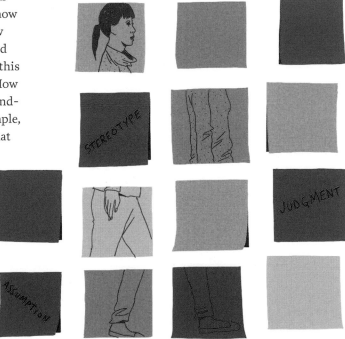

Take your "How might we?" questions and come up with some ideas for solutions and tools to improve your work by identifying and addressing these biases.

End with a reflection. You know the exercise has gone well if you feel or hear others using words like "empowered" and "hopeful."

This assignment is all about uncovering negative assumptions and unconscious bias. I'm from Chicago, where it's super segregated. Being an anti-racist also means being an integrationist. I'm always trying to figure out ways to incorporate integration into design. I just truly believe that if we're going to have a civil society, we have to be together.

I created this activity because many of my students are international, and the narratives they hear from the media or in their home countries says, "Don't go south of a certain part of that city because it's dangerous." And now we're asking them to go there to do their design work. I know they've been clouded. But how can we design for people if we think negatively about them? We need a way to get our biases out.

One time I ran this exercise with college counselors who were trying to improve their services. The prompt was to identify assumptions about the students they work with. When the data visualization was complete, Black and Latino students had a lot of negatives, very few positives; White students had a lot of positives, very few negatives. And transgender students had only negatives, despite this being a pretty progressive and younger group of folks. I know they don't feel negatively toward trans students, but the counselors could not think of one positive stereotype to say about this group, which was kind of telling. As a result, the counselors started to really focus on the trans students they worked with.

Another group of counselors created a self-reflection tool for evaluating racial bias that they planned to use right after sessions with students. "Was I influenced by this stereotype? Did I say something that might have unintentionally conveyed it to that student?" With a good reflection tool, they believed they could start to plan for better interactions and counseling from the start.

If you're doing this assignment with a group, be intentional with your language when giving instructions.

For example, to set the context of the activity, make an opening statement like, "We live in a racist system," then invite the participants to discuss. People really tune in to the word system, because it requires them to think about their role within it and whether or not they perpetuate, ignore, or disrupt the system. This statement is the right framing for the work I lead in Chicago, but you may need to set a different context where you are.

Remember that no one should attribute the assumptions and stereotypes to anyone's personal beliefs. The activity helps expose dominant narratives in society and shouldn't be taken as "this is how I feel." Without attending to this aspect, you'll find that people are too self-conscious and afraid of giving offense to get much out of the assignment.

—*Chris Rudd*

Practicing Metaphors

Featuring the work of Nihir Shah, with inspiration from Jane Hirshfield

In creative work you routinely venture into the unknown. You make big leaps to figure out what your work will do, look like, or feel like when it's done. Can you get good at describing where you're headed even before you fully know it yourself? You can! And reaching for a metaphor can point you in the right direction. A metaphor serves as a cognitive bridge that helps you leap ahead but still feel like you're standing on familiar, solid ground, not hovering precariously in thin air.

Metaphors allow you to experience or understand one thing in terms of another. In a beautiful short video called "The Art of the Metaphor," poet Jane Hirshfield notes that if you've ever felt like you were *drowning in paperwork,* you've done more than simply describe a large volume of documents; you've offered a visceral feeling of the experience. Metaphors help you think with your imagination, your feelings, and your senses all at once. Here's another one: *it's raining cats and dogs* conjures an image of torrential downpour and perhaps even the smell of damp fur or the sound of hissing felines.

Metaphors are more than just colorful language to describe something already known. You can also use them to express emerging ideas or come up with new perspectives on complex challenges.

This assignment helps you use metaphors to understand the problem you're trying to solve or to define the opportunity for your creative impact. (There are many other ways to creatively use metaphors: check out *The Solution Already Exists* on page 114 to work with metaphors to come up with ideas, or *Tell Your Granddad* on page 181 to use metaphors to communicate abstract concepts.)

You can do this entirely on your own or with a group of people to develop common language around the thing you're trying to discover together. »

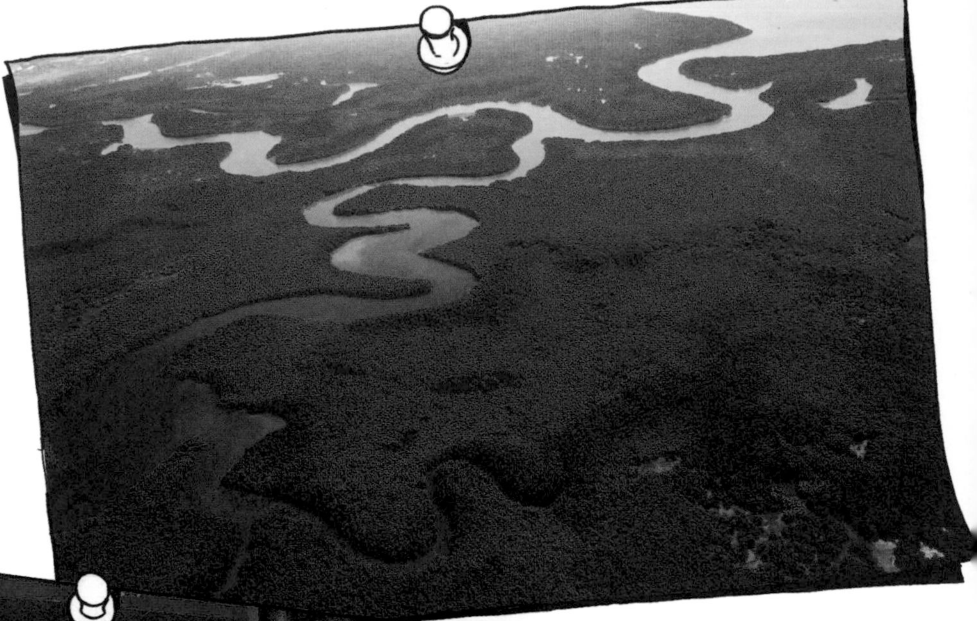

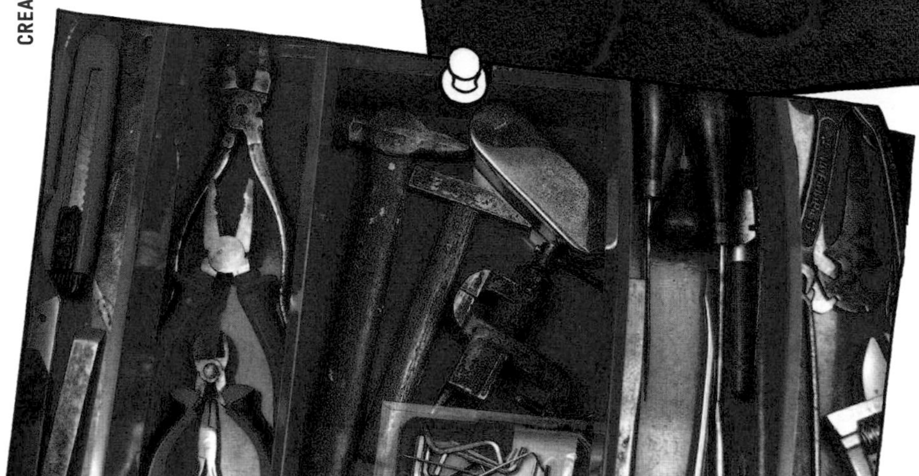

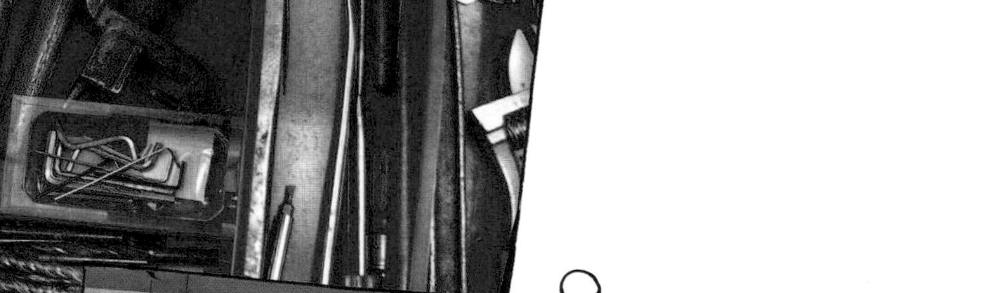

Think about a challenge that you are currently facing in your life or work. Look at the photos opposite and pick an image that captures the essence of your current problem in some way.

If you're struggling, try picking the image—or metaphor—that:

Best captures how you feel about the current situation

Best captures how you want to feel (or want others to feel) after you've designed a solution to the current issue

Seems like it's the closest to what your intervention or design might be like

Once you've chosen an image, start by making a list of as many different parts of the system or object as you see or can imagine. For example, for the airport, you might list lots of different jobs and roles, like pilots, food service workers, and baggage handlers; types of equipment, like engines, trucks, and conveyor belts; types of experiences, like delays, anticipation, earaches, fears; and types of formal and informal relationships, like concessions contracts, gate allocations, and seatmates. This list barely scratches the surface; each of these illustrations has been chosen for its richness and the huge array of interactions it can describe. Potential metaphors abound; if another one comes to mind, feel free to use that one.

Now try to connect the different components on your list with the aspects of the challenge you're working on. In your world, who or what is represented by the pilot-copilot relationship or the experience of watching your luggage disappear after you check it? What would you want those elements to represent in your solution? You might find yourself immediately connecting the dots: *Oh—I know exactly what that endless line at airport security represents*

in my project! or you might have to push yourself by methodically going down your lists and making connections. Do this for fifteen to twenty minutes, making as many connections as you can.

Then step back and ask yourself three questions:

What new insights do I have about the challenge I'm addressing?

What new ideas do I have about the types of solutions I need to consider?

How can I use parts of this metaphor to more easily describe what I'm working on?

———

Bringing creativity to any challenge involves looking at it differently. Metaphors are a quick and easy way to look at something through a different lens. And they help you organize fuzzy thoughts into a familiar frame. If you're ever feeling stuck or overwhelmed by the ambiguity of the challenge you're trying to address, thinking with metaphors will help the different tumblers fall into place as you strive to unlock the problem. Metaphors can also inspire you to build solutions based on deliberate, positive models. What would it be like if walking into your doctor's waiting room felt like walking into a coffee shop? How about an auto repair shop that takes care of your car the way a spa takes care of you?

If you'd like to build your own set of metaphors to use in your work, just look for images of systems. Ecological and natural systems almost always work well, as do transportation hubs, collections of objects, or highly designed experiences (like the circus, a fancy hotel lobby, or a professional basketball game). Print these images and make a set of metaphor cards you can use in your current and future work.

21 Direct Your Curiosity

Featuring the work of Eugene Korsunskiy, Kyle Williams, Bill Burnett, and Dave Evans

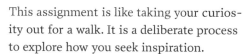

This assignment is like taking your curiosity out for a walk. It is a deliberate process to explore how you seek inspiration.

It's helpful because these days you can get inspiration from just about any corner of the globe, and that's a lot of input to make sense of. You may feel like you're constantly missing out on something incredible. You need a way to shut off that little internal voice crying *FOMO! FOMO!* by giving it something better to focus on: inspiration that really lights you up and fuels your creative fire.

Discovering just what does it for you is what this assignment is all about. Use it any time you're feeling overwhelmed by too many options for what to pay attention to or, the opposite, whenever your well of inspiration has run dry.

This activity takes about thirty minutes. You'll need a notebook and a pen. Go to a museum, a mall, a bookstore, or any place with a lot of objects to interact with and look at closely.

Walk around until one object draws your attention. Attend to that object for a moment or two. What is it about this object that you find interesting? It could

be the form, the colors, the materials, the scale, how a subject like gender or food or sport is depicted, and so on.

Write down one aspect of the object that jumps out at you and what you like about it. Then go wandering again and look for an object with this same characteristic.

Hang out with the new object and just be with it for a couple of minutes. Write a few notes about what's interesting to you about this one. Maybe you came for the bright colors, but now that you've spent some time, you're getting excited about the interplay between smooth and rough textures. That's your next mission: go wandering and find something with *that* characteristic.

Keep going. Make six or seven jumps, each time pausing to think about what draws you in. What is it about each object that calls to you?

Once you're done, reflect.

First, you've created a mini-catalog of visual values that you're drawn to. That's very useful to know! Second, think about how you normally act in a museum (or mall, bookstore, and the like). If your answer is something like, "I feel like I should be enriched culturally, but I just

wander aimlessly," how was this different from how you typically navigate?

Here's the big follow-up question: Is this experience a microcosm or metaphor for anything else you're navigating? A challenging project you're working on now? A relationship? Your experience in your new job? In what way is that new job experience like the one you just had?

Maybe your other experience has some parallels, like aimlessness, or hurriedness, or feeling unsure. How can your new insights about what stokes your curiosity help you take more control and focus your attention in your current situation? What did you love about the assignment experience? Where else in your project/relationship/job can you find things that share that characteristic?

––––––––

This assignment is designed to give you a visceral, tangible way to learn how to get more out of an experience, not by actually cramming more in, but by being intentional.

A museum has a ton of stuff. You can't see all of it in the thirty minutes allotted for this activity. This creates a situation of imposed scarcity. You are then guided through a process that provokes insights about your own practices of exposing yourself to new things, whether that's deliberate or random, and how that makes you feel.

With intentional curiosity, my hope is that people can use what they learn to become less anxious about their trajectory. And that they can invoke and feed their curiosity in deliberate ways.

—*Eugene Korsunskiy*

Remember That Time . . .

Featuring the work of Dan Klein, Patricia Ryan Madson, and improvisers everywhere

To come up with novel, compelling concepts, it helps to build on the ideas of others. An idea that is bouncing around between two or more brains might just be cooler, weirder, or more insightful—all good things that put you in the position to consider a wide range of potential solutions. This process requires you to listen and then respond, as opposed to just generating new ideas internally and then saying them out loud.

Too often we forget to follow each other. Maybe it's when you want to be a hero and come up with the "best" idea. Maybe you just don't want to be seen to misinterpret, go too far, or look silly. Whatever the cause, you can train yourself to harness the cognitive magic that comes from connecting things together in unexpected ways.

This assignment is like doing a few reps of the most fun mental exercise you can imagine. Do it right before you launch into a brainstorming session or any moment when you want to be generative. It will help you understand how to achieve a core principle of creative collaboration: building up ideas rather than cutting them down.

This activity requires a partner.

Round 1: Agree to Disagree

With your partner, pretend that you are old friends who always disagree about details. While using your imagination, "recall" an activity—a fake shared memory. It can be boring or exciting; the only rule is that you can't say something that you have *actually* done together. One person starts off: "Remember that time when we . . ."

> *. . . got coffee?*
> *. . . went to the bodega on 5th Avenue?*
> *. . . couldn't find any Band-aids?*

The other person says yes, but disagrees about some of the details.

Go back and forth, adding to your shared memory, but continue to disagree. "No, that's not true at all." And sometimes,

"Oh yeah, I remember. But it was not quite like that."

Keep the fictitious memory going for a minute or ninety seconds, and then cut it off.

Round 2: Agree to Agree

It's the same game, with the same partner. But now, miraculously, you wholeheartedly agree about everything. Whatever your partner says is exactly right.

If you catch yourself disagreeing, just say, "Oh no, wait, you're right. I forgot. We did get kidnapped!" or whatever it is. It's important to make your partner look good in your shared fake memory. It's made up, so you might as well make them into a hero.

Keep round 2 going for a few more minutes.

Now compare the two rounds. How did you feel about round 1 compared to round 2? »

You've likely just experienced several types of interaction: full-on blocking, when someone flat-out disagrees; partial blocking, when someone negates part of an idea (a partial block is still a block—it shuts down a channel of creative energy); and accepting, when someone starts building on your ideas. Did you feel genuinely excited and enthusiastic toward your partner when they kept agreeing with you? That's the wonderful contagion of positive energy, and the goal is to have it spread throughout your work.

You might feel you know this principle cognitively, but experiencing it creates a kind of embodied knowledge that helps you notice and correct your own bad habits. It helps you make more space for others. Nothing constrains the flow of ideas more than faltering confidence after someone is blocked, so make it your number one job to make your partner feel good. In this part of creative collaboration, it's not about you.

Awareness of blocking and accepting is valuable far beyond brainstorming. It's useful any time you need to be constructive with someone else. A lot of creative conflict happens when one person is blocking while another is trying to accept and explore. Being able to see this while it's happening is an ability that will help you succeed with minimum friction, whether you are trying to come up with the best new widget at work or trying to decide which couch to buy with your roommate.

This activity is one of my favorite ways to help people feel and understand that how they respond to others is just as significant as how good they are at generating ideas themselves.

—Dan Klein

The Monsoon Challenge

Featuring the work of Jim Patell and Scott Cannon

Preparing to take on a big creative challenge is exciting. It requires stamina, resilience, and a tune-up of the specific skills required by the work at hand. It can be useful to wake up the behaviors you'll need over the long haul by doing a short, intense starter project before you dive into the main event.

This challenge was created for people designing in resource-poor settings, but it can be useful to anyone on a budget who needs to push their level of resourcefulness to the limit. It's an ideal first project for a new team, because it helps you learn quickly about your instincts, strengths, and blind spots. For many, it also gives a quick taste of failure that reinforces how essential it is to prototype and test your work before it has to perform for real. Plus, you get to get wet.

This assignment was created and first taught in 2005 for the course *Design for Extreme Affordability.* It is described here by David Janka, who experienced it as both a student and an instructor. Ideas for how you might adapt and run the assignment yourself appear at the end.

The goal was simple, as were the criteria for winning against the other teams: collect the most "rain" during a simulated monsoon, which was actually a sprinkler mounted on a ladder. Each team would set up their device and have five minutes to collect water while the sprinkler was running. The measurement was basic: a collection bucket with a ruler stuck straight down to read the number of inches. The designers had less than a week and a team of five to design the device. The members of the team were from all different departments and backgrounds, and the assignment helped everyone meet new collaborators and observe how everyone in the group worked in depth.

Each team received $20 to cover prototyping expenses. The hard-and-fast rule was to spend no more than $20, but we encouraged students to spend no money if they could find or reuse whatever materials they needed. The time allowed for analysis and preparation was minimal. The intent was to (gently) force the students into full-scale prototyping mode, using readily available materials: duct tape, PVC pipe, zip-ties, plastic sheets. Students *would ingeniously come up with a world of additional parts because everyone had to just jump in and go for it.*

A clear pattern emerged: some teams planned, sketched, and discussed, but didn't actually build their device until competition time. By then they were stuck with one set of materials and a concept. Teams that quickly started building and testing with actual water got much further along, often iterating on their original ideas dramatically. This turns into an incredible lesson, of course, because some of the solutions would fail catastrophically! People tend to forget how heavy water is. They'd build elaborate funnels and use tarps to collect the water, which would then pool in a corner and cause the entire structure to crash to the ground. You can easily discover this, but only if you test your idea. Building and testing is the quickest way to find out what you don't know.

One year, a team used a whole bunch of umbrellas as a kind of drainage system. They went to restaurants and bars and asked if

there were any umbrellas in the lost and found they wanted to get rid of. They collected a few dozen umbrellas and built their contraption. They placed some umbrellas upside down with holes and other umbrellas right side up to distribute the water across many vessels. They did not get first place, but they were the winners in my mind because they were resourceful and creative about the materials. I knew this would serve them well going forward in their bigger projects.

We also saw really boundary-pushing solutions, like when a team used the $20 budget to buy beer for a road work crew that then used their crane to bring in a bunch of equipment that the team adapted to build their monsoon catcher. On Monday morning after the assignment was over, the road crew craned all the equipment back onto the road.

It was amazing to see students come up to speed in an unfamiliar domain much more quickly than they thought they could. Every year at the end of the assignment the course leader, Jim Patell, would give a short, inspiring speech: "Today we saw many different approaches. A few succeeded to varying extents, and many failed. Of course they did. We gave you seventy-two hours and twenty dollars. But having seen these attempts, you all now know that if we gave you another go, you could crush this challenge."

—David Janka

You can adapt this assignment for many different contexts and skill levels.

To replicate it fully, divide a group into teams of four or five, and give each team a few days and $20 to build a device to catch as much sprinkler water as possible in a five-minute period. Host the group in a rural location or parking lot, and hold the competition at the end of that week.

Allow sufficient time for the teams to set up their devices; ideally you can divide up your space so that each team has a dedicated area and everyone sets up at once. Run a hose with a sprinkler attached to the top of a ladder. It's even better if you have more than one, so that you can easily move the hoses and sprinklers around the lot to the different prototypes, as this will save time. Determine who will judge and how they will gauge how much water has been collected. (The winner may be very obvious, but if not, it's good to have an agreed-upon method.) You may find that the competition element melts away, and that's fine: it also works when teams cheer each other on.

Have the teams go one at a time by running a sprinkler for exactly five minutes. After all the teams have had their turn, declare the winner!

As a group, reflect on what made for a successful device, and what failed. Then shift the conversation to your process. What did the more successful groups do differently from the others? What new strategies for prototyping or group collaboration will you bring into your next project?

If you have limited time, budget, or participants, you can easily run this as a solo project, competing against yourself by building a few different prototypes. If you don't have a yard or sprinkler, build your devices and wait until it actually rains. Or you can scale it way down by using a shower instead of a sprinkler and build mini-devices.

If you live in place that is dry or experiencing drought, you can alter the specifics of the challenge but keep the structure. You could have everyone build a device that can transport something heavy between two points, or retrieve objects placed inside a large area of dirt or grass without physically stepping inside a marked perimeter. Get creative so you don't waste water in a place where it is not abundant.

24 ABC Sketching

Featuring the work of Ashish Goel, with inspiration from students at the Nueva School

When you and I are chatting, we both have ideas in our heads. Our words are creating more ideas, also in our heads. When communicating with spoken language, you are creating dual concepts—at least one in each person's brain. They might be similar, or they might not. That willow tree in your mind might be a palm or a redwood or even a family tree in mine.

If our ideas are fundamentally different, it skews our understanding of what we're discussing. You and I might each misinterpret a lot of what the other is saying.

Drawing, sketching, making chicken scratches—whatever you call it, representing your ideas in a physical form is incredibly helpful for clearer communication. When you draw something, the idea moves out of your brain and into someone else's with less chance for it to drastically mutate, helping you avoid misinterpretations and wasted time. As soon as you visualize something externally, you know what you're working on together.

Adults are oddly scared to make something visual in front of others, but if you can draw the alphabet, you've already got some basic sketching skills. A great way to get started with visualizing is by sketching stick figure people, and this assignment helps you turn the alphabet into every form of person you'll ever need to draw.

There are lots of resources out there to refine your drawing skills if you've already got the basics. This assignment is for taking your very first steps.

———

Letters of the alphabet are great building blocks for drawing stick people. Don't even think of them as drawing.

Start by writing your name in the middle of a sheet of paper. Use whatever pen or pencil you want. Then write each letter of the alphabet three times, all upper case.

Do the same thing with all lowercase letters.

AAA   BBB   CCC
LLL   OOO   ZZZ
WWW   ddd
UUU   ooo

Okay! You're ready to start combining letters (and a few other strokes) to form the basis of your stick people. Here are a few Z people and U people:

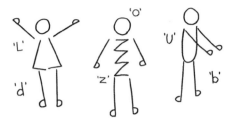

You're about to bring your stick people to life and get them to do things.

Look in a mirror. Get into the pose of a confused person. Or an excited person. A person on the phone. How about a person in love? Look at the shapes your body is making each time.

Look back over your alphabet and pick a letter that resembles the body shape you were making, or draw a new shape based on what you saw.

Now that you've practiced a bit, assign yourself a mini challenge to use your new skills. Over the course of the next day, find three moments to communicate something visually that normally you would express verbally. Add a few instructional stick figures to the family chore board at home, sketch a little message of thanks to a friend and snap a photo of it rather than sending a text, or make a visual shopping list.

———————

If you routinely practice your drawing, it will become second nature, and you will find that the more you complement writing with visuals, the more people will tune into and remember your ideas clearly.

I learned this brilliant technique from a group of fourth graders who once visited the d.school, and I've never needed another one.

—*Ashish Goel*

25 Reflections & Revelations

Featuring the work of Michelle Jia and Michael Barry

There are often inconsistencies or gaps between the story we tell about ourselves and our own behaviors and beliefs. For example, I am likely to tell you that I'm a pretty healthy eater. After all, I've been a vegetarian for most of my life (a preference I will readily articulate). These things together are a story I have about myself. But if you observe me closely or have me write a food journal, you'd see that, on many days, I eat more bread and cheese than vegetables. That's actually not so "healthy." So what have you learned? Since you're not my doctor, the details of my diet don't matter much, and if they are self-reported, you still don't know if they are factually true. But now you know that the idea of being a healthy eater is important to me. It's how I want to be seen. That is an implicit need, and it has bearing on why I might make certain choices. If you were to try to design anything for me in the areas of food, diet, or even overall health, the knowledge that being seen in a certain way is part of my identity—a trait potentially shared by many others—would be crucial.

When you design, you are constantly trying to understand why. The better you grasp the desires, interests, and needs of others, the more likely you are to create something that will meet those needs. Explicit needs can be recognized quickly because they're on the surface and are often addressed by making things easier to use or find. Implicit needs, like my desire to be considered a healthy eater, are invisible to the naked eye. It is easier to observe what people do than to understand why they do it. You can witness the actions people take and hear what they say, but you cannot see their motivations or what they think or feel. What drives human behavior is hidden; even our own actions, decisions, preferences, and beliefs can be hard to understand. But if you can sense them, you'll be better able to reframe a problem and come at it from a new direction: one that matters to the people whose needs you're trying to meet.

This assignment helps you learn how certain questions take you beyond basic information so you can start to understand the "why" beneath the surface. Although you can't just inquire about these deeper whys, you can ask many questions that are "why adjacent." What you encounter at the surface are specific behaviors and spoken preferences: people can tell you step by step what happened or what they did, and they will talk freely about what they like and dislike. This is a good starting point. Hidden inside these stories are beliefs or attitudes that are difficult to express in words. These stories are deeply grounded in how people find meaning and make sense of the world, and their personal values.

Having a repertoire of questions that helps you uncover implicit needs can be useful to you whether you want to be more effective at creating things for other people or simply to be a better friend, parent, leader, or teammate. You want questions that leave room for interpretation, give someone space to think out loud, or provide the opportunity to organize ideas in a new way. However, the magic is not actually in the questions themselves. It's all about how well you've created and maintained space for and trust with the person you're speaking to. For that reason, this assignment has a prerequisite. Make sure you've spent time trying out the fundamentals of interviewing in *Interview Essentials* (page 56) before you work through this assignment.

This will help you develop reflection questions that you can use during an interview aimed at discussing the larger context, meaning, and implications of someone's experiences or actions. These questions serve as a metaphorical mirror in which someone else can examine their own comments or views, reflect on what they see, and engage in sensemaking. Sometimes the questions provoke emotions and reactions or yield previously unstated beliefs, which in turn may result in catharsis. Because of these possible outcomes, the questions are valuable (and appropriate) only toward the end of an interview when sufficient trust has developed between you and the person you're talking to. The understanding you've gained during the earlier stages of the conversation gives you the context to understand the later responses; without that context, you won't know how to interpret them.

Getting at implicit needs is the key that unlocks so much potential for creativity and change. But people often perceive a direct "why" question as a personal challenge, resulting in a fight or flight response. You need ways to redirect challenging why questions into reflective ones that result in compelling stories.

In this assignment you'll find five categories of reflective questions, listed in order of increasing difficulty. This means you need higher levels of trust and rapport with your interviewee before you ask the questions further down the list. »

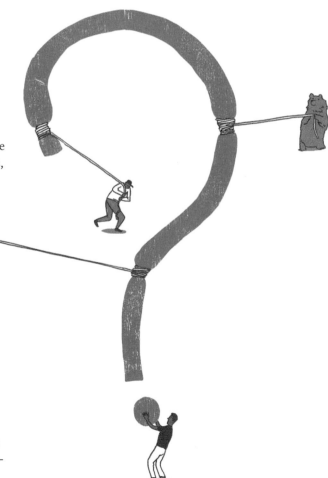

For each question below, write down how you'd adapt it to an interview on a topic of your choice. If you aren't currently working on a project that requires this, imagine that you are tackling *The Haircut* (page 254) design challenge. Each question includes examples to show how you might think about adapting it for *The Haircut* assignment. After that, it's up to you to flex your ability to craft new questions within that category.

Characterization

These questions encourage your interviewee to examine previously unremarkable things or ideas in detail, describing their distinctive nature and a personal relationship with them. Asking someone to organize their world often reveals the difference between your (or the existing industry's) way of thinking about segments or categories of offerings versus how people really experience things.

What are the ways to characterize all the different stylists you've had?

How would you categorize the range of haircut experiences that are out there?

Which category is your preference and why?

You can always end a characterization question with, "And where do *you* fit in all this?" to bring it back to a personal place.

Projection

Typically you should avoid asking someone to speculate, especially about impossible-to-know details like, "How much would you pay for this if it were available in the future?" The abstract predictions people make don't accurately indicate what they will do once the concrete situation arrives. One exception is using a question to foster a suspension of disbelief. This helps someone put themselves into a different context and speculate how things work for others.

How do you think other busy moms deal with this haircut conundrum you're describing?

What do you think would happen if no one in your office could get a haircut for the next year?

What do you think I will think about that?

Projection is a safe way for someone to explore and try out different judgments or perspectives, and then you can bring it back to their own opinions.

And is that true for you too?

Clarification

Clarification is a softer way to approach "why" questions. It is particularly useful when you've noticed a generalization or a contradiction in what someone has said. For example, a clarification question could help you help me untangle my "healthy" eating habits versus aspirations. In the context of a haircut interview, you could try:

Help me understand why you think none of the barbershops around here are good?

What exactly do you mean when you say, "too fancy to believe?"

These questions help you go deeper—not to gather more detail, but to get at personal beliefs. You can always try these with a very humble opener, like, "I know this sounds like a dumb question, but . . ."

Labeling

This type of question can land badly, so use it with caution. But when solid trust exists, you can use labeling to give explicit voice to your interviewee's emerging thoughts or feelings and run it by them. Good labels take a form like:

It seems like . . . you're pretty uncomfortable getting your hair cut by someone of a different gender.

It looks like . . . this topic is making you anxious. How are you feeling right now?

It's very important when labeling to use a third-person voice, which is neutral. Avoid saying, "I think you look upset," as this subtly puts you above the other person.

Challenging

The final category is the toughest. Use questions like these carefully even when you have a very good rapport. Challenging questions force a reexamination of an explicit situation, belief, or excuse.

It's hard to believe that you "just don't care" about your appearance, given what else we've talked about.

Why do you let your daughter pick out your stylist?

Challenging is tricky because you are using judgment yet need to come across as nonjudgmental. But this category is worth attempting under the right conditions because it sometimes results in epiphanies, both positive and negative.

After you've written down a few examples for each of these categories, try using a few of them during your next long discovery interview. Remember that while you're learning, it's perfectly fine to say to someone mid-interview, "I've got a few more questions and I may fumble them a bit. If something doesn't land well for you, please stop me at any time."

————————

An important mindset to bring to conversations like these is the idea that people make sense. Their decisions and behaviors are governed by their worldview, needs, and past experiences. Judgment or preconceived ideas you bring to the conversation will get in the way of you trying to understand. Set those notions aside while you're engaging people this way because these types of questions lead to conversations that are more than data gathering. You

must be ready to hear new things and be changed by them. Your direction and creative point of view may be altered by a deeper appreciation of how others see and experience the world. You could discover something that matters more to people than the goals you have for your work, which causes you to stop and take stock of your process and aims.

Be sure to capture your interview in some way. Recording on video or audio or having a second interviewer serve as a scribe are all great approaches depending on the situation. You want to be able to deeply listen and react in the moment; having a way to record the discussion will help you stay present and engaged.

Over time, I've started taking visual notes. It came from a desire to give back in the moment because the information from an interview like this is such a gift. I take the notes on index cards and it's usually a little caption of something the person we were interviewing said with a few important words highlighted. At the end of the interview, my interview partner and I go through all the notes with the respondent. I hold up the cards and say, "This is what we're taking away, and I want to make sure we're representing your experience authentically. If there are any corrections, please let us know." We also have them pick two cards that strongly resonate with them, and we mark those as the most important. We save fifteen to thirty minutes for this interaction. It's a key part of the interview. We don't want to get the data wrong, but even more, we often learn new things because even if they confirm that what's on the card is accurate, they often share more detail that shows us what was actually missing. It's a really powerful tool and it makes me feel good about what I do. Sometimes people ask to keep those cards. It's like you're giving them the knowledge they synthesized in the moment.

—Michelle Jia

26 The Girl on a Chair

Featuring the work of Michael Barry, with commentary from Adam Royalty

Finding the most meaningful opportunities for your creative mind and skills involves thinking about all the different problems or needs that might be present in a situation. Often the first problem you spot has a pretty easy solution. Can you learn to see beyond the obvious?

Beloved by many generations of students at the d.school, this short assignment will help you learn to analyze a situation and think more deeply about what needs might be lurking beneath the surface.

Use it when you want to tune up that part of your brain that needs to think critically about whether the problem you're working on is really the challenge you ought to be tackling. How you frame the challenge is often why breakthroughs happen; changing the frame changes your whole direction.

———

Look at the image on the opposite page.

Ask yourself, *what does this girl need?* You might have a number of different answers: *a ladder, a Kindle, shoes, a teacher.*

For most people, everything that comes out initially is a noun.

Nouns tend to be solutions. If you decide she needs a ladder, you're kind of stuck with that.

Try again, but this time generate needs that are verbs. *This girl needs to _____.* Needs that are stated as verbs keep more potential for innovation and creativity open. Some examples: *she needs to reach, to learn, to know.* Try to come up with at least six more needs.

Pick one of the verb needs and ask why that need exists. This might help you speculate or infer an even more fundamental need, for which a solution might help someone on a profound level. This is just a thought experiment, so don't hesitate to really go for it and use your imagination, even though you don't know anything about this girl. If you picked "to learn," your why could be: *she's a really curious kid, she wants to show off for her older sibling, she's not challenged in school,* and so on.

This *why* level may illuminate an issue in the broader context, not just for the individual girl. Follow the thread and envision a few different solutions you could test to address one of these deeper needs.

Now try this exercise again from the beginning with an image of your own: from today's newspaper, a magazine, or the scene outside your window right now.

———

When you push your analysis to get to a deeper why, you start to approach what we call "implicit" or "latent" needs. These are rarely expressed explicitly by someone, but they often exist at a deep level of emotion and motivation. Striving to understand people at this level helps you reframe what might at first appear to be a simple problem into a more powerful area where your creative efforts can make a bigger difference.

Because it's not always possible for someone to explicitly connect their own actions (standing on a chair to reach for a book) with a deeper need at this level (not feeling challenged in school), you are in the uncertain realm of inference. Treat these inferences lightly. Do not fall in love with them—you are quite possibly wrong. Instead, reflect your thinking back to a person you are designing for or with, or build a prototype solution that speaks to this

need. If your person responds positively, you might deepen your conviction that you're moving in the right direction.

The English language in particular is saturated with nouns. Other languages, particularly non-Western languages (like Mandarin Chinese), are richer in verbs. So it can be very important for primarily English speakers to think beyond the language-based frame of "needs are nouns." Thinking beyond nouns often leads to a more interesting set of solutions later on.

This is a classic way to sharpen your capacity for reframing a problem. I use it often, even with experienced designers. I want everyone to remember that they need to push beyond the obvious to get to deeper insights. Ultimately, that ability is inside all of us, if we're conscious about pushing ourselves to use this approach.

—Adam Royalty

27

How We Are

Featuring the work of Barry Svigals

Barry Svigals is an architect and sculptor who has worked closely with communities that have experienced trauma. He's best known for leading the redesign of the Sandy Hook School in Newtown, Connecticut, following a mass shooting there. Barry's words are a reminder that your creative process changes your creative output and that your process isn't just the steps you take, it's how you personally engage with the work and with others along the way. If you're not joyful or inclusive or collaborative, your work won't be either. You can never hide the traces of yourself and your way of being: they always show up in your work.

Think about something you produced recently.

How did you feel and act while you were creating it?
What traces of yourself and your way of being showed up in that work?
What traces do you want to preserve and what traces do you want to change in your next project?

How we are is what it becomes.

—*Barry Svigals*

28 Bisociation

Featuring the work of Hannah Jones, with inspiration from Arthur Koestler

Many people love to brainstorm; it's a widely used ideation technique that, when done effectively, leads to a broad range of ideas. Tutorials for how to brainstorm well are readily available, including the basic rules, how to get started with good prompts, how to regulate the energy of a team (if you're working with one), and how to develop and select the best ideas that are generated.

But don't get stuck thinking brainstorming is the only way to generate new ideas. This assignment is a great addition to your routine. Even experienced brainstormers need a palate cleanser sometimes: a break to inspire and invigorate their thinking. This activity is perfect for that moment when the energy starts to wane and the pace of idea generation begins to falter. It is a fun way to practice making spontaneous, creative leaps.

Arthur Koestler's book *The Act of Creation* inspired this assignment. Koestler coined the term "bisociation" while writing about creativity in the mid-twentieth century. It combines ideation (coming up with new ideas) with synthesis (connecting two previously unrelated things). The activity is a good way to help train your brain to challenge the regular boundaries between apparently incompatible frames of reference, which helps you come up with bolder, more novel ideas.

You can use this assignment on your own or with a group, any time you need a way to (literally) mix it up.

————

Pick a moment in your process when you've already come up with a lot of ideas but the energy and concepts need a boost.

If you're working on your own: Out of all the concepts that you have generated so far, choose eight or ten ideas (any even number works) and write them on separate cards or scrap paper. Turn the ideas so they are face down, shuffle, and create random pairs.

Turn the first pair right side up. Set a timer for ninety seconds to create a third idea out of those two cards that somehow draws on the two original ideas. This is a bisociation, in which you bring two seemingly unconnected ideas together. Our instinct is often to search for commonalities across our individual ideas; here you are explicitly encouraged to play with the differences.

The new ideas can be fanciful or crazy, constrained only by your imagination. Ninety seconds go fast, so be impulsive! Capture your third idea on a new card.

Keep going with ninety-second efforts until you have exhausted all your pairs, and then go through the ideas and cluster them, creating a few super bisociations. Can you even link all of the ideas together in some way? If so, congratulations. Your bisociation muscle is strong!

If you're working with a group: Start by having everyone choose two or three ideas from the original ideation session, and then line everyone up in two rows so each person is facing a partner. Ask your partner to randomly pick one of your cards, and then you pick one of theirs. All the other pairs in the room do the same thing, simultaneously.

With your partner, read your two cards out loud, and then take ninety seconds to come up with a bisociation together. Capture your pair's third idea and add it to a nearby group pile or box. Keep going until you've used up all your cards.

Share the new concepts that have come from each pair and do the final clustering and super-bisociation step together as a group.

The new ideas that come out of this practice aren't necessarily meant to be put into development. Experiencing this assignment helps you change the way you look at something for a while so that when you go back to it, you might see it from another perspective and with some fresh energy.

————

This assignment is a way to cross-pollinate ideas (and people) and to help you free up your thinking. It's a chance to break away from trying to solve the problem and to express yourself in a very rapid and imaginative way without worrying about where it is going to go.

The rules of brainstorming are meant to break down hierarchy and power dynamics, allowing even the most junior person on the team to contribute to the ideas being generated. However, sometimes you need a more radical way to collapse any power dynamics in a group. This is one such way. The playful structure and rules mean that people can't be precious about their ideas, but everyone is being acknowledged. As a member of the group or its leader you can encourage the tension and awkwardness inherent in uniting two very different ideas in order to help people get to something completely different or new.

29 The Secret Handshake

Featuring the work of Dan Klein and Lisa Rowland, with commentary from Ashish Goel

Before you can collaborate with someone else, you need to be comfortable with each other. You need to connect on a human level.

This assignment is all about quickly creating the conditions for collaboration. You are trying to accelerate the bonding process by changing the inherent social contract between the people in the room. You are going to have to (1) stand up, (2) interact with each other, and (3) be silly. Everything about this is different from the way we "normally" act as adults. By breaking social norms, you open up space for new norms to be created, ones that foster closer connection, trust, and vulnerability.

This assignment is an opportunity to model courage, energy, joy, or whatever the new norms are that you want to see in your work and those you work with. Seeing a model and then personally practicing that behavior gives people a bodily experience of what it's like to be in a creative culture.

Use this assignment to introduce new collaborators to each other for the first time or reignite an old group with a new spark.

First, imagine a shared scenario that happened in the past. Address the group to set the stage with something like: "Remember how, when you were in school together, you and your best friends had a secret handshake?" Any fictional shared setting that conjures a little nostalgia works, like growing up in the same neighborhood or working the same job as teenagers.

Next, you and a partner create your secret handshake. It helps when someone gives an example or you look one up online; professional soccer players are great inspiration. You just need a model of a goofy handshake to get going—the more elaborate the better. It's important that you model

the behavior you want the participants to show.

Invite the members of your group to pair up and create their own secret handshake that is unique to each pair. Give them one minute to make and practice their secret handshake with their partner to be sure they've got it down. If you have an odd number, a group of three works fine.

Then say, "Individually, go to different spots all over the room. Imagine that you have graduated, and it's been years since you've seen your partner. You are at a class reunion, mingling around, and you see each other. As soon as you see your long-lost friend, break into the secret handshake."

Pause, so they can migrate to different areas.

And then yell "Go!"

Everyone will start to slowly gravitate toward their partner. Then the whole group erupts into a physical movement that engulfs the room.

At the end, you can ask a few pairs (or everyone, if you have time) to show off their secret handshakes.

————

This assignment is a good reminder that playfulness opens us up. Even if you're working on your own, you can think of ways to bring a little playfulness or humor into your own work every time you sit down. Maybe it's a favorite cartoon you read, a daily sketching exercise, or a dance move you do right before you settle in.

This is one of my favorite activities because it creates a sense of community between everyone in the room and between each pair of individuals. Co-creating a goofy secret helps people feel a sense of connection to each other. You'll even see people doing their secret handshakes later on.

It also works because you are being stupid as a group and stupid individually. It's structured stupidity!

And that's so important in creative work: you are being playful—even silly—with intention. A playful atmosphere allows novel ideas to emerge because it is an environment where judgment is not present.

—Ashish Goel

30

Map the Design Space

Featuring the work of Carissa Carter, Megan Stariha, and Mark Grundberg

Almost anything you design these days is part of a broad landscape. Take your smartphone. It's easily recognizable as a designed *object:* a nice shiny physical thing you can touch and hold. But that's just one layer. Inside, it's got lots of different materials and technologies that make it run. It has an operating system and constantly updating software. Streams of data flow invisibly through it every day. It's connected to a platform that determines what kinds of applications are allowed on it. It helps you have wonderful experiences like documenting your daily life with photos and listening to music nonstop or paying a parking meter when you're nowhere near the place you left your car. And it contributes to many serious implications for society as a whole, like increasing isolation and depression among teens, in turn fostering new ideas like "digital detox." All of these layers contain many examples of different types of design work.

Despite a vast, almost unlimited canvas, when you set out to put your creative skills to work, you're still most likely to think about making things that fall into more traditional categories: products or experiences. How can you push yourself right at the beginning of any new project to consider the whole landscape?

This assignment helps you identify a wider array of opportunities for design across the layers of data, technologies, products, experiences, systems, and implications that make up the totality of any one thing, whether you can see them immediately or not. You can use it to expand your field of vision, thereby spotting new opportunities you might want to focus on in that landscape. And you can uncover new connections or implications that help you orient your skills and time toward the things you care about the most.

Plan to spend thirty to forty-five minutes exploring a topic of importance to you. It could be based on your work or something closer to home, like your own experience as a student in a school or that of your kids. To try out a practice topic, read any of the design challenges in the final section of this book—such as *The Haircut* (page 254), *Thirty-Million-Word Gap* (page 259), or *Post-Disaster Finance* (page 266)—and use one of them as an example to work through.

With the d-shaped map shown here as your guide, draw a larger-scale version of it on a board or a big piece of paper.

Prompted by the word in each layer, think about how your topic shows up in each layer of the map. You might be naturally drawn to start in one of the layers in the middle—and that's fine. Most people find it easiest to begin with Products or Experiences. Use whatever sequence stimulates your thinking the most. You don't need to go in a set order, but be sure to respond to all of them. Toward the end of the allotted time, step back and make sure that you haven't left any category blank.

Implications (positive, negative, intended, unintended, predicted, unexpected): *What societal changes or phenomena do you see?*

Systems (platforms, movements, schools, governments): *What systems are connected to your topic? What systems make the things in the other layers possible? What problems might be related to these systems?*

Experiences (events, spaces, moments, feelings): *What are some known problems with the current experiences? Hypothetical opportunities?*

Products (digital, physical, form, function): *What physical or digital products are part of the current experiences?*

Technologies (emerging, essential, standalone, integrated): *What technologies are currently used in the landscape of your topic? What's needed? What's missing?*

Data (sources, algorithms, big data, qualitative data): *What types of data might be available that are related to your topic?* »

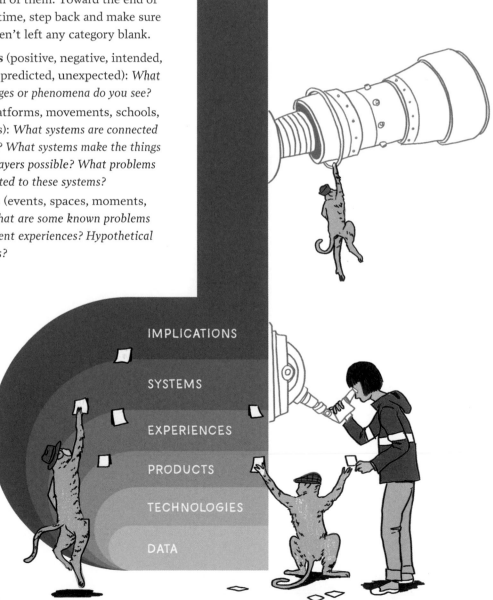

IMPLICATIONS

SYSTEMS

EXPERIENCES

PRODUCTS

TECHNOLOGIES

DATA

On sticky notes, write down as many examples as you can for each layer of the map, posting them directly on the map as you go. For most layers, you'll be able to come up with ten, twenty, or even more. You might find yourself coming up with things that existed in the past, are current phenomena, or might happen in the near future—all of these are fine.

Now that you've populated the map with many examples, reflect on two things: framing your work and thinking about implications.

First, imagine you could work on anything. Think about all of the new or unexpected places that you might focus on that could bring new value or a fresh approach to designing within this space. What intrigues or inspires you? What are nontraditional ways to apply your creative skills within this space? What more do you need to learn to move forward? If work constraints limit or proscribe what you can focus on, can you use your new insights about how these layers connect to start a conversation about a more holistic approach that's within your mandate? What would have to be true in a different layer to make your current work most successful?

Second, now that you have thought more about the upper layers of the map, what implications are happening or could happen that concern you most? Excite you the most? How can you orient your own creative efforts going forward to drive toward the future of this topic that you most wish to see?

This assignment is a jumping-off point for you to recognize how interrelated all of these layers are and to realize that design applies to many issues within each one. Everywhere there is design, there are values and choices to be made. Each time you work on something creative that sparks change, you're changing things in multiple layers at once. Even the tiniest project or application of your creative skills has implications or makes a ripple. You can be quite powerful!

Revisit your map from time to time as your work progresses. The more you know about your topic, the more nuance you will see in the relationships between different elements and layers and the more easily you'll be able to navigate the design space you wish to be in.

31 Rock Paper Scissors Tournament

It's possible that nothing pumps a group full of energy quite as much as the rowdy, warm-hearted competition in this assignment.

So widely used that no one can remember who first started playing it at the d.school, this magical warm-up has you locked in an intense battle with a mortal enemy and then, ten seconds later, becoming a full-throated supporter of that same enemy. A parable for our globally challenging times if ever there was one, it's also a subtle reminder that it's possible to 100-percent support your team members if a decision is made in their favor, even if you disagree with or oppose their ideas.

Mostly, though, it's just fun, loud, and the type of barely controlled chaos that everyone should get to enjoy from time to time.

Try this assignment to wake people up after lunch or to break up a long day and inject some fresh energy.

This activity requires a group of any size, from ten to a thousand.

Everyone in the room finds a partner. Your partner is now your opponent. Each pair plays Rock Paper Scissors (also known as Roshambo).

Face each other and speak the name of the game ("Rock! Paper! Scissors!") on each count by raising your playing hand in a fist and swinging it down on the count. After the final count ("Scissors!"), both of you "throw" by extending your hand to each other in the form of either Rock (a closed fist), Paper (a flat hand), or Scissors (two fingers in a sideways V shape).

To score the round:

Rock breaks Scissors.
Scissors cuts Paper.
Paper covers Rock. »

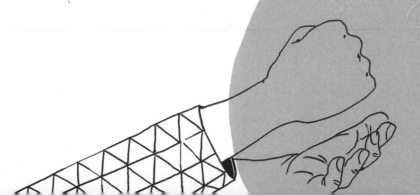

After playing for the best two out of three rounds, the loser of the duo becomes the winner's biggest fan. They holler, cheer, encourage, clap, stomp, and yell the winner's (their former opponent's) name.

The winner finds another winner to play, and their biggest fan follows, rooting for them all the way as the tournament proceeds. As the number of winners gets smaller, the number of cheering fans increases.

By the time there are only two remaining players, each with roughly half of the room cheering passionately for them, you've staged the most remarkable inverse of a mob you can imagine.

————

When the tournament wraps, everyone is beaming as they return to the task at hand.

32

First Date, Worst Date

Featuring the work of Carissa Carter

Many people lack experience building their ideas in a physical format. If this describes you, you may be hesitant to try it, or even skeptical that you can do it or that it will be valuable to your design work. But this is not something you should just leave to engineers or already-skilled craftspeople. You can unlock new ways of thinking when you get comfortable working with objects as a regular part of your creative process.

We call this "thinking with things." Handling things, making things, and externalizing your ideas all help your creative work in a few crucial ways. These actions provide inspiration and emotional satisfaction that you're getting your ideas across, and they even expand your cognitive reach by allowing your ideas to temporarily rest outside of your brain.

This assignment is an unexpectedly fun and disarming way for you to try expressing your ideas using one of our favorite materials. Working in a tangible format with the most basic tools helps you build more complex, serious prototypes later on. Over time, you'll get used to using a wide range of physical materials when you're working creatively.

Make a pile of maybe twenty-five to thirty LEGOs. Don't worry about the exact number.

Using just those LEGOs, make a model of the worst first date you've ever been on. Don't steal more LEGOs! Challenge yourself to work within the constraints of your materials. Give yourself a specific time limit, like eight or ten minutes. Time pressure can help you get unstuck if you have a slow start.

This is a really fun activity to do with a friend or a team. In that case, share your model with a partner and explain all the details. Then you get to hear about theirs.

Somehow, absolutely everyone has a funny story within this theme. Sometimes they are romantic dates, and sometimes not. These stories are even more humorous when built out of LEGOs. People represent their dates in a range of ways. Some people show a scene. Some make an object that was part of their date experience. Others build a mosaic about how they felt during the date or an exaggerated metaphor: the date was like scaling a sheer cliff face that would never end!

This assignment takes you to a different place than the usual verbal storytelling experience. When you bring in a physical medium to support storytelling, it puts you into an "I can make something" mode. As you refine your skills and explore other materials, you'll grow increasingly able to tap into that capacity, regardless of what you're designing.

33 The Solution Already Exists

Featuring the work of Matt Rothe

As a kid you were probably taught that stealing is wrong. (And it is, most of the time.) But the following saying is also true: "Good artists borrow. Great artists steal."

The world just loves to tease us with contradictions.

Don't shy away from building on others' ideas when it comes to your own work. When you try to come up with new concepts in isolation, you're unaware of what's already out there and your ideas are less likely to be new. Rid yourself of the myth that creative genius is a solo act of conjuring original thought from thin air. It really doesn't work that way.

A stream of ideas is all around you, if you know how to look. This assignment helps you seek relevant inspiration when faced with a creative challenge and encourages you to steal the ideas of others in just the right way.

Use this exercise when you already have a pretty clear idea of the problem or opportunity you're trying to address and are starting to think about solutions. Just keep in mind that the solution (or some piece of it) already exists.

As you might have guessed, the idea at the foundation of this very assignment already exists too! To dive deeper, check out the work of Kirby Ferguson in the video series *Everything Is a Remix,* or read the books of Austin Kleon, who offers lots of practical advice for ethical creative theft.

———

To start, come up with an analogue for the problem you're trying to solve. In this case an analogue is an example of how someone else has solved a problem similar to yours but in a different context. It gives you a point of comparison. With a decent analogue, you get to borrow from something familiar to help you envision the new and unknown.

To find an analogue, think about your challenge and its core attributes. For example, imagine you're trying to design a new way for kids to keep at it while studying.

What kind of challenges come up? Dealing with repetition, boredom, and distraction? Great. What other activities have similar facets? Unless you're a passionate ultrarunner, one that immediately comes to mind is exercise.

Luckily for you, there's a huge industry that specializes in finding creative solutions to get people exercising (and to pay a lot of money while doing it). An interesting analogue might be the rise of aerobics in the 1980s or the more recent popularity of SoulCycle or hot yoga. Choose something obvious: you're looking for examples where someone else has solved a similar problem in an effective way and where the hallmarks of the solution are pronounced or even exaggerated. This makes for great learning.

Armed with your analogue, conduct some research. Read articles, interview existing customers, or call up a few companies. Find enough information to take a crack at the following questions:

Why did the analogous solution work?
For whom?
How do you know it worked?
How did it transform people's feelings?
What are people able to do now that they couldn't do before?

Now apply some of those learnings to your problem. What jumps out of your research as the most interesting? Use your insights as the starting point to explore new ways to tackle your problem and come up with approaches that fit your context.

––––––––

Looking into similar problems that have been faced and creatively conquered brings in a rich set of potential material. Sadly, it is an underused approach. It is the most effective way I've found to get new designers to come up with sophisticated, surprisingly novel outcomes in their initial stab at developing a new concept.

—Matt Rothe

34 How Are You Doing, Really?

Featuring the work of Julian Gorodsky

When you invite people to contribute to any task where imagination is required, you are playing with human fire in the best sense, hoping to ignite something new. You are also asking people to let down their guard. The more you can establish safety and shared experiences, the more likely people are to take creative risks with each other.

Yet all too often, we hide our true selves or what's really happening for us in the moment. The professional has been detached from the personal, or what we call the home space, which we consider to be more real or authentic. I think it doesn't have to be that way.

One fundamental tenet at the d.school is that a less-judgmental atmosphere is an essential condition for collaboration, whether for creative work or any other purpose. Scientists who study teams have a name for this: "psychological safety" (which you can read more about in *The Feeling of Learning* on page 161).

This assignment is a simple, friendly way to make feelings that usually stay on the inside visible on the outside. The shared human experience of expressing feelings can help a group of any size feel more comfortable taking risks together.

—————

To start, each person takes a handful of sticky notes and writes down one thing they are feeling on each note.

To get people to reveal a bit more than just polite conversation, it helps if you demonstrate a few: I'm feeling "worried about my son who is struggling," "happy that today is my last day of work," "irritated with my neighbor," "confused and preoccupied about the situation at the border."

This is how you get from "How are you doing?" to a place of interpersonal honesty where the "really" comes in. Be explicit that you're aiming to go beyond what people think others might be totally comfortable hearing. You're asking people to take a risk. It's just a small one, but it's a risk nonetheless.

Then stick all of your "feelings" onto yourself where they're visible. Walk around the room and find someone to connect‧ with. Have a conversation about what's on their notes, and then what's on your notes. Actively listen to your partner and be mindful of the little risk they're taking. If there's time, circulate some more and chat with someone else.

—————

If you step back to see what's happening in the room, you'll notice that people have warmed up and a more familiar feeling in the gathering is palpable. This activity works whether it's a group of eighth graders or world-class engineers. You can tailor it to a limited span or take more time with it. No matter how much time you have, it will help create deeper connections.

Everyone has a lot going on, and getting that out in the open helps the group focus on the real task at hand and support each other while doing so. It's often hard to get people to stop talking. Even strangers, once you set the conditions, want to meet each other. At our essence, we are social animals.

—*Julian Gorodsky*

Widening Your Lens

A little over a decade ago I took my first scuba dive, and if I didn't have to surface periodically for air, I'd be pretty happy doing nothing else. Many people like adventures that are fast, like roller coasters; my idea of the perfect adventure is to descend into the salt water near a beautiful reef, swim as slowly as possible, and look at everything in great detail. The visual beauty and complexity, the different symbiotic relationships, the paradox of a reef's strength and fragility—I just want to take it all in and keep learning more and more.

Once I became a good diver, I started bringing a camera along. Sometimes, when I want to capture a whole reef or another large scene, I use a very wide, fish-eye lens, with a field of view that spans 180 degrees. When I review these shots later, I sometimes see creatures, interactions, or details I didn't even notice in the moment, which changes my perspective or helps me understand the ecosystem in a new way. The trick to these images is making sure that at least one interesting thing is prominent in the foreground, and that means I have to get really close to it. If I don't, then nothing stands out. It's a funny paradox: the way the glass in this lens works means that I can get a broad view and a very close one at the same time, and they work together to produce an image that is memorable.

Changing your lens to alter your perspective also plays an important role in design, and this often involves meeting and interviewing people and observing different processes and activities. The concept of *empathy* as part of design has been around for several decades, part and parcel of the growing emphasis on being human-centered. This is a valuable orientation, especially in contrast to using technology as the driving or sole starting point in your work. ("What cool thing can I build based on this new piece of tech?" doesn't really address whether anyone wants or needs that thing, nor does it include enough contextual awareness to see whether there could be unintended consequences if that thing spreads.)

What or who you place at the center of your work matters, because it sends you off in a particular direction. We value the practice of placing humans at the center of our design work in part because it guides us to prioritize the *other* humans whose needs and interests are being considered, rather than our own. This is vital, because no matter how diverse or skilled your team may be, no one individual or group can represent the complexity of others' lives, and an active practice of seeking empathy and insight about others narrows (though doesn't close) this gap. Whatever your topic, the opportunity or need for creative work is considerably larger and more nuanced than any one person's lived experience, so developing empathy for others' needs and perspectives is essential to framing problems in new ways that lead to better outcomes.

In 2014, the creativity scholar Justin Berg published a fascinating paper, "The Primal Mark: How the Beginning Shapes the End in the Development of Creative Ideas," in the journal *Organizational Behavior and Human Decision Processes.* His research indicates that if you start out in familiar territory, you end up producing familiar ideas. If you start out in novel or unusual territory, you come up with far more interesting ideas, and you can always dial back their strangeness if you need to place them in a more familiar or mundane context to start. Berg's paper specifically looks at the process of coming up with new ideas, but I find the concept very useful throughout design work. Where you begin determines, to some degree, where you end up.

Over many years of guiding students to go beyond their own impressions and ideas and to interview people or observe real situations throughout their design work, I've seen time and again how they depart campus with conventional, fairly obvious ideas for what to create. But they return after their research with a messy pile of divergent—and quite possibly useful—new directions they could pursue, directions that are now far more likely to be tuned in to the interests of the people they want to serve or to care about their work. When they continue to engage the perspectives of others throughout their creative work by testing rough ideas, taking feedback, and iterating, they get closer and closer to work that is meaningful, effective, and sometimes quite innovative.

Students and alumni tell me that although this practice was hard to master at first, it ultimately feels freeing. Katy Ashe, from the founding Noora Health team, says, "People are always surprised by what we make. They ask, 'How did you ever come up with this?' I just think, *You did it. You told us.* We just listened and made what people needed. So much of what we're usually trained to do is be correct, to have the right answers and prescribe those as solutions. With design, we learned to be brave and put things out there that didn't match our perfect vision, as opposed to pouncing on people with our so-called right ideas."

Putting humans at the center—or as the only center—can also be incomplete. For example, if you imagine the survival or thriving of humans *and* all other animals as the worthy center of your design work, you might think differently about creative solutions to pressing environmental problems like mass species extinction or climate change. If you adopt a design practice based on the seventh generation principle of the Haudenosaunee (Iroquois) people, you would be just as concerned about the impact of your work seven generations into the future as its impact on the people who might first experience your designs today.

A shorthand version of empathy, often described as "walking in someone else's shoes" or "feeling what someone else feels," is now widespread in design (in part due to frameworks popularized by the d.school in our early days). But there's a lot more you should know about empathy; the simplistic version doesn't quite get at the full range of what empathy is about, its pitfalls and limits, and its relationship to your own creativity.

As neuroscientists, social psychologists, and designers become more precise and knowledgeable about how empathy works in the brain and between people, we are learning that empathy has multiple, distinct facets—and that those facets work together. Three different aspects are shown in this diagram, adapted from a 2012 paper in *Nature Neuroscience* by Jamil Zaki and Kevin Ochsner. The best-known aspect of empathy relates to *experience sharing,* in which you pay attention to others' emotions, resonate with them, and perhaps start to feel something you think is similar. If you've ever told someone a personal story and thought you could see your emotions reflected in their face, that is an expression of this part of empathy.

THREE FACETS OF EMPATHY

MENTALIZING

COGNITIVE EMPATHY

PERSPECTIVE TAKING

THEORY OF MIND

EXPERIENCE SHARING

AFFECTIVE EMPATHY

SHARED SELF-REPRESENTATIONS

EMOTIONAL CONTAGION

PROSOCIAL CONCERN

EMPATHETIC MOTIVATION

SYMPATHY

EMPATHETIC CONCERN

The second aspect is *perspective taking,* in which you reason through and infer what you think another person might feel or think about something. For example, you take someone else's perspective when you interpret their crankiness as a feeling of being underappreciated or surmise that they might need some time off. (It's important to recognize that you might or might not be right about your inference or the conclusion you are drawing from it.) Another example is when you find yourself saying, "Given your experiences, I think I understand why you're voting for that person, even though I don't feel the same way." Perspective taking is essential to the connection between design and empathy. By taking someone else's perspective you are more able to understand a problem or opportunity and describe it to yourself or others, which puts you in a position to begin to address it. Perspective taking is about understanding, rather than caring or compassion, and it is rich with potential for creative action.

A third facet of empathy is starting to receive greater attention and study, which is encouraging because it just might be vitally important for design work. It turns out that resonating with and understanding the emotions that others are experiencing creates what's called "prosocial motivation," which means that you develop a feeling of wanting to help other people. I didn't always know what to call it, but for years I observed that students who had meaningfully connected with someone during their research clearly felt compelled to create something that could meet that person's needs. Those students worked harder and were often more successful than others in my classes. To me it appeared that they were motivated by a genuine sense of urgency, not just the regular incentives of finishing the course and doing well academically. And perhaps I've been noticing a real phenomenon. A 2011 study on the link between empathy and creativity, published in the *Academy of Management Journal* by management and organizational behavior experts Adam Grant and James Berry, shows a connection between perspective taking (the deliberate effort to understand what others need) and actually coming up with ideas that are both novel and useful. It appears that the desire to help others can help you persist during difficult creative tasks.

How do you put your capacity for empathy—in all three of its forms—to work? Practice through a short experience like *What's in Your Fridge?* (page 68), spend a day *Shadowing* (page 41), or set aside time to really stretch your skills through *A Day in the Life* (page 156). Write yourself (or your team) a bold project brief that inspires you as you're diving into an opportunity, just like the challenge descriptions for redesigning the *Organ Donation Experience* or *Post-Disaster Finance* in the final section of the book, starting on page 251.

As you do these assignments, you'll also have an opportunity to reflect on the limits of empathy. As the founders of the social-impact design studio Civilla note about their assignment, *Immersion for Insight* (page 38), it is a privilege to *choose* to experience a process or system in order to understand it and design improvements for it, when some have no choice but to use that same system to access something vital that they need. Someone who can drop in and out of a situation cannot have precisely the same understanding as someone who has no choice but to be there. Empathy is not a magical tool for mind reading that you can adopt for an hour or two to divine exactly what's going on inside another person. A sense of bonding or understanding doesn't mean you have the whole picture, although it can feel like that in the moment. And since everything you and others experience bends through the individual prism of race, gender, history, geography, and culture, be humble about your level of conviction for any conclusions you draw about others.

Another important limit of empathy: it's not moral or immoral; it is amoral. Empathy doesn't automatically put you on a path toward doing good or bad in the world. In fact, the Grant and Berry research noted earlier indicates that by taking others' perspectives you can develop prosocial motivation on behalf of people who are so different from you that helping them achieve their goals might not align with your own values. That is how good it feels when you connect with and begin to understand other people! You can develop insight, ideas, and motivation through your connection with others, but tapping into empathy is no substitute for stepping back and asking questions about the work you're doing, who it will help, and what other effects it could create. Great ways to practice stepping back include *Your Inner Ethicist* (page 218), *The Futures Wheel* (page 221), and *Map the Design Space* (page 106).

Finally, think about the way in which developing empathy for others affects how you view yourself in relation to them. In the moment you might feel humbled, or compassionate, or impressed, or excited. Over time you will become better at translating your empathy into insights and design directions. When you build confidence in these creative tools and abilities, you may feel very empowered. And when we feel empowered, and important, and maybe a little bit like an empathy hero, there's a line that's easy to slip over, into a mindset described as the "creative savior complex" by artist and technologist Omayeli Arenyeka, in an excellent piece in the online guide *The Creative Independent*. Her work emphasizes the many ways to avoid this pitfall by being explicit about your objectives (to yourself and others) and clear about who is benefiting from your work and by thinking through your relationship with the people who might ultimately use or live with the results of your work.

Despite all these complexities, there is value in developing your ability to experience all facets of empathy. It can help you bring useful creative work into the world in a respectful way. The important thing is to *seek* empathy. Set your compass in that direction; just don't assume that you will ever fully arrive at the destination. Use your caring and compassion for others to bring purpose to your creative skills and insight to your design work and to increase the chances that someone else might actually find what you're creating to be useful.

In this context, unlike in photography, you can't rely on a special type of lens to help you understand something up close and simultaneously view the broader context in which it sits. You must hone your skill and work to see both the details *and* the landscape, the individuality of the different people involved *and* the social context in which we all exist. The flexibility to actively shift between these different views is the perspective you're after, as it will ultimately help you produce creative solutions that work on all those different levels.

35 Fresh Eyes Sketching

Featuring the work of Maureen Carroll

It's easy to know intellectually that it's important to look at the world through different perspectives, but that's very different from actually doing it. Yet it's a pursuit worth engaging in throughout your life: being able to turn on fresh eyes at will is key to expanding your curiosity and inviting in new ideas.

This assignment starts as a simple sketching activity but has a twist: you briefly take on the persona of someone other than yourself. It is a gentle way to warm up your mind or start your day, and it helps you practice mindful attention and observation. It will also remind you of the value of seeking diverse perspectives throughout your creative journey.

You can do this on your own or with a group of any size.

———

You'll need notebooks and colored pencils or pens. Then create a list of different types of people or roles, and assign each one a color from your collection. To get started, you might choose some of the following:

A seven-year-old kid (orange)
A gardener (green)
A poet (red)
Someone with a recently broken leg (pink)
Someone living in a climate very different from yours (blue)

Now go outside and find a place to sit and observe.

If you're on your own (or with a very small group), pick a subset of the personae you want to try. Spend ten minutes drawing what you see as if you're seeing the world through one of the personae. Then do another, and another. Draw with the color assigned to each persona, and then switch colors when you switch personae. You can draw right on top of the previous persona and create a layered scene until you have a complete drawing as if made by different people. Or you can do them side by side. You will see new things emerge in your drawings depending on the perspective you are taking.

If you're with a larger group, plan a fun method for assigning roles using different colors so the role assignment is random and people can literally take on a token aspect of their role. There are a million ways to do this: colored dots that stick on someone's shirt, bandanas, sunglasses with different colored temples, or hats. You'll end up with several different people taking the same role.

Each member of the group takes one role-assigning artifact (dots, glasses, hats, and so on) that tells you which role you will play, and you all spend ten minutes sketching what you see through the eyes of your persona. Use your imagination. What do you see?

Return to the group and find someone representing a different color and persona and share your sketch with them.

While sharing, you'll uncover how much the lens you adopt affects what you see and how you see it. For example, the seven-year-old kid might see a bench that all of a sudden becomes a roller coaster. The gardener notices how the plants are arranged. The poet writes an illustrated poem. The person with the broken leg notices alarming cracks in every sidewalk. You are looking at the same things but seeing differently.

The work produced by each of the individuals, filtered through their adopted lens, becomes a jumping-off point for a great discussion about training your attention throughout your design process.

You can structure this along a theme. For example, if you or your group is designing within the education system, perhaps each color represents a different role in that environment (student, parent, principal, janitor, and so on).

Although you are adopting a new lens, it's important to remember that what you see in this activity is still just filtered through you, one person with one specific set of experiences and frames. Consider how different this activity would be if you did it with people who actually represented each different persona. Or how it would be at different moments in your life when you were actively living the experience implied by the persona. It's a great way to stretch your imagination and also a good reminder of those limits.

The phrase that always comes to mind when I do this activity is "capture meaning as you see meaning." The inspiration for this assignment came from the words of Elliot Eisner in The Impoverished Mind: *"Each symbol system sets parameters upon what can be conceived and what can be expressed. Thus, through painting we are able to know autumn in ways that only the visual arts make possible. Through poetry, we can know autumn in ways that only poems can provide. Through botany, we are able to know autumn in ways that only botanists can convey. How autumn is conceived, and hence, what we know about it depends on the symbol system we use or choose to use."*

This exercise is a concrete way to explore that idea. It helps you narrow perspective to really zoom in, and then zoom back out when you see the divergent perspectives across the group. These are the skills of a designer.

—Maureen Carroll

36 Unpacking Exercises

Featuring the work of Susie Wise and Thomas Both, with inspiration from Michael Barry

Interviewing or observing people and contexts is like taking an incredible trip to a place that introduces you to new ways of looking at the world. It sparks your imagination, and you return home lugging a suitcase full of incredible gifts and treasures. And now it's time to unpack and see what you've got in there.

It might sound strange, but unpacking your observations so they lead to insights often takes three or four times as long as the experience you are unpacking did. This process is as important as the trip itself, because it's how you make sense of all the wonderful data you've collected in your suitcase. First, you have to take out all the obvious stuff that everyone notices—the equivalent of souvenirs from the airport gift shop. Then you think about any personal stories you heard, and you spend time examining each one to try to understand more about what they mean and what they tell you about the situation and the needs that are present. Finally, you discover some very special things underneath everything else at the bottom of your luggage. You might not even remember picking them up, because your brain was too busy enjoying the sights to notice. These insights take time to access, but the excavation is worth it.

This assignment offers a simple framework for unpacking your observations. It will help you avoid jumping to the first solution you think of based on the stuff you've noticed at the surface level. Time and patience are essential to this process. Most people wish for a shortcut, because unpacking is inherently uncomfortable— you don't know what you'll find, and you don't know exactly how valuable it will be. But stick with it.

It's much easier to understand unpacking in the context of a specific challenge. This assignment is described by someone who has experienced it many times: serial entrepreneur and education leader Jill Vialet.

A certain problem had been following me around, and I finally got a chance to tackle it when I became a fellow at the d.school. For many years I'd been running a successful, growing organization that supplied expert coaches to public schools to run activities during recess. There's growing evidence that a well-run recess contributes to kids' developing skills in conflict resolution and leadership and positively affects classroom behavior. Principals kept asking whether they could "borrow" my coaches to fill in for various teachers, and that led me to realize that schools face a chronic set of problems around substitute teaching.

Despite the fact that 10 percent of classroom time in the United States is spent with substitute teachers, the problems hadn't been well defined as far as I know. So I embarked on a creative process to try to figure out what could improve the situation and began engaging with a complex web of stakeholders that I needed to understand.

Once I started interviewing teachers, substitutes, principals, and others involved in the system, I quickly moved past the simplistic framing that a lack of substitutes was causing the main problem.

Every interview added new complexity, potentially taking the project in new directions. I started working with several designers at the d.school who coached me through the process of synthesis, beginning by unpacking each of these interviews in detail. I would describe a highlight of an interview, and they would ask prompting questions to get me to go deeper into making meaning of the things that were most salient. There were certain things each interviewee had said to me that felt important, but I hadn't yet considered why they stood out to me so strongly.

We often started with a basic physical description of the person I interviewed. I tried to recreate a visual scene, noting if interviews were in person or by phone. I'd walk through the questions I had posed, call out things that

were either similar or different from other interviews, and then dig into any divergence, since those responses signaled the possibility of new insights. We talked a lot about the emotions that people exuded when describing their experiences and looked for things that felt like inconsistencies.

For example, one interview with a substitute teacher made me realize that she typically entered the classroom in which she was subbing with a whole bunch of preexisting plans. I was already imagining that the need for subs is like the wildfires in California because those needs pop up unexpectedly. These two things combined made me wonder if it made sense to frame subs as firefighters who always show up with an emergency pack. This got me thinking about what the subs would need to bring with them to the classroom to be successful.

Based on this, one of my first prototypes was a backpack with a bunch of age-appropriate games and activities. I took that backpack with me when I interviewed principals. To test the idea, I would ask, "What if we train subs as if they were like firefighters, and they come in with a particular set of skills—how would that work?" On some level, that interested them and got them to be open to the possibility that more could be expected of substitutes, but they weren't enthusiastic about subs being the drivers of their own content. So that tiny thread that came out of my synthesis process led to

several important new insights after I tested it in the form of a prototype.

During one of the coaching sessions, I expressed my surprise that, while I thought the greatest resistance to changing the way we handle subs would come from school leaders, I actually heard much more negativity from classroom teachers. I started questioning the very idea of exactly what a substitute teacher is. For example, as a mom you want other grown-ups to be in your kids' lives, but you don't want a substitute mom. No one wants to feel replaceable. This was another major reframing moment. I realized there is no such thing as a substitute teacher! These people can come in and play an important role in a classroom, but they aren't a substitute for anything.

Once I realized this and said it out loud, it felt blindingly obvious in retrospect, but I couldn't have gotten there except by taking the long road through the process. It reminds me of that quote by Oliver Wendell Holmes Jr.: "Simplicity is the other side of complexity."

Humans need time and space to make meaning, whether in a specific creative process or when trying to deal with everyday life. In the absence of having a dedicated space to do so, they will hijack other spaces to make that happen. When I translate this idea back to my work life, it reminds me that our need for synthesis often shows up in the form of

derailing meetings intended for some other purpose. This might be why I'm not a person who likes meetings!

To get to great synthesis, you need to give it time and space. During my time working on this project, I stayed open, and I had this feeling that if I just stuck with it I would get to something good. And I was able to do that, time and time again.

Working closely and having these dialogues with others gave me permission to dwell in that uncertain, but productive process. I learned that getting to something concrete is not always a straight line. The purpose is not always immediately apparent, but that doesn't mean there is no purpose.

—Jill Vialet

———

To unpack stories and data that you've gathered in your creative research, first write down eight to ten highlights from a specific interview or an observation experience. These could be quotes that stood out, tensions or contradictions about the situation, things you found disappointing or exciting, or places where you saw people solving their own problem with a home-made solution.

Write each highlight on a separate card or sticky note.

On a bigger piece of paper or a board, for each of your highlights write down responses to the following prompts:

Why did this stand out to you so much?

Why is it interesting in light of the challenge you're trying to address?
What does it tell you about what this person believes or cares about?
Why is this highlight important? What does it mean?
What other types of situations does that make you think of?
How does this help you see the problem or opportunity in a new way?

Keep it going until you feel you've exhausted what you can mine from that observation and move on to the next one.

Over time, you'll develop a repertoire of unpacking questions that you really like to use. Be aware that the type of questions you gravitate toward probably reflects something about you and your instincts or biases. All of this work is subjective: the underlying stories, your approach to unpacking them, and your conclusions. Your interpretations flow directly into your framing of the challenge and into the solutions you propose.

Subjectivity is essential to creativity; you can't run away from it. But just as Jill did, keep going back to test your ideas and what you're learning in order to check your assumptions. You'll eventually realize, just as she did, that you've found the treasure at the bottom of your suitcase.

37 Frame & Concept

Featuring the work of Perry Klebahn, Jeremy Utley, and Scott Doorley, with commentary from Yusuke Miyashita

Receiving constructive reactions and feedback is like getting assists in basketball: it's harder to score without them. But getting an assist to your perfect layup requires you to know how to gracefully accept the pass.

Sometimes people hesitate to ask for feedback because they are not sure what receiving it means. Does it mean you are obligated to implement it? Does it mean your role as designer is less important? Of course not. You are obligated to exercise your judgment about what to do with any feedback. Receiving feedback is the act of learning about the difference between how you intended the work to land and how it is being perceived.

When you share your work, one person might like the color, while another thinks the topic isn't very relevant. You don't want to limit the candor or range of feedback being offered, so you need a structured way to evaluate what you're learning. This assignment gives you a way to decipher the feedback from a testing session. It helps you distinguish between information about your understanding of the challenge (the frame) and the quality of your proposed solution (the concept).

Frame & Concept is a simple method for interpreting how people are responding to your work. It's so simple that it might expand what you consider to be a prototype worth testing. So, what else do you want to start getting feedback on in the early stages? A grocery shopping list? A plan for a family vacation? Almost anything gets better once you start seeking early input.

———

Before you ask for feedback on your creative work, put it in some kind of form that can be shared. Sketches, physical prototypes, writing—all work well. Then think to yourself, *what is my frame, and what is my concept*?

The frame is the need you are trying to address or the broader idea you are playing with. The concept is much more concrete: it's the specific solution you've come up with.

For example, if you're testing your family vacation plan, your implicit frame might be "to instill a sense of adventure and joy for life, especially after a tough year as a family," and the explicit concepts you're testing might include "roller coaster theme park" and "white water rafting." If you're working with a bank to design new services for people who've just lost their home in a natural disaster, your frame might be "to become the 'first responder' in finance and strengthen trust in a time of crisis," and your concept might be "immediate, no-interest loan of $1,000 for housing and food."

Use these principles to start your testing session, share your sketches or prototypes, and get feedback:

Be clear that you're sharing early-stage ideas and that you're genuinely seeking input. State that your feelings won't be hurt by honest feedback.

Don't try to explain yourself, your entire vision, or just how great the final version of this thing will be once it has all the bells and whistles. Doing so shows how invested you are, and people are less likely to give you candid feedback in fear that it will hurt your feelings. In other words, it's best not to share your frame *with your testers, just the* concepts—*at least at first.*

Carefully document the reactions of your tester(s). Record comments and note their body language and affect.

If you adopt the right posture of inquiry and humility, the person you're testing with may feel encouraged to tell you how to make your concept better, which also helps you learn more about the underlying need and might result in a new idea you hadn't thought of. You might get into a deeper discussion that leads you to better understand what's in your frame. And it's fine to share more about what you were aiming for after you get the initial feedback.

When you sit down to digest the reactions, draw two vertically stacked circles in your notebook or on a large piece of paper. Label the top one "Frame" and the bottom one "Concept." This provides a visual reminder that the frame is more abstract—the thing that everything has to add up to. Use these two circles to categorize the feedback you've received. Write down all of the comments you heard (or body language you noticed) and place them in the top circle if related to the frame and in the bottom circle if related to the concept. »

FRAME

CONCEPT

Now evaluate:

How close are you to meeting the needs of the situation in the way you have articulated your frame?

Are your insights about what matters to people powerful and relevant?

For the concept, are people loving it? Or is it getting a polite, disinterested, or downright negative reaction? What's really driving the emotional reaction, and why?

Here are some common findings:

Your concept was poorly received, but by putting it out there for feedback you got to understand much more about the frame. For example, "Roller coasters terrify me, but I like the independence we'd have if we could each choose our own rides," or "I don't want to spend my vacation being wet, but I like the idea of all being together in the wilderness." Your solutions might not be meeting the need, and in your next cycle you can work harder to refine the concepts.

Sometimes the concept looks amazing, and testers really respond to its aesthetic qualities. But after going through the reactions, you find that it didn't really ring the bell or connect to the needs implied in the frame of the project. For example, people might have liked the concept of a $1,000 no-interest loan but think it would be more useful during everyday situations. So you still haven't addressed your core frame in the natural disaster project. Time to go back to ideation and develop some other concepts.

The myth of the solo genius perfecting something alone and then unveiling it to the world could not be further from how we work at the d.school. Our mantra is: share your work early and often. Other people's reactions make your work better because they show what's missing, help you make sure you're not designing just for yourself, or call attention to potential unintended effects that you might have missed. Feedback is a huge help, even when it's temporarily deflating.

This is probably one of the most satisfying and useful tools that I have encountered in more than a decade as a designer and teacher. Being able to evaluate your insight and then assess the quality of your prototype independently sets you up to make really good decisions about how to move forward. Is your frame good? Is your concept good? You immediately know what to do next.

—Yusuke Miyashita

Making Morning Coffee

Featuring the work of Seamus Yu Harte,
Scott Doorley, and Bill Guttentag

This assignment helps you hone your visual communication skills. To do so, you're going to make something before you feel ready. Doing something quickly reveals the gaps between what you can do and what you think you can do. You'll also find out what you already know—but might not know you know—and you'll feel a lot more ready the next time. In this case, you're focused on making a tiny movie, but you can apply the concept more broadly for any situation. This assignment gives you a visceral way to explore learning by doing. (How? By learning by doing!)

When you work with media like video, your message or idea will live on without you being there to explain it. The best way to learn the difference between what you are trying to say and what people are actually taking in is just to make something and see how it plays.

———

Your goal is to shoot a one-minute video of a process—in this case, making a morning beverage. Find a willing friend or roommate and gather any supplies you need.

The first step is to make the movie— literally. Pick up your smartphone and record the process of your friend making

coffee (or tea or a smoothie). It doesn't matter if it's good, decent, or incredibly, laughably bad (the movie, not your beverage)—that's not the point.

Try to use the different shot styles shown on page 135 (wide shot, extreme close-up, and so on). To narrow the endless possibilities, adopt the following constraints and get going quickly:

The title of your movie is Making Morning Coffee.
It should be exactly one minute long.
It should include less than a dozen different shots.
It should be silent, not narrated (you can add music only, but that makes the assignment more complicated). »

Now, watch your first attempt and think about what works and what doesn't. Was it too long? Why? What's not essential to the narrative? Was it dizzying when you zoomed in too fast on the coffee grounds? Did you have trouble fitting in all of the different shot styles? What feeling did it leave you with?

Prepare to record it again. This time make a loose plan by sketching out a rough storyboard first. Simply draw a series of empty boxes on a page of your notebook and fill them in with the sequence of shots you plan to record. If you don't want to edit your final movie, you can pause the video recording to break up the action into different scenes. Or use the cheapest, easiest smartphone video editing app you can find. Don't get fancy; just string your shots together and trim here or there to get your movie down to one minute.

Record again, and edit. When you're satisfied, upload your video to a video sharing site and make your friends (or family) watch. See if they understand the coffee routine. As you do, notice how *you* feel. Your gut will tell you what's working and what's not.

The strict constraints in this assignment (time, topic, and format) allow you to focus on the fundamentals. The assignment helps you try the video medium and then reflect on it afterward. This is the opposite of the traditional path of first attending lectures on cinematography and theory—or worse, enduring a technical explanation of how to use a camera before you ever touch one. It is a mindset shift from thinking you need to acquire a skill to knowing you have a way to activate one.

Periodically throwing yourself into something in which you have little expertise has a huge value you might not expect. This assignment helps you quickly learn how to shoot video, but it also gets at a simple idea that you can use for any skill you want to improve. When it comes to making something, you never know what you don't know until you try it. Have to deliver something in a format you've never used? Try out a simple—almost silly—project first to get the hang of how to put it together.

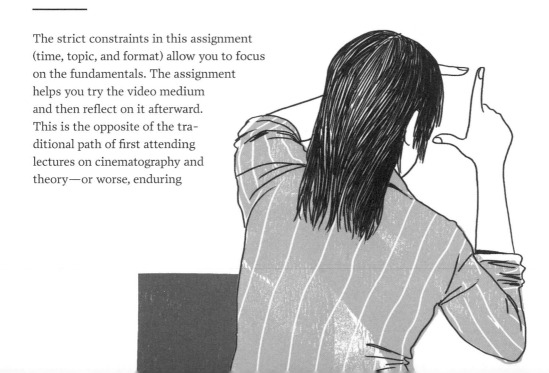

PAN

SHOT
ANGLES

   ZOOM

SHOT
SIZES

TILT

39 Five Chairs

Featuring the work of Grace Hawthorne, Charlotte Burgess-Auburn, and Scott Doorley

We're often encouraged to walk into a situation and act like we already know what we're doing, but that facade makes it harder to listen, harder to course correct, and harder to operate with humility. It also means an awful lot of people are projecting something false at any given time. One way that design can help free you to do your best work is by giving you tools to embody the reality that, most of the time, "I don't know the answer yet" is the truest thing you can say.

This assignment is a way to experience one of those tools: rapid prototyping. First, think of *prototype* as more a verb than a noun, although of course it's both. The core of prototyping is to create multiple representations of the same concept, which shows you and others that the final manifestation of your idea is not a fixed, known certainty; rather, it's just one of many possible variations. Not only is prototyping an important way to expand your own exploration, but it also gives you concrete artifacts to share and test with other people who care about or experience the challenges you're designing for.

To make prototyping easier, it helps to become familiar with the properties of different materials to inform your intuition about how to build things. Some materials are really good for articulating lines, others for creating volume, and still others for making something small or something big.

This assignment is also literally mind expanding. When you pick up and handle objects, they inspire you with new ideas for how to develop and refine your core concept in new directions. It's a good reminder that your brain contains many more variations of an idea than you're conscious of at the outset; you just have to give yourself the nudge to explore in multiple directions. Use this assignment any time you want that nudge. Regardless of what you're working on, it will help you get into the rapid prototyping mindset.

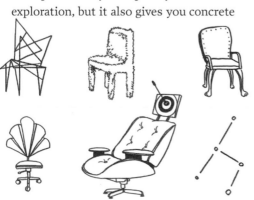

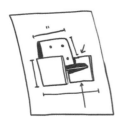  

Using a piece of paper and a marker, draw the chair of your dreams in two minutes. It should be a chair that takes your needs perfectly into account.

Get a piece of cardboard and a pair of scissors and build a model of your chair out of the cardboard. (At this point, you might groan and ask yourself why you designed the chair the way you did!)

Admire your chair and then get some new materials, like pipe cleaners.

Build your chair out of pipe cleaners.

Then modeling clay.

Then chewing gum and toothpicks.

Line up all of your chairs in a row.

Here are some great questions to ask yourself:

What was it like to create different iterations of your design?

What did you change along the way? Why?

Which material did you enjoy working with the most or least? Why?

Which material best expresses the essence of the chair you drew? Why?

Sometimes it's useful to just try working with new materials. You're never going to use these materials in your "serious" work, but they can teach you a lot.

The cardboard is very much about the surfaces.

The pipe cleaners are all about the lines.

The chewing gum and toothpicks force you to be really strategic about small connections.

You might find working with some materials really enjoyable, so they become your go-to for rapid prototyping. Every material has intrinsic physical qualities; to know them, you have to experience them physically. You have to put your hands on the stuff to know how it will behave. The more "stuff" you put your hands on, the more your brain has to work with.

It's really fun to do this with a group—it works equally well with a team at work or on game night at home with friends. You can pause between each round to line up everyone's chairs according to material. You get to see how a roomful of people make their chairs in all different ways. There's a fun moment of tension after the cardboard chairs are lined up and people think they are done; that's when you tell them to take out another medium.

If you're doing this on your own, make sure to commit to making all of the different variations. Use a two-minute time limit per material if you find yourself getting stuck. Part of the magic of stretching your creative abilities happens when you don't take the opportunity to talk yourself out of being able to do something.

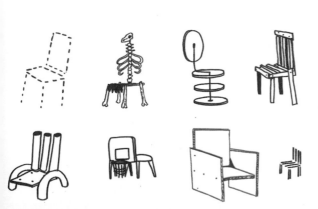

40 The Hundred-Foot Journey Map

Featuring the work of Lena Selzer, Adam Selzer, Claire Jencks, and Michael Brennan

Think about what happened the last time you asked an airline to find your lost luggage, renewed your driver's license, or went to the hospital for a small procedure. The process was made up of many small moments—ones that might have made you mad, left you confused, or given you a sense of relief. No one means to make complex systems that are bad or frustrating, but these systems often are just that.

Most systems build up layers of complexity over time, like haphazard additions to a house never planned by any sane architect. Unless the organization has recently gone through a human-centered renovation, you may have to set off on a heroic quest just to navigate what should be a simple process. Step by step, you feel your way

through, find information, make decisions, and have interactions you'd never predict.

Now imagine that every public or private system you encounter was designed to make difficult moments brief and bring you quickly to the triumphant conclusion of your journey. This would be extraordinary!

Often systems are far more complex than they appear to the casual observer. It's natural to think, *Why can't they just fix the DMV? Why can't that take half as long as it does?* This assignment helps you navigate

the workings of a system and allows you to see all the different parts as well as the shape of the whole. It takes you through the process of making a map that reveals all the complexity and detail that prevent quick fixes, while identifying a few places where improvements would start to change the system for the better.

Part of what makes systems-level challenges so daunting is that it's hard to know where to start. One way is to look for specific places where changes can improve outcomes for both the people who run the system and the people who need to use it, because the two are closely related.

Use this assignment to try out the approaches of a systems designer. Maybe you're launching an ambitious effort to redesign a whole system, or perhaps you want to develop creative ideas that equip you to advocate for change in a system from the outside. Or perhaps you simply want to gain insight into the human experience of getting caught in the intricate complexity of the systems we tangle with every day.

Pick a system that you interact with: a customer service department, your local pharmacy, that kind of thing. Make sure it's one where you can connect with someone on the inside: your favorite bank teller, a call center operator with some time on their hands, your cousin the surgeon, or your neighbor the postal worker.

You are going to map the experiences of two people within this system—an outsider and an insider—to see how they intersect.

Part 1: The Interviews

Conduct two in-depth interviews: the first with someone who needs something from

the system, like a customer, patient, or beneficiary, and the second with a person who makes that same part of the system work (and who interacts with those customers): a caseworker, loan officer, mechanic. During each interview, ask the interviewee to relate in chronological detail a specific experience with this system. Take copious notes. Be very specific and go slowly. Start with their motivation from the beginning.

For the person using the system: Why did they go to the bank, airport, or doctor's office in the first place? How did they get ready to go? How did they get there? What's the first thing that happened when they arrived?

From there on out, it's pretty much:

What happened next?
What happened next?
And what happened next?

Pay attention to body language and tone. If something sounds like it was scary, ask why. If a particular step provokes a smile, find out about that. You're trying to capture more than just the mechanics; you want to soak up the human experience.

For the person inside the system, start with their overall motivation. Why did they take this job? What does a good day look like to them? Then zoom in and ask about the moments that stood out from your first interview to understand the corresponding activity; you want to hear about the outsider's journey from the insider's perspective.

Then ask your insider to tell you about a particular interaction of this type they've had in the past week. You'll get much more detail if you ask about specifics rather than people's idealized version of what they think generally happens. You can amplify this even further by spending another hour or two observing this person in action. You

might notice things they don't register as significant, like getting interrupted by frequent phone calls or struggling to find an answer in a complicated manual. That's the part of a system that no one ever captures—that's the lived experience of it.

Part 2: Visualization

Now that you've got your data, you can begin to visualize the journey. It is a challenge to weave those two different experiences together, but creating one map (instead of separate ones) will generate the biggest insights.

Chronicle each person's story on sticky notes, one step per note. Place your outsider's story in order in a single line of notes. Then do the same for your insider, lining up the notes underneath the first line, with enough space between for inserting additional notes. Yours may or may not stretch for a hundred feet, but you'll need plenty of space!

Look for the intersections. Wherever you see that your interviewees have described the same activity but from two different points of view, sketch an icon and name that moment on a new sticky note, and place that in between the two lines so that they connect at that spot. Often, those are key places to start designing for. For

example, if you are looking at the experience of losing airplane luggage and also mapping the airline's system for finding lost luggage, there might be an intersecting moment when the outsider (customer) is reporting that they've lost their bags, and the insider (service agent) is filling out a form to document the problem. You'd name this moment based on something one of them said, like "The Mysterious Lost Luggage Form" or simply "Filing an Alert." And you would sketch a quick icon that showed this moment in action.

When you've done this for the whole story, go back and add visual notation to the sticky notes by sketching all the individual moments that are experienced alone. This gives you another opportunity to unpack and process and to add any emotional qualities that may be missing from notes that only capture the sequential action. Add headlines or other notations to help someone who's not part of this system be able to understand what's happening along the way.

Part 3: Telling the Story

Your goal is to use your map to reveal all the complexity and detail that prevents quick fixes and to identify a few places where improvements would start to change both the outsider and the insider experience. As

you step back and analyze your map, notice how connected all the pieces are.

Transfer your map to its final format: an extra-long piece of butcher paper works, or you can break it up across separate pieces of paper and tape them together. Show your map to someone in the system who can advocate for change, or make a digital version and post your work online to start a discussion about the problems and opportunities you've found.

———

We call this the hundred-foot journey map, because that's how long ours was when we mapped out caseworker and client interactions for people applying for Michigan public benefits like food assistance. It blows people's minds to see how involved and detailed the journey is. It helps illuminate all the invisible, overlooked ways that systems fail and customer experiences suck, even if you don't intend them to.

Every institution or organization has all the steps in their business process captured somewhere in their office, and that's how people get trained to perform those actions. But it never happens in that exact way.

One time we observed a caseworker begin to review an application. They started reviewing a case and then got a phone call. While they took the phone call, the computer timed out. Once the computer timed out, they had to log back in. When they logged back in, they had to click sixty-eight times to get back to where they were in the application. Then they found out they had another client waiting, so they had to go downstairs to meet that client. The computer timed out again. That's the lived experience. They might tell you they have to deal with a lot of interruptions, but until you actually depict all of the individual details, no one can quite grasp how significantly those things are detracting from the system being able to function for everyone.

—Lena Selzer

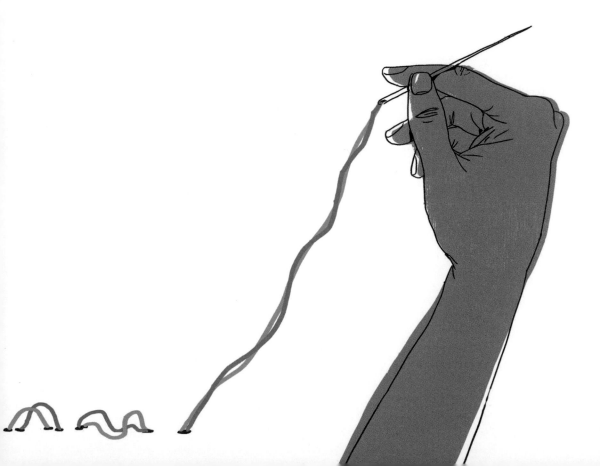

41 Everyone Designs

Featuring the work of Kareem Collie

Kareem Collie's words embody an essential principle: design is about being intentional and deliberate. This is true whether you are designing a meal to delight your child, a room that inspires play, a logo to evoke nostalgia, or a doctor's visit that builds trust. All you have to do is choose to consider the context surrounding whatever you are designing—the situation, people, and needs involved—so you don't produce something random.

Can you be more increasingly intentional when exercising your creative skills?

What is something you've been thinking about making?

What needs are you instinctively responding to?

What else do you want to learn so you can be deliberate about what you make and how you make it?

Borrowing from Kareem's metaphor, what is your "weather" and what is your "attire"?

Everyone designs.

When you wake up in the morning and look at the weather…you get dressed appropriately. You just designed your attire for the day, right? I want people to look at the weather of more things.

There is so much clutter in the world that lacks intention. Stop, think, and look critically at the context in which you're designing to find your way toward intentionality.

—Kareem Collie

42 Protobot

Featuring the work of Molly Wilson

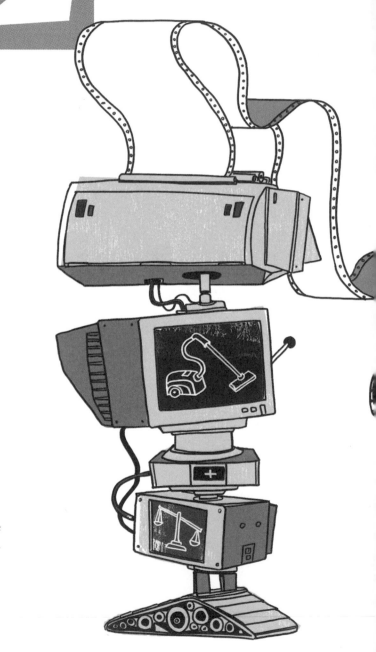

There's a not-very-old, not-nearly-famous-enough saying: "The person who brings a prototype to a meeting gets all the attention." And it's completely true. If you bring a prototype of your new concept, everyone will be curious. People will start to weigh your idea and talk about how to bring it to life as if it's already happening. That's the power of making an idea concrete: it already feels real, especially in comparison to ideas that remain words, air, or gestures.

It follows that one of the most useful skills you can learn is how to build things. Not just for the sake of what you create and the attention it garners, but also because of the thinking you do as you make it. Translating an idea into something physical is an active process of exploration and elaboration, not only execution. As you build, the idea becomes more of what it ultimately could be.

You actually already know how to build. You used to do it all the time as a child. But somewhere along the way you stopped practicing it in your daily life, and now you're probably rusty. When you have a complicated new idea, it can be hard to envision how to start building it, even when it's just a little model to share with others.

This assignment isolates and strengthens your building muscle—that little corner of your brain that used to reach for the blocks even before you knew what you wanted to make. You can use it any time you want a spontaneous design challenge. It's also a great way to launch a creative session with others, especially when you want to loosen people up and get them ready to build something new together.

———————

Have the following materials close at hand:

Something long, thin, and flexible, like string.
Something semi-flexible, like wire.
Something stiff, like a stick.
Something that sticks things together, like glue or tape.
Something that separates things from other things, like scissors.
Something that marks on things, like a marker.
Something that is flat and flexible, like paper.
School supplies in general.
Materials with lots of different properties.
No glitter. (Unless you love vacuuming.)

You're about to build something that doesn't make any sense at all, so you don't have to worry about whether it's a good idea. In fact, it's almost guaranteed to be a bad idea, because a computer named Protobot came up with it. Protobot lives online, and you can visit it anytime at https://protobot.org. But to get started, give it a shot with any of these Protobot-generated suggestions:

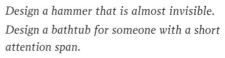

Design a hammer that is almost invisible.
Design a bathtub for someone with a short attention span.
Design a picnic blanket for a rock star.
Design a lawn mower that changes based on your location.
Design a vacuum cleaner that creates a more equal society.
Design a scarf that requires at least twenty people to use.
Design a bench that teaches another language.

Choose the one that appeals to you most. Or pick one that feels weird, funny, or stupid. You spend a lot of your life trying to pick the best idea, but this is a very low-pressure exercise! Maybe pick the worst idea now just to exercise that part of your brain.

You have eight minutes to build your prototype using anything in the room. That's it. Enjoy the build!

And if you're working with a group, have everyone share their absurdist, wonderful creations at the end.

———————

This is for people who don't consider themselves designers. It's useful to have a source you can go to when you really want to get your team brainstorming with their hands. It's very accessible and democratic, and it's a little mysterious, bizarre, and stupid. Robots are funny. That's why I put "bot" in the name.

I think it helps release tension or apprehension about building because you're not judging what you make. You don't have to come up with the idea. I'm isolating one step of the dance, and you get to practice it as much as you want. You don't have to worry about other people, their needs, testing, or implementation. It's just the work and pleasure of building that you get to focus on.

—*Molly Wilson*

43 Experts/ Assumptions

Featuring the work of Carissa Carter and Sarah Stein Greenberg, with inspiration from Craig Lauchner

Experts are usually experts for a good reason. They have been immersed in or studied a topic for a long time. They've had years to gather facts, make observations, and form opinions. Maybe they've produced a documentary on the subject or written books and articles. Maybe they are the person in a neighborhood or organization who everyone thinks of as the "institutional memory" of the place.

Experts' knowledge is critical to unlocking complex challenges. Chances are you won't be successful in your creative efforts if you completely ignore what has come before. To bring new ideas to a challenging problem or project that needs an innovative approach, first steep yourself in the preexisting knowledge about the space you're working in.

At the same time, you do not want to become overly constrained by the current modes of thought. You need to strike a balance; to take in, but not cling to, all the beliefs and assertions of experts.

Experts feel authoritative. They have a well-developed point of view, though it's still just one perspective. Listening to them can save you time and money and help you get closer to focusing on the right

opportunity to make something better. Long experience can bring wisdom. You, on the other hand, might bring a fresh approach and still be naïve about the topic. This frees you from prejudice, but it also means you don't know what you don't know. It's a fine needle to thread.

This assignment helps you learn how to take in and digest what experts have to offer, while cultivating your ability to question those frames and dream about what is possible. It begins training you to be able to seek expert perspectives without hearing them as absolute truths that dictate how much room is available for creativity.

Begin by interviewing two or three experts on a topic of interest to you. If you can't interview someone directly, read or watch their work and take careful notes.

Next, write down all the assumptions you think are being made by any of your experts about how your topic does or should work. Truly, *all* of them. Make as long a list as you can.

Here's an example. You're a volunteer at your local library, and you're trying to find more creative ways to use the lobby space. In addition to interviewing many people in the community who both do and don't use the library and observing how the different library spaces are currently used, you also seek some contextual expertise. You might watch a documentary about the history of a big public library system in another city, interview a professor at a nearby community college who studies the role of libraries in neighborhoods, and read a lengthy article you found online about how librarians in some towns are playing a surprising role as front-line workers in the nationwide opioid crisis.

Using a separate sticky note for each assumption, you might write down:

Libraries serve people of all ages.

Libraries have times they are open and times they are closed.

Libraries have many different kinds of content.

Libraries are for people who like to read.

Libraries are for absolutely anyone who lives nearby.

You must have a library card to use a library.

Libraries are accessible in everyone's neighborhood.

Libraries are dying out.

Libraries are more important than ever.

Libraries are publicly funded.

Ninety-eight percent of libraries in the United States provide internet access.

Libraries are the only place where some people can access a computer.

Libraries are quiet!

Libraries are staffed by people with specialized academic degrees.

Libraries are . . . etc. »

Even a casual reading and watching of a few different pieces of content will help you generate a list much longer than this; perhaps fifty to a hundred different assumptions or more. Not all assumptions have to agree with each other. Since you're focused on the lobby space, you might even zoom in and create a list that contains all of the assumptions you can think of about the nature and use of a library lobby.

Once you've got your list, sort your sticky notes into three categories: facts, opinions, and guesses.

The statistic about the percentage of libraries that provide internet access is a fact, and you won't need to spend much time deliberating about it. The assumption that libraries are the only place where some people can access a computer might be an inference based on a film or article you watched or read. Perhaps it's true in some places but not others. Maybe right now it's best labeled a guess. Is a library, by its nature, quiet? That's an opinion. This circumstance is common, but is quiet essential to how a library has to work? Not totally clear. Sorting your list into these three categories will also help you probe your own opinions and guesses about the work you're doing, which helps you advance your ideas because you don't get too rooted in your own beliefs.

When you're done sorting, take a longer look at the stickies in your opinions and guesses categories. Choose three to challenge. Ask yourself *What if this were not true? Or even What if the opposite were true? What would I design then? How could a library overall (or the lobby specifically) be different?* Come up with a list of ideas for each of the assumptions you've chosen to challenge.

Some of these ideas may find their way into your solution, and some may simply be helpful in opening up your thinking.

This practice of examining popular or expert assumptions in a considered way will help you remain creative and flexible while deepening your understanding of the broader context and how others view it.

This assignment is based on Craig Lauchner's practice of "assumption storming," which can be used in many different ways. You can use the same approach to review all the assumptions about a service or product you're about to launch or the way you've framed a problem. You can use it to help a longstanding group identify and challenge its operating norms or methods or its focus. This can help the group identify places where long-held assumptions might be preventing it from taking innovative steps forward.

As you become more confident in your experience of finding and addressing opportunities creatively, you won't need as much structure to judge how to hear and interpret expert views.

Knowing something about previous approaches can spark your imagination— just be sure you don't wholly defer to them. Don't be reluctant to grapple with the past and the present, while designing for the future.

Stakeholder Mapping

Featuring the work of Durell Coleman, Libby Johnson, and Ariel Raz

An idea alone is rarely enough to change the status quo. You need a group of people to get behind the idea, clear the way to try it out, and sometimes retire old or competing ideas in the process.

When your goal is to improve or redesign experiences within large, complex systems, you focus first and foremost on the people whose lives are most affected by that system. But trying to improve a system with only that one group of stakeholders in mind won't be sufficient. A stakeholder is anyone affected by or involved with the work you're doing, and in some situations, support from several different kinds of stakeholders is key to getting things done. Just because you believe your creative change is an improvement doesn't mean that everyone will see it that way. If you don't recognize the broader ecosystem of stakeholders, you risk designing things that get blocked or torn down by an opponent you didn't see coming.

If you're working to improve the education system, the health care system, the foster care system, or the legal system or you're simply operating within a large corporate structure, you're familiar with this. (Even a small neighborhood, local community center, or extended family can have some of

the same dynamics.) Most efforts to make lasting change require creative approaches to both the concepts and the solutions that will improve things, as well as sensitivity and insight toward building a coalition of like-minded people who can help you accomplish your goals.

This assignment helps you explore and assess the power structures of the system you're operating in. It will help you see the places where you might partner with stakeholders to accomplish your goals. If you're at the start of a project, and you can't yet name all the people you're trying to engage, it will help you gather more information.

———

On a large board or giant piece of paper, draw three concentric circles and label the center circle with examples of the people who are your primary focus. For example, if you are mapping an ecosystem for criminal justice reform, the person who has been incarcerated would likely be at the center.

One tier out from the center, write down all the folks who are allies in what you want to accomplish. These people support your vision or mission or have similar goals. In our criminal justice reform example, the allies might be the Office of Reentry Services, Catholic Charities, organizations focused on helping folks not return to prison, faith-based organizations, family members, and so on.

In the third circle, indicate all the people or organizations you can think of who are not aligned with your mission or goals. In fact, perhaps they benefit from the status quo. In our example, this could be someone who runs a private prison, a company that profits from prison labor, or a specific local politician who wants to be seen as "tough on crime."

In a final tier, which is actually outside of the circles you have drawn, indicate the people who are affected by or connected with this challenge, but who are unaware or disengaged. They are not currently part of the conversation, but they could be. This might be citizens, the populace in general, a church that many folks in an inner tier attend but that isn't part of the process, or family members of any of the stakeholders.

Next, annotate your map to add more detail about relationships between the different groups. Draw lines to show existing connections between the stakeholders. Label those lines to describe the type of relationships happening. Ask yourself: *Who is not connected to anyone?*

You'll notice that there are more people you could consider your design work to be "for" than you previously realized, whether that means designing a part of a solution to involve them, ways to communicate effectively, or strategies or policies to offset the strength o the opposition.

Your map is now a springboard for further research, during which you'll seek to empathize with a wider group of people: ideally people who represent each stakeholder type. Set up times to meet with

each of them and listen to their needs and interests. Ask for feedback on your ideas. Your goal is to identify how to lean on your allies and where your goals and their help might be aligned.

For the disengaged, you're trying to learn about their motivations, uncover previously unseen opportunities to involve them in your work, and discover their reactions to what you are trying to design.

Over time, you'll need to come up with strategies to interact with those who are against you. Sometimes a group you assume is opposed is not as opposed as you think. Find out what is motivating them. If they are worried about resource scarcity, how could they benefit economically from your solution? Other times the approach might be to figure out how to form a coalition that can overcome their power to resist change.

This assignment has been a crucial tool for how my team and I tackle systemic change through design. For example, we once worked with four school districts in the Central Valley in California, seeking to understand the barriers preventing many immigrant families from enrolling their children in prekindergarten. The goal was to help more of these young kids gain the benefit of early childhood education.

At the center of our map we put the children. Family members and school administrators were those aiming to help educate these kids. Amongst the disengaged from the conversation was the local church, which many of the immigrant families attended.

Once we had mapped out the ecosystem, we sought to understand why families weren't enrolling their children. One school district formed a collaboration with the church to share the benefits of prekindergarten while addressing families' concerns. Part of the solution wound up being a registration drive at the church, which led to an increase in the number of parents enrolling their kids.

In our work, the "aha!" typically comes when we identify who else could contribute to a solution who is not yet at the table.

—Durell Coleman

45 The Banana Challenge

Featuring the work of Thomas Both

This assignment helps you explore the idea that while solutions you design must respond to people's needs, they also come from your own creativity and personal experiences.

The Banana Challenge is framed around the concept of an obsession. It's about connecting your own passions, biases, and interests to the process of coming up with ideas. (There are a lot of obsessions at the d.school: motorcycles, sneakers, old radios, sharks, Swedish pastries, calligraphy, marine invertebrates, bananas, awkwardness, dragon boat racing, and esoteric gummy candy. You can imagine some of the ideas that come out of that mix!)

This is a useful assignment when you want to explore and discover new things about your own unique perspective. You can do it on your own, but it's fun when done alongside others. The range of individual passions that come out can help you to learn more about people you already feel close to or to find commonalities and respect for collaborators.

————

Have a bunch of bananas on hand. Yes, real bananas. (More green than ripe, if possible. Squishy ones are harder to work with.)

Identify an obsession you have and think about why it matters to you or what you

enjoy about it. What do you engage with, learn about, and ponder far more often than others do? What does it say to others about you? If that question makes you feel nervous, remember that this is an exercise in running toward whatever makes you different and special.

Now, imagine that you have been hired for a hot advertising campaign to sell more bananas. Take about thirty minutes to develop a print advertisement to help accomplish this goal.

Use the following rules to create constraints and structure:

Your advertisement must be conveyed through one photograph and a pithy tagline.
You must use something about your obsession to generate the idea for the advertisement.
You must feature at least one banana in your image.

Grab a banana, then scout the perfect location anywhere in your environment or create a scene to place the banana in. Take a photo and create a tagline.

Reflect. How did you leverage some aspect of your obsession—or your relationship to it—as a spark for your banana advertisement? How can you use what you learned from this activity to generate new ideas in the future?

If you're with a group, have everyone upload their photos to a common sharing platform and have a viewing party. It's nice when everyone can see the results immediately. Can you discern other people's obsessions?

One subtle benefit of this assignment is that it gives you a nudge to cross between the physical world and a digital space. Today people go right to digital tools like Photoshop or a slide deck to make visuals. The more people start out in the same flat, two-dimensional medium, the more everything starts to look the same. In this assignment you first have to create something physical, which allows you to take advantage of the serendipity of what's around you to make something even more unique.

Having constraints can help you generate ideas. In this exercise, I give you some general constraints about the format, the medium, and the idea of selling bananas, and then you add a more specific constraint based on your own obsession. Because it's your obsession, your knowledge base helps you think of more ideas. That information lets you make mental connections that someone else couldn't.

By not saying what the advertisement should be, I'm giving you the autonomy and ability to decide. This experience is an opportunity to recognize the unique perspectives, leaps, and inferences of which only you are capable.

—Thomas Both

Micro-Mindfulness Exercises

Featuring the work of Leticia Britos Cavagnaro, Maureen Carroll, and Frederik G. Pferdt, with inspiration from Keri Smith and Jan Chozen Bays

Where have all your daydreams gone?

If you are reading this in the 2020s, you are likely suffering from the modern ailment of imagination insomnia. Common symptoms include being unable to locate a creative mindset. If this is happening to you, it could be because your daydreams have gotten lost in your smartphone.

When you reach for your phone during every idle moment, you are never just bored or thinking. When you walk through the world in a hurry without noticing it, you're missing opportunities for your brain to make magical connections on its own time. Those connections and ideas are important fodder for all of your future creative endeavors.

You already have a way to describe the deficit created by nighttime insomnia: you *lose* sleep. It feels bad, and you know it's damaging in the long run. Well, just as your body needs sleep to renew, your creativity needs daydreams to refresh.

If you're looking to find your way back to your daydreams, this assignment is the map. Follow it to some mental space and bring new attention to the world around you.

Your daydreams will hurry to find you again. They are missing you, too.

———

First, find a notebook in which to write down what you notice during these activities and make it your own. Purposely mar, scar, or otherwise injure the first page or two using whatever is on hand: coffee, stamps, tape, or pens. The goal is to preemptively free yourself from any hesitation later that you might ruin your pristine new journal with your imperfect ideas. Try out Keri Smith's wonderful ideas in *Wreck This Journal* to make a new journal less precious.

Then, starting in the morning, try one of these micro-mindfulness activities.

Put It in Your Pocket!

For a whole morning, don't reach for your smartphone while walking, in transit, or while waiting in line.

In the afternoon, reflect: How did the challenge go? What did you do and how did you feel in those transition/wait moments without your phone in hand? Are there things you noticed—about yourself, others, or the environment—that you might not have otherwise noticed? Write it all down.

Entering New Spaces

A shorthand for this mindfulness practice is "mindfulness of doors." For a whole morning, before you walk through a door, pause, even if only for a second, and take one breath. Be aware of the differences you might feel in each new space you enter. Once you master doors, try bringing awareness to any transition when you leave one kind of space and enter another.

In the afternoon, use this journal prompt: Did you discover anything new about the physical (or mental) spaces you entered (or left behind) today?

Photo-Free Day

See the world through your eyes, not your screen. For a whole day, do not take any photos with your phone. If taking photos is not your thing, then instead do not send any messages.

Afterward, describe and write about any feelings you experienced as a result of this challenge.

Smile!

For a whole morning, allow yourself to smile. Notice the expression on your whole face. Notice how it feels from the inside. Are your lips turned up or down? Teeth clenched? Frown lines between the eyebrows? When you pass a mirror or reflective window, take a look at your expression. When you notice a neutral or negative expression, smile. This does not have to be a wide smile; it can be a small smile, like the smile of the Mona Lisa.

In the afternoon, write about this: What effect did this challenge have on you? What effect did you notice in others?

————

These exercises pair two powerful actions that are important for creative work: noticing and reflection. Reflection is a critical tool you can use to take control of how you improve your own skills. For the full benefit of this series, challenge yourself to do one of these activities per day over four consecutive days. If you use the full sequence, you get closer to establishing a rhythm of reflection that will stay with you.

47 A Day in the Life

Featuring the work of Jules Sherman, Seamus Yu Harte, and Dr. Henry Lee

In general, design work is for and about others, not the self.

If you understand the breadth and complexity of other people's lives, you're much more likely to create or offer things that meet others' needs. This is true whether you're a designer, a teacher, a doctor, or a neighbor. Even if you're designing for your customers, students, or patients—even when you explicitly have influence in their lives or they've asked you for professional help—keep in mind that they don't wake up in the morning with the sole purpose of using your object, studying the subject you've assigned them, or following your prescription or therapy. They wake up trying to accomplish their own goals and priorities in life.

As you embrace this mentality, you'll start to intuitively understand how to shape your work so it fits into the lives of others rather than expecting them to change in order to adopt what you produce.

Of course, this isn't easy. Human beings are complicated. You need to understand their big picture. If you know only the part of them related to your work or to their relationship with you, you will never understand the most fundamental aspects of people and what makes them tick.

This assignment helps you try on one way to get close to another person's life. It pushes you to understand more of the whole human by helping you tell a story that connects the dots: motivations, beliefs, behaviors, and daily habits. Try it when you are ready to advance your ability to learn from and about others and can commit significant time to understanding a particular person or family. The activities involved were originally developed for doctors-in-training to build their capacity to empathize with patients, and they will get you to go beyond relating to someone else based only on your goals for them or the situation. This assignment helps young physicians develop compassion beyond the normal eight- to ten-minute patient visit, and it will be eye-opening for you too.

———

Your goal is to make a day-in-the-life video about someone else that is five to seven minutes long. You'll build up to this slowly: first spend a few days capturing their routines with photos, then go back and conduct video interviews based on ten key images.

Find someone who will agree to be the subject for your short video—a person

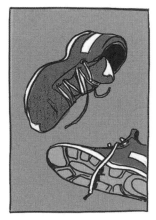

whose daily life contains challenges, ideally related to the work you do. If you design for athletes, maybe you find someone who is training for a marathon. If you work in health care, perhaps you connect with someone who is dealing with chronic illness. You could choose your elderly relative or someone with a brand-new baby. That person will need to fully consent to this project, so before you embark together, make sure you explain its entire scope as described here (at a minimum, how long it will take, the personal nature of the interactions, and how you plan to share the video).

With permission secured, shadow this person for three days, four to five hours per day, documenting what you observe. Spend most of that time in their home. Yes, this is a lot of time. But life happens in the daily details and the in-betweens. If you record and observe only the "notable" moments, you can't see the big picture. (For another take on this practice, try out *Shadowing*, page 41.)

Your goal is to learn about what's happening in this person's life, their strategies for handling it, how they interact with others as a result, and what they think and feel about it all. But it's not just about the details you're trying to unearth to accomplish your storytelling goals. Throughout the experience, you want them to feel heard, seen, and cared for.

Take frequent snapshots throughout: these will serve as essential prototyping materials for the video. Where does he keep his running shoes, and how does he care for them? How does she organize her medicines, and how does she feel about the help she needs to take them?

After those three days of shadowing, review all the photos. See what stands out as important elements of your subject's life. This process allows you to discover and react to what's true and meaningful for your subject, rather than viewing them through your own preconceived lens. Build a rough arc of the story you will ultimately present through video by arranging and rearranging ten of those photos until you know the ideas you're aiming to bring to life. Digital photography is an easy medium to use for rough drafts and to experiment with content and structure before you start to work with the medium of video.

Unlike a fairy tale or a famous hero story, the arc of this story might not have a tidy resolution at the end. It might end with a subject asking a question or saying something that shows how they make sense of their challenges. A day-in-the-life story is about showing the details and the humanity of your protagonist.

After your shadowing is complete and you've made a prototype of the arc you hope to portray, interview (on camera) all the people who matter in this story. That might be only the protagonist or perhaps others they interact with daily. Use whatever editing software you can access to put together your day-in-the-life video. You might integrate the photos and intersperse them with the video clips, or you might not need them any more if you have captured all the main ideas on camera.

Share the video with your subject as well as other people who would benefit from understanding daily life through this person's eyes.

———

We created this assignment out of an interest in the connection between storytelling, empathy, and the practice of medicine. I teach a lot of medical students who are also interested in design, and I want them to gain empathy for patients with chronic illness. They are being taught how to ask good diagnostic questions, but can they ask the right questions that help them understand vital information about the broader context of these people's lives? They shouldn't just ask, "Did you take your medication?" They should know what the rhythm of someone's day is like so they can ask a better question, which might be "How can we set up reminders during your day that help you stick to your prescriptions?" A person and a disease aren't the same thing.

You have to set this assignment up with sensitivity and care. For some of my students, it's the first time someone has asked them to understand the world through a patient's eyes. And at first, patients are tentative to interact with these students on such a deep level. But there's an outpouring of emotion after the patients watch the finished videos with the students. "This is what I deal with every single day, and you're the only one who cared enough to see what this looks like."

I don't want the patients to feel analyzed. I want them to feel heard and seen. When somebody feels seen, they have a deep feeling of recognition for what they are struggling with. That's my goal. Then any further design work becomes a co-creation between the students, the patients, and their families.

—Jules Sherman

The Feeling of
Learning

On any given day, the phrase most likely to be uttered by anyone at the d.school is "How did that feel?"

If this makes you immediately skeptical or slightly annoyed by us touchy-feely California types, this essay is particularly for you. There's a good reason you have that reaction, which will become clearer in a minute.

"How did that feel?" is a typical prompt a group of students might use to launch a discussion after a challenging assignment. It's an open-ended question posed to someone who has just tested a work-in-progress prototype. It gets people thinking about the *how,* not just the *what,* which leads beyond a surface-level discussion to better insights. We're curious about feelings, because they just keep hitting us all in the face.

Feelings are everywhere in creative work, from the elation of generating something new or useful to the tangle of effort and disappointment at moments of setback or failure. Feelings are also vital to how people learn. Scholars like Mary Helen Immordino-Yang and Rebecca Gotlieb—who are working to bridge the gaps in our understanding of how the brain is structured, how we learn, and the role of emotions—write, "It's neurobiologically impossible to think deeply about or remember information to which you have no emotional connection, because a healthy brain does not waste energy processing information that does not matter to you."

Despite this, emotions are rarely seen as vital to producing work or learning. Even if they are acknowledged, they are viewed as something to be managed and diffused, rather than a contributor to better outcomes.

Culturally, we've separated thinking and feeling, as if cognition is the business of the brain and emotions are the domain of the heart. If you take this phrasing literally, it suggests that these actions originate from different parts of your body! Biologically, of course, it's not that simple. Emotions are made in your brain, just like thoughts, but it is possible we understand them even less. Compounding the complexity are the physiological effects that manifest in your body in response to different feelings or ideas. It's highly connected, but that principle is not always embedded at the center of how we teach and learn.

Gendered thinking from earlier eras is still wrapped up in this idea: a tacit (and sometimes explicit) belief that emotions are soft and more female, while thoughts and ideas are objective and more male. That's both a false dichotomy and a false attribution. However, this stubbornly enduring inheritance of a patriarchal society shows up in norms that prize work and learning done by thinking and exclude work and learning done by feeling. These ideas limit all of us from developing our abilities to the fullest.

At the d.school we are proponents of integrating ideas and emotions because this combination facilitates effective learning. It feels natural and familiar to us because this framing also corresponds to how design works: design requires a combination of *thinking, observing, feeling,* and *doing.* This model has been elegantly described through the work of education researchers Alice and David Kolb.

A sad result of the bias toward thoughts and away from emotions is that people place more value and focus on building skills around the part of learning that involves *thinking* and *observing* and leave their capacity for *feeling* and *doing* underdeveloped.

My colleagues Leticia Britos Cavagnaro, Meenu Singh, and sam seidel use a great analogy for this when they teach. Imagine going to the gym, and day after day you work out just one side of your body. Soon, one arm will be muscular and defined, while the other stays relatively puny. It sounds preposterous, but the truth is that most of us have done this for roughly a decade and a half of our lives (or as long as we were engaged in formal education).

Drawing from the work of the Kolbs, James Zull, Paolo Freire, and many other scientists and educators, it's clear that to take full advantage of your faculties you need to strengthen all of your muscles because they support each other. For example, the Kolbs describe how these different abilities motivate learning because they are like voices in a conversation with each other. When one voice dominates the other, learning is stalled. In a 2018 article in the education journal *AEL,* they wrote, "Hyperactivity or withdrawal into reflection both inhibit learning. Dogmatic beliefs leave us closed to new experience while total immersion in experience clouds clear thought. On the other hand, the 'shock and awe' of an intense experience can cause reconsideration of an entrenched belief while a new idea can reshape the way we experience things. Reflection on the consequences of action can serve to correct errors and refine future actions while acting on reflections can stop incessant rumination."

Part of the reason that d.school experiences strike people as unusual is because they emphasize the two "muscle groups" that are typically the least developed: *feeling* and *doing.* These are the aspects of our assignments that provoke the most skepticism and discomfort. However, since both feeling and doing are so vital to design and creativity, we highlight and enrich the ways people can use them. Get a taste of this by trying any assignment in this book that helps you *feel* through concrete experience or *do* by engaging in active experimentation (see *How to Talk to Strangers,* page 32; *Party Park Parkway,* page 61; or *The Monsoon Challenge,* page 89).

Tom Maiorana, a frequent d.school instructor and design professor at the University of California, Davis, tells his students: "When I'm teaching I want to give you a visceral experience of different aspects of design, especially the more abstract phases. I want you to have an experience that helps you observe your own behavior when confronted with uncertainty, for example. If you can observe it, then you can start to pay attention to it and develop stronger skills. If you're in my class, I want you to jump in, and regularly use your body as a thinking tool. I want you to see that whether you're in class or in life, you often need to look at things from a different vantage point."

The other two muscle groups—thinking and observing—deserve exploration as well, since working and learning like a designer requires them. You need to take time and have specific approaches to make sense of complexity and visualize what's really important in the data you're gathering. This helps you to focus your work and find creative new ways to address challenges. To try out design-based approaches for making sense of complicated issues, see *Practicing Metaphors* (page 81) and *Map the Design Space* (page 106). These assignments help you practice what's called abstract conceptualization, allowing you to link disparate examples, stories, or small bits of information by showing how they're all connected to a bigger idea. If you know someone who is really good at "connecting the dots," it's likely that they are generally good at abstract conceptualization.

Of course, none of these modes occur completely apart from one another. You can't really have a creative action that completely isolates one muscle, even if one way of working is your primary focus at a given time. In particular, once you've opened the door to embracing all of your different abilities, you'll start to notice how frequently emotions can affect the quality of your learning or making. As the title of this essay suggests, *the feeling of learning* is central to any creative practice, and becoming aware of it gives you more control over strengthening and applying your creative abilities.

In the course of your lifelong journey of expanding your creative capacity, you will experience many feelings, both highs and lows. Knowing what triggers these and how your behaviors intersect with the feelings of those around you will help you get better at setting the conditions that allow for both emotional and intellectual engagement with the work you're doing. "Setting the conditions" means that you take a deliberate action to affect the physical or interpersonal environment in which you're working. This could be very simple, like moving the chairs out of a room to get people who are able to stand to do so when you want their full attention, or creating a ritual to stretch or have a meditation minute right before you sit down to work. Or it could be a long-term effort to design a large collaboration space or cultivate a particular culture in an organization.

Three special conditions are crucial to the learning and creative outcomes we aim for at the d.school. Each of these sets the stage for more creativity to emerge. When you build these conditions into the environments where you learn and work, they help you unblock and support your own creative abilities as well as those of the people around you.

If you work closely with others, you already know that the range of different ways people relate to emotion can be wide. This can be due to factors like cultural difference, gender socialization, and biological neurodiversity. There's no right way to feel or express emotion, and gaining more fluency in how it operates for different people in a team or group gives you additional ways to be intentional as you experiment with the following levers. You'll learn the most by experimenting with the ideas below, debriefing with your group, and seeing how they work in your environment.

At the top of the list is *safety*. Safety means both *being* safe and *feeling* safe. When physical safety is assured, then the focus is on *psychological safety.* This is all about experiencing the feeling of interpersonal trust that allows you to be vulnerable. Trust is important between collaborators when outcomes are uncertain, so it's especially true in any kind of work where creativity is involved. Your fear of being judged inhibits your willingness to risk offering new ideas. As Steven Johnson writes in *Where Good Ideas Come From,* "Oftentimes the thing that turns a hunch into a real breakthrough is another hunch that's lurking in somebody else's mind." If you can't get the hunch out into the open, you can't learn what it might bring out in someone else.

Fears about how your work or ideas will be perceived are strong enough that they can act as a self-censor. You may have experienced this even when creating something entirely on your own; this doesn't confer immunity to worry about how your work will ultimately be perceived. If you feel creatively constrained, take some time to figure out where those feelings might be coming from. Being stuck is often the result of a lack of either inspiration or confidence. Inspiration abounds; confidence you must build from the inside. The more you are able to trust and feel safe when you are in the process of creating, the more fully you can explore new and unusual ideas. You've got a lot of options just from this book, since trust is at the core of many d.school assignments.

It's especially important when starting a project or launching a team to develop trust and foster psychological safety. To do so, build a repertoire of warm-up activities that you like to use. In choosing assignments for this book, "warm-ups" was the hardest category to narrow down and select from; designers at the d.school cannot stop inventing new ones. You will find over time that you have particular favorites you love and that are most effective in helping you and the people you work with get ready to be productive, collaborative, generative, or connected.

To get the most out of warm-ups, tie them to the work or the moment at hand. This is what makes them more than just "ice breakers." Breaking the ice is an okay concept, and starting off any activity or meeting with something fun or interactive is usually better than nothing. But when you link your choice of warm-up directly to something meaningful that you want to see happen during the rest of the work or learning experience, it helps you embody the same behavior you are hoping to see from yourself and your teammates in the creative work you are about to do. A few examples: *Blind Contour Bookend* (page 30) will help you locate your inner critic so that you (or your group) can be more freely generative. *First Date, Worst Date* (page 112) will help you turn something abstract into something concrete by building a physical object with your hands and telling a story all in one assignment. When you use a warm-up in an intentional way, you get to rehearse the very themes and habits that apply to the work you're about to do; then you'll carry this sensitivity directly into your next creative acts.

No structured activity or ritual alone can maintain psychological safety; you also need to commit to showing up for whatever feelings present themselves, whenever that happens. People are emotional animals, and you can't get too far working creatively without real feelings emerging. If you establish a routine to warm up (or to reflect or debrief), you create a release valve to let off the emotional steam as you go. But still, even when you expect and plan for emerging feelings, sometimes a strong emotional reaction to uncertainty or a strong conviction of joy and celebration takes over at an unscheduled moment. Be there for yourself and others when it happens. It's not getting in the way of the work; it's part of the work.

The second way to use feelings as a canvas for creativity is to *have fun* in order to provoke glee, wonder, or joy. This sounds utterly simple, and it is. Creativity involves play, improvisation, surprise, and (hopefully!) delight. And considering the hard work and uncertain struggle it takes to produce great work that meets the needs of the moment, often you have to make the fun happen.

Fun and joy show up at the d.school in many ways, and you can adopt any of the ones that appeal to you or make your own. For starters, there's a whole cluster of warm-up activities that are sometimes called "stokes." The main purpose of a stoke is to fan a flame that might be burning low after a lot of exertion, and in doing so, bring renewed light and heat into the effort. Stokes almost always involve a combination of *doing* and *feeling,* a counter balance to fatigue from a long session of *observing* or *thinking. Rock Paper Scissors Tournament* (page 109) is a great example: this classic experience of near mayhem and good-hearted competition helps you pick up and move yourself and your spirit any time you play it. To try a stoke on your own, you can move your body in a one-person dance party, send a quick note of appreciation to a friend, or close your eyes and listen to a song that always makes you feel something. Just find a way to experience a brief moment of contrast to *observing/thinking* with a *doing/feeling* break.

Fun can also come from surprises and "reveals" that you plant along the way. *This Assignment Is a Surprise* (page 238) serves the specific goal of temporarily suppressing your inhibitions so you can see how capable you are well before you think you might be. It fits within a tradition of many types of surprises that show up periodically at the d.school: a special guest speaker, a new design challenge topic, or an unexpected reward for great work.

For the final presentation of a large-scale design project around innovating the future of the undergraduate experience, we once surprised hundreds of exhibition guests (including Stanford's trustees and president) with a playful invitation to enter the event by going through a time machine to visit the university of the future. This was fun with a purpose: we hoped to help the participants suspend their disbelief about how radically a university could change. We also knew that few of them would show up if we announced the time-travel theme in advance. Everyone opted in to the surprise experience, and the whole event was richer for it. In addition to the sheer fun of these moments of surprise, when you design them with care, joy, and optimism, they help you overcome skepticism or fear and step into new behaviors that you might not try with more expected methods.

It's a little harder to design an elaborate surprise for yourself if you're working on your own. However, you can draw on the long tradition in certain art practices of using randomness to create a very similar effect. Try out *Protobot* (page 144) for a never-ending supply of hilarious and unexpected prompts for proto-typing, or *Bisociation* (page 102) to build off of ideas in combinations you could never predict.

The theory behind what's happening with stokes and surprises is the way that excitement creates a greater capacity for learning and doing certain kinds of complex tasks. (Technically, this is called "arousal," but not the kind you're now thinking of.) When your mind is aroused you are better able to complete certain tasks. Short, energetic activities or surprises may even help you the most because they are not about sustaining a high level of energy (which over a long period of time becomes draining); rather, they create a rapid change in your environment that excites your brain to respond.

Establishing safety and sparking fun both speak to cultivating positive emotions. Since design work will take you across the full spectrum of highs and lows, it's important to know how to set the conditions to productively engage in the third emotional attribute we focus on (and celebrate): *struggle*. This is such an important part of creative work that it gets its own section, which you can find on page 207.

If you go back through the story of the founders of Noora Health at the beginning of this book, you can appreciate the many ways that feelings flowed in and out of their creative work. They consciously built psychological safety on their team by addressing challenging dynamics and tensions. They injected fun and humor into their prototyping process, which wound up capturing a spark of authenticity that resonated halfway around the world. They went through many highs and lows throughout their learning and design journey. And they became passionately dedicated to their work through their openness to hearing and seeing the perspectives of people going through very different life experiences from most of the team members.

Whatever your starting point, it takes time to develop confidence in your ability to embrace emotions in your work, cultivate your faith in the value they can yield, and hone your ability to judge when to use these approaches in thoughtful, ethical, effective ways. The ups and downs you experience along the way are core to the feeling of learning: it's an often exciting, sometimes scary, always fruitful way of engaging with the world when you don't yet know the answers or outcomes, but have a hunch that your creativity can contribute in some way.

48

Tether

Featuring the work of Carissa Carter, with inspiration from Jennifer L. Roberts and commentary from Laura McBain

Observation is a critical tool for good design; you have to be good at noticing. But it's a skill that's steadily disappearing, lost amid the scattered fragments of our attention across multiple screens and the fast pace of modern life. That's not to say that moving quickly is always bad, but having facility at the slow end of the spectrum is a valuable way to stretch your ability to see and make sense of what's going on around you.

This assignment will help you learn to notice better. It slows you down to watch, think, and internalize something new.

The things you notice right away are what's on the surface; interesting reflections come later. You'll start to understand the process you need to *see* something that is insightful, meaningful, or even profound.

That takes time.

That's why this incredibly simple assignment might also be one of the hardest in this book. Use it when you want a transformative experience. You just have to give it the time.

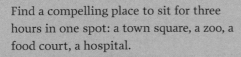

Find a compelling place to sit for three hours in one spot: a town square, a zoo, a food court, a hospital.

You can choose a place that's familiar if you're excited to see it in a new way—or pick a location new to you. Regardless, you're about to learn something powerful about how you observe the world and what you tend to notice.

Once you settle down in your spot, don't use your phone except to track the time (or use your watch). Silence all notifications so that you're not distracted.

Bring a notebook and do your best to write constantly about what's happening around you. You will go through different phases of processing.

First, you will notice a bunch of things right away.

Then—I can't lie—there's a terrible trough of boredom. It's almost a nervousness. A little internal voice that says, *How much longer do I need to be here?* might start to whisper in your ear. »

And then slowly you'll realize how liberating it is just to have time to watch what is. Especially when that's the only thing you have to do.

Over the course of three hours, there will be boring moments.

But those are the moments when you notice the interplay of shadows.

And why someone decided to place an object in this particular spot right here.

And why those people moved just over there instead of standing where the path is.

Sometimes you actually watch people. Other times there might be an absence of others, and you contemplate what factors might affect your space in invisible ways. You start to deconstruct what happened in your space before you got there . . . maybe before you were born. You reach insights that you can't get to without long, slow, intentional observation.

When you're bored with seeing, try listening. What other senses can help you make new observations?

You've tethered yourself to one spot. Don't forget to keep writing. A bathroom break is fine to take if you need it, but don't jolt yourself out of your attuned, focused state of mind by checking your phone or doing anything else.

Afterward, look at your notes. Examine your trajectory. When were you patient or impatient? How did this affect what you saw, heard, or perceived? What problems did you observe? The next time you embark on a creative project, how might you evolve your approach to noticing?

———————

It's important for designers to understand context and get granular in their observation.

Once I took students to a lake with no water. Weird, right? I gave them the historical context of the place, but didn't allow for any questions. I wanted them to get into noticing and observing without conversation. Could we just sit in this place and really observe the sounds?

Oftentimes we jump directly into conversation with our design work. It's natural; we're curious about people! But it's important to take time to really look at context. An activity that starts with more inward focus and quiet allows you to get into another space of imagination, and that's important for your work.

—Laura McBain

Solutions
Tic-Tac-Toe

Featuring the work of Rich Crandall, Adam Royalty, and Shelley Goldman

So you've got an idea! You've seen a need in the world that no one else is addressing. You think you've got a shot to create something new, and you want to get it going as quickly as possible. At this point, it seems logical to get right down to work building a mock-up of your idea and starting to shop it around.

But watch out. This is a very common trap.

Design defies the regular laws of time, space, and efficiency; the best way to the finish line isn't always a straight shot. Considering more than one way to solve your problem may seem like a waste of time at the start, but it's essential. It's the difference between seeing the full landscape and heading down a fruitless path with your eyes closed.

This assignment helps you think more expansively about what to make and how to make it in order to bring your idea to fruition. It reveals the many different forms that your core concept could take. It helps you navigate that tricky gap between your first idea and your best idea. And it even helps you gain a better understanding of your problem or concept. At this

moment, you want to stay in a learning mindset when it comes to your solution and consider many different ways to bring it to life.

For example, maybe you need to design a method for keeping something cool. A freezer, a fan, a mountain stream, a shade, the nighttime, or a sensor to identify the coldest spot in your house could all do it, depending on the specifics of your cooling needs. Your idea and the form it takes in the world are not the same thing.

You can do this assignment on your own, but it's far more productive to invite others to help. When you can build off of others' ideas, you'll end up with more variety.

First, think about multiple ways to bring your idea to fruition. Sketch out at least nine forms that your idea could take, putting each idea on a separate piece of paper or sticky note. (If you want to do a practice round, use the "keeping things cool" example I've offered. But let's make it specific: come up with nine different ways to keep an ice cream cone from melting too fast.) »

Copy the tic-tac-toe board on the opposite page onto a large piece of paper or a whiteboard. With your idea now embodied in nine different sketches, place your variations on the tic-tac-toe board. Use one board to capture all the different versions you're considering. Put your ideas wherever they fit.

For ideas that don't naturally fit on the board, ask yourself if there's something you could do to nudge them into underrepresented categories. Pay attention to squares that don't have much activity. Sketch out all kinds of approaches! If most of your sketches fall in one square, you'll have learned you have a natural bias toward conceptualizing in a certain medium. Stretch your thinking and engage your co-conspirators to come at the idea from a different angle.

Ultimately, you want full coverage across the board. This increases the odds that you'll learn something vital and spark many new ways to successfully implement your idea.

After using this tool to stretch your concept in new directions, share a few sketches with people who can give you feedback: ideally, folks who have experienced the need you are designing for.

When you're reflecting on what you learned from testing these concepts, ask yourself these three questions:

What are you learning about the person who might use this?

What are you learning about how you've framed the problem?

What are you learning about the different concepts specifically?

You'll be amazed at how much you're able to develop and strengthen your idea and how much ground you've actually covered just from hitting the categories in these squares. Most important, you'll have gained confidence that you know which direction to go.

————

Using these prompts and provocations helps you elaborate on your original idea. Those squares on the board that you aren't naturally inclined toward help you leap into unexpected territory and further develop your concept. Nobody wants to do unnecessary extra work, but getting in the habit of injecting divergent thinking into your process will help you flex your creative muscles in many settings. The beauty of the board is that if you think of it as a little game, you'll do this automatically. When you look back you'll realize it wasn't "extra" and it got you to a better place. It's a little trick to stretch yourself to generate new possibilities.

A Briefcase Viewpoint

Featuring the work of Charlotte Burgess-Auburn, with inspiration from Wim de Wit and David M. Kelley and commentary from Kareem Collie

Whatever you're making, do you know who your audience is? What they care about, how they'll use it, and what it will help them achieve? Just as important, can you say who your creative work is *not* for?

At the d.school we use the term "point of view" to describe the clarity you have when you can say exactly who your work will serve and what need it fulfills and can show that you have a unique perspective on a direction in which your solution might lie. Your work can never be for "everyone" or "anyone." These broad descriptions won't allow you to get specific enough to make your work really meaningful to someone in particular. Creating things that try to do too much at once—or for too many different kinds of people—hold you back from doing your best work. It's far better

that a small number of people love it than for everyone to just say "meh."

Declaring a point of view is like putting a stake in the ground; it sounds definitive, but you can in fact just pull the stake out of the ground and move it to another spot later if you find a better place to pitch your tent. As your work develops—and long before you finalize it—you want to be able to answer the questions in this assignment clearly and succinctly. Often, clarity about your point of view sharpens over time as a result of learning more and more about the need you're addressing, the people you're designing for or with, and the context you're in.

This assignment draws on a legendary lecture given by d.school founder David M. Kelley, during which he invites people to explore his unusually large collection of briefcases to experience what it's like to have a strong point of view. You might not think so, but many briefcases have a surprisingly specific point of view. There are briefcases made out of recycled truck tarps for people concerned about the environment. There are expensive hand-made Italian briefcases for individuals whose knowledge of the rare materials or techniques involved make the object—and

them—feel special. There are briefcases with many compartments, for folks who are meticulously organized. There are bags that function as briefcases that bear a conference logo, signaling membership in a group. And more. Exploring David's briefcase collection makes you realize just how many specific choices the designers of these different briefcases made and how clear they were about who they were making them for.

Try this assignment to experience what that level of clarity feels like, so you can know what you're aiming for in your own creative work.

For this activity, you'll need to print out a set of images you find online, and have scissors, tape, some thick paper or cardstock, and a wall to work on.

First, make your own collection of briefcases. Unless you have many years and lots of closet space to acquire them in a physical form, you're going to do so with online image searches or by cutting out images of briefcases you find in magazines. "Collect" twenty to twenty-five briefcases by searching for ones that appear most different from each other. You'll find briefcases with exquisite leatherwork, briefcases with

wheels, briefcases in the brightest color, and briefcases with tech built right in. You can expand your search to a broader category, like "work bag," if you choose.

Once you've found a collection of interesting briefcases, print out an image of each one. Spread them out on a table. Start with one that you find really interesting.

Who do you think it's for? What makes you say that? What kind of details do you notice? What kind of choices do you think were made in the design and manufacturing process? Take notes as you go; you'll want to keep track of the main attributes. Go through this process for at least ten to fifteen of your briefcases.

Now, create your own meta-level point of view by curating an "exhibit" of briefcases.

Choose four or five of your briefcase images and prepare to mount your exhibit on a wall. Imagine you are going to take someone on a tour of this exhibit after you've prepared it. You want them to be able to understand why this set belongs together and see the connections between your chosen cases. This is a curatorial point of view: a perspective on how a group of things are related based on a deep understanding of the attributes of all the individual artifacts involved.

Use these guiding questions to develop your point of view.

Why do these briefcases belong together? What is the through line? (This forms the first part of your point of view.)

Who is the audience for your exhibit? What do you hope to communicate to your audience? (This is the second part of your point of view.)

How does each briefcase support your point of view? What aspects of the briefcase show how it belongs with the others?

Now decide how you will express your point of view so that your audience can experience it. How will you present your artifacts? Consider the order you put them in, the spatial relationships, and any extra images or material you want to add to them. The decisions you make will affect your audience's experience: a chronological arrangement feels different from one based on affinity or contrast, for instance. A curatorial point of view is a sort of story, and your briefcase story will be memorable if your curation leads your audience to some kind of new insight.

On small pieces of paper or cards, write or print out some text for each briefcase to explain or engage your audience. Then mount your exhibit on a wall, arranging the images of the briefcases and any additional information or images in an intentional way to communicate your point of view as clearly as you can.

If possible, invite someone else to your museum opening, and find out what they see in your collection.

––––––––––

This assignment is a simple and effective example of how having a strong point of view creates meaning. Identical briefcases can be used in multiple exhibits and express very different meanings depending on the point of view. And regardless of the designer or curator's intent, a part of the meaning can be made only by the viewer. For instance, David's favorite briefcase in his whole collection is one that belonged to his father. The personal meaning associated with having his father's briefcase far outweighs whatever the original designer's point of view was.

The point of view of any creative work is the initial stake that hints at where the solution lies. Without a point of view, you communicate confusion. With a sturdy point of view, you can craft clarity. But the beginning also presages the end. Your point of view is both the start to finding your solution and the constraints you place around what your solution might be. When you point your telescope at the sky, you can see only a small fraction of the stars and constellations that exist. There is still a breadth of possibility for your solution, but it is no longer as infinite as the universe. When the solution you need or want falls outside of these constraints, you have to change your point of view.

If the advantage [of a strong point of view] is clarity and momentum, the caution is that you are taking a point *of view, not* the view. *To make the leap in design is to stand in one vantage point in relation to the question you're trying to address. But there are always multiple vantage points that one could stand in.*

—*Kareem Collie*

51 Instant Replay

Featuring the work of Eugene Korsunskiy

Since every team is made up of a unique combination of humans, every team is different, regardless of your professional or personal circumstances. Creative tasks in particular require you to have exceptional skills for interacting with others: qualities like generosity, flexibility, and resourcefulness. And your team dynamic isn't fixed. It grows and changes over time as team members influence and affect each other, much like a family does. Scientists who study organizations call this "emergent diversity." It can be a huge asset for creative exchange—and it also increases the potential for misunderstandings and friction.

One surprising solution to that friction is to lean right into the messy misunderstandings and do something even more awkward: video record your team in action, and watch it play back—together.

This assignment helps you bring self-awareness to any group that has been together for a while and wants to tune up its collaboration and communication. It creates space to observe unconscious aspects of your teamwork that can be hard to see without this small, but deliberate effort.

This assignment works best when a team is comfortable letting their guard down and isn't in the midst of a crisis. Everyone needs to be on board to try this out. (If there's already an obvious problem, work to resolve it, not to study it further.)

During a group meeting, set up a video camera (or smartphone) in a place where you can see everyone. If you do this with a distributed team using videoconferencing, you already have this capacity built in.

It's important to capture body language in addition to verbal exchange. Body language is the subtext of any human interaction; it often carries significant clues about emotions, hierarchy, or conflict.

Record ten to fifteen minutes of your team meeting. Then watch the clip together, review, and talk about what you see.

Note: This video is just for you and your team; it's not meant to be used as an evaluation. If it is for evaluation and the team knows this, the video won't capture the natural workings of the team. Everyone must be clear that it's solely an internal reflection and analysis tool.

Now, together, write a written reflection of all that you observed about yourself, other individuals, and the whole team.

Consider the following:

What were some of the best, most fun, or most productive moments? Why?

What were some of the worst, least fun, or least productive moments? Why?

What roles did the team members play? Who was the formal or de facto facilitator, devil's advocate, timekeeper, team clown, and so on?

Who spoke the most? The least?

Who interrupted the most? Who was interrupted the most? The least?

For each person: what surprised you about seeing yourself on video in this way?

What insights do you have for improving your team process going forward? What are you doing well that you want to pat yourselves on the back for and double down on? What do you want to try tweaking about your process?

Once you've finished writing, talk as a team about your insights. Be sure to discuss the behaviors that support and the ones that block; behaviors that help the team diverge and explore many ideas, and behaviors that help you converge on a smaller set of concepts to develop further. Refer to body language that's confident and comfortable and any that signals the opposite. Approach the conversation with a tone of inquiry: "What's your interpretation of that interaction?" "Why does that stand out to you?"

Write out some resolutions that the team wants to make to improve the collaboration going forward.

When you are done, delete the video together. It makes for a nice ritual and helps build trust. »

You may hear some hesitation from others when you propose this idea. The idea of seeing yourself as others see you makes most people feel truly vulnerable. Remind people that everyone else is seeing them in action all the time; this is an opportunity for each group member to have a way to observe their own behavior from outside of themselves. Also, you're in it together.

Like high-performing athletic teams that obsessively review game-day tape to find ways to improve their abilities, great creative teams can gather the courage to identify their own strengths and weaknesses in an honest and direct way.

When I first developed this assignment, I wondered whether people would be their genuine selves, or if the video would distort their behavior. Even though they know they are recording themselves, their reflections and comments after the assignment were so insightful that it convinced me of the value of the activity.

I often hear realizations that one person was interrupting another team member a lot. Or that someone observed how little they actually speak in the team. I've heard powerful insights, like "People have told me that I'm quiet and I didn't believe them, but I saw it on the tape and I think I can explain it better now. I'm sitting there processing, so when I do say something, it's sparse but insightful. Now my team realizes that they don't need to push me to speak—that's actually interrupting my train of thought."

—Eugene Korsunskiy

52 Tell Your Granddad

Featuring the work of Grace Hawthorne and Seamus Yu Harte

Work that is risky, bold, or novel needs a compelling, clear explanation to survive the trek from idea to reality. The trick is to find the essence and share it in a way that someone else can easily understand. Sometimes there's a big gap between what you think is completely clear and what others actually find relatable.

This assignment builds your ability to generate metaphors quickly and develop the cognitive flexibility to reimagine and even rebrand a concept in different dimensions.

This rapid-fire, high-energy game is useful for teams and groups who are moving from an abstract phase of work (like gathering a lot of information or deciding on a design direction) to a concrete one (like building models or writing copy), or back again. It's so fun that even if you are working on your own, you can probably get some friends to play this with you at home.

————

Your goal is to take an abstract concept and attempt to express the idea in as many concrete ways as possible using metaphors, analogies, and similes.

To do so, first imagine an audience of someone you know well and understand but who is very different from you. For the purposes of this game, call him Granddad.

Granddad probably grew up in a pre-digital technology era. He may still prefer a toaster to a panini press. He reads the newspaper in print and always buys his movie tickets in person, at the theater. He's a smart guy, but he's just not into all this modern stuff.

Your goal is to make sure your communication has reference points Granddad will connect to and immediately understand.

Make a list of some abstract concepts that are nonetheless important to talk about. Here are some examples:

Climate change

Smartphone addiction

Student debt

The Beyhive

Robocalls

Plant-based meat

Ocean acidification

Why Harry and Meghan left their posts as royals

Absentee ballots

Emojis

Reality TV

Doomscrolling

Giving Tuesday

If you're working solo, give yourself a time limit of one or two minutes per topic and challenge yourself to come up with as many metaphors as you can for each topic. If you're with a group, the activity becomes a competition. If your group includes people from different countries, the primary language being spoken may not be everyone's first language. Be aware that this makes a highly verbal activity more challenging. You might try pairing up two non-native speakers, or pair people across language differences to level the playing field.

Step 1

Form teams of two and connect with another team so you are standing in a group of four people. Within your quartet, Team A is the team with the shortest person on it; the other is Team B. (Repeat this pairing of teams for as many people as you have in your group. If you have an odd number of people, make a trio.)

Step 2

Each Team A has one minute to use as many analogies, similies, or metaphors as possible to explain *climate change* by starting each sentence with the phrase, "It's like . . . _____."

While Team A goes, Team B captures each of Team A's metaphors on a sticky note. (For example, a great metaphor to explain climate change to someone who's never heard of it is, "It's like being stuck in a car with windows that won't open and no air conditioning on a hot day with a dog that won't stop farting." Try to top that!)

Step 3

Next, each Team B has one minute to use as many analogies and metaphors as possible to explain *smartphone addiction* by starting each sentence with the phrase "It's like . . . _____." While Team B goes, Team A captures each one of Team B's metaphors on a sticky note.

Step 4

Play as many rounds as you have time or concepts for.

Step 5

Tally the sticky notes from each pairing of teams to determine a grand winner from across the whole group.

Step 6

Share the work by posting the outcomes from all the teams, categorized under each respective prompt. If your group has non-native speakers, you can adapt the exercise by asking the pairs to share their best analogy rather than all of them. If you're feeling playful, nominate someone to play the role of Granddad, and give them the task of awarding a prize for best metaphor.

Debrief the experience as a whole group. Which metaphors really sang? Which ones tanked? Can you figure out why that might be? Does everyone react to them in the same way?

Getting better at generating the right metaphor can help you explain something complex or new when it really counts.

This assignment came from the desire to help people become increasingly fluent in moving between concrete solutions and abstract concepts. It's something you see strong designers do, but rarely taught as a specific skill.

A sense of urgency is deliberately created by the time limits and competition: they either force you into action or freeze you up. The more accustomed you get to the feelings, the better you become at reaching for the right metaphor to explain something while under pressure.

There's an art to coming up with good topics that the whole group can use. Smartphone addiction works well because it's very abstract, conceptually complex. Perhaps within some fields, it's very technical, but it's a big topic and there are lots of angles and elements that you can latch onto. That's what helps you generate lots of different ways of describing the concept, which is the purpose of the game.

—Grace Hawthorne

Distribution Prototyping

Featuring the work of Sarah Stein Greenberg

Think about the last time you bought a new toothbrush.

Your purchase may have felt simple, but in fact a very long chain of decisions and events had to occur between the time your new toothbrush was made and the moment you were able to use it. It was packaged, stored, transported, selected, priced, marketed, and displayed, and then you made the decision to buy that particular one and paid for it.

The same goes for the last time you got your teeth cleaned at a dentist's office: many actions by many different people had to happen in order for you to receive that service. After your dentist was trained, they had to create an environment that made you feel confident about their skills and qualifications, assemble the machinery and tools they need to clean your teeth,

and alert you that their services are available in a way that made you choose them over the dentist down the street. Each of these steps was essential: one broken link in the chain and you would be using a different toothbrush or dentist. And each of these links is an opportunity for creativity.

When you think about the process of creating and designing a product or service, you naturally think about where to find inspiration, how to figure out if the idea is meaningful to others, and how to build it. If you're entrepreneurial, you might also consider whether there will be demand for your idea, if it will be profitable, and where you might get the money to scale it up.

But even folks who aim to revolutionize a whole industry with their incredible new creation often overlook one of the most interesting parts of bringing something

new into the world: how on earth it's going to get to the people who want to use it.

You don't want to leave the activities required in distributing your product or service as an afterthought. You need to envision the way in which something can be distributed early on in your creative process, because it might have an important effect on what it is or how it's made. For example, IKEA furniture is cheaper than other furniture because customers put it together themselves. It's also shipped flat in boxes so the company can cram much more into one truckload, lowering the transportation cost per dresser or bed. The distribution model that the company developed has a huge upstream effect on how every piece of furniture is designed.

This assignment will help you think through the distribution challenges you may face with a mindset of creative experimentation. Use it whenever you're working on something that you want a large number of people to discover or purchase without you interacting with them face to face. (In other words, you don't need a complicated system to "distribute" a small number of holiday gifts to your immediate family members, but projects on a larger scale will benefit from having one.) If you have an idea that you might turn into a business or

side hustle, this assignment will help you uncover creative challenges to address early in the process, not after your concept is fully baked.

———

Grab ten to fifteen index cards or small pieces of paper, a length of string as wide as your biggest room or as long as your hallway, and a bunch of paper clips.

Take two cards from your pile. On one card—let's call it Card A—draw a picture of your product or service, and write down a few notes about what it is and how it works. On the second card, Card Z, describe who you hope will use your product or service. Create a specific persona (one of your future satisfied customers) and make up the following information: where they live, their age and occupation, where they buy things similar to your idea, and any other demographic information you think is relevant. Sometimes this persona is based on a real person you know or have interacted with while doing research for your creative project. If not, use your imagination to come up with a realistic character.

Tape one end of your string to a wall or chair, and tape the other end at the farthest point of the room, again using the wall, a chair, or whatever is handy. At one end,

use a paper clip to attach Card A—your concept—and at the other end, attach Card Z—your customer. The length of string that stretches between Cards A and Z is your distribution channel, representing the distance your product or service will have to go to reach the person you hope will use or benefit from it.

Use the remaining cards to write down, step by step, all the different hands your product must pass through (or steps your service must take) to become available and appealing to your customer.

For the purposes of this exercise, we're assuming that your product has already been manufactured or that your service provider can be trained. Consider these questions to help you identify each step:

How will the product be transported from the place it's manufactured or assembled to the place where your customer can buy it (a product like a toothbrush) or use it (a service like a dental cleaning)?
Is the product bulky or small? How is it packaged?
Does it get stored for long or short periods of time along the way? If so, where?
In what kind of retail environment will the product be sold? Where will the service take place? Is that environment digital or physical? How does the space look and feel?

How will potential customers find out about your product or service? How will they become convinced that your offering is better than someone else's?

Add more cards to your string until you have a convincing distribution channel. If someone in your life knows about business, ask them to walk along the string with you and point out any gaps or weak links. Refine your channel until you can imagine "shipping" your product or service all the way down the line.

This assignment helps you generate a list of questions that you may not have answers to yet. Once you have the questions, figure out how to learn more about those issues and respond to them before you try to launch your concept. You might discover that you can change the dimensions of your product so it can be shipped and stored more cheaply, which will make it more profitable. You might realize that you don't yet have any ideas for what kind of retail environment might best display or promote your product, so you start to research that. You might recognize that even if you believe your service concept is likely to give people a better experience than what's out there, you'll have to invest in building up its credibility through a marketing campaign or endorsements.

Whatever the nature of your work, building a prototype of your distribution channel will help you increase the odds that it actually ends up in the hands of people who want it.

———

I created this assignment for students who design goods and services in emerging markets, which often don't have robust distribution networks. A lot of great health, educational, or agricultural products have been created with the needs of people in these markets in mind, but they never actually reach the people in question because the designer didn't think about that part of the challenge and apply their creativity to the whole distribution and business model. If designers don't think through these issues in advance, they are less likely to understand the market context and constraints in which they are designing, and their creative efforts around the solution may go to waste.

This activity is based on a practice called bodystorming, in which you walk through or act out a process or experience before it actually exists. In this case, you're using yourself, space, and some basic materials to create a model of something you can't really experience: the interconnected chain of people, spaces, and interactions that form a distribution channel. It's a way to make this highly abstract yet fundamentally important part of design work into something you can see and touch physically, which in turn gives you lots of insights and ideas about it.

Creating physical representations of abstract things is a great habit to develop, and you can apply this tactic to many tasks that require creative solutions. Try using this idea the next time you need to make a budget, starting with LEGOs or blocks to represent different expense areas. Or, if you're hosting a party that involves complicated family relationships, use stuffed animals, pairs of shoes, or books to represent all the different personalities to make a seating chart most likely to keep everyone exhibiting good behavior. Moving physical objects around allows you to think about and react to them in ways that drawing or writing about them cannot; this tangible practice will help you solve many intangible problems.

54 When to Change Your Mind

Featuring the work of Erik Olesund

Erik Olesund draws on his skills as a comedic improviser to inhabit different states of mind when he's designing. He can rapidly shift his approach from one of great conviction to one of total uncertainty. By "acting" with confidence when he's working on a solution, he gains momentum. By "acting" with complete humility while sharing his work with others, he can listen for—and really hear—honest, valuable feedback that helps him improve his work.

How do *you* practice these different postures?

Think about the last time you developed and shared a new idea.

How did you act while you were coming up with it and building it out? How did you feel at the time?
How did you act and feel when you were sharing it?

Think about the two sides of a coin. Imagine that behaviors and emotions that help you when you're building are one side of the coin, and those that help you when testing are the other. Pretend that coin is in your pocket whenever you're working on something creative. "Turn" the coin over to help shift your mental state whenever you need to move into the other posture.

Prototype as if you know your solution is right … and test as if you know your solution is wrong.

Knowing you're right gives you the confidence to put your work out there. Knowing you're wrong makes you open to changing your mind.

—*Erik Olesund*

55 Embodied Prototyping

Featuring the work of Zaza Kabayadondo

Every once in a while, it's important to look around and realize that everything surrounding you has been designed by someone. Go ahead and try it right now.

Someone designed the style of window you're sitting nearest to, decided whether or not you can open it, and therefore whether or not you can use it to affect the temperature of the room. Someone designed the electrical system, the wiring, the switches, and the presence or absence of lampshades, which are all responsible for the quality of light you're currently experiencing—perhaps vibrant, perhaps peaceful. Over time, many someones have designed the idea of "living room" or "bedroom," and now we generally share an understanding of what that is, at least within a given culture. Someone designed your house or apartment relative to the other houses on the block or apartments in the same building or buildings nearby. Someone designed how many people should "fit" in your neighborhood, and now it feels either dense or spacious as a result. Sometimes design decisions on this broad level are called "policy," though this does not make them any more neutral or detached from human values than any other type of design.

Each of the people or groups involved in the design of these physical objects, environments, and social spaces (like neighborhoods) were influenced by their own experiences, values, and social context, which in turn affects your experience of their work. Whether those embedded values were accidental or intentional, the effects are substantial. Your sense of belonging or exclusion in your own neighborhood, for example, may be a result of design decisions made long ago. For instance, many post-WWII suburban housing developments in the United States were designed to create "idyllic" and affordable communities through the architecture and arrangement of homes. This produced environments that some people love and others feel smothered by, and that many were not even permitted to access due to explicit preferences or restrictions on the race of prospective homeowners.

The social and physical spaces and objects we interact with in everyday life play a role in shaping our feelings and experiences. These experiences can be powerful or subtle, affirming or negative. And you can bring these insights to bear with anything you are creating. When people use design, they most often consider the tangible attributes of what they create; for instance, what a product looks like or how it operates. But you can actively design the intangible ones as well. For instance, a window that gives you a sense of control, a light that restores your good mood, a neighborhood that is welcoming to newcomers or helps children feel safe. You don't have to just hope that a certain emotional attribute will radiate from your work; it's possible to get in there and design your desired emotional attributes into it. This assignment gives you a way to explore how that's done.

Through this prototyping assignment you will design an experience that provokes a feeling. You're not concerned at the moment with functionality or even the larger concept: you just isolate the emotion you're seeking to spark and focus all of your attention on it. This allows you to actively play with and shape a feeling or value that is often produced by accident (rather than on purpose) by seeing how different people respond to your prototype. By prototyping with this "medium," you bring more intention to this subtle, but powerful, area of creative work and improve your ability to design these experiences from the beginning.

Make a list of some emotional qualities that you want people who come in contact with your work to have. It helps to think of a specific project or challenge you're currently addressing. This could be anything, either professional or personal. It doesn't matter if what you normally work on is physical, a service, or an experience: you're going to be exploring feelings that arise from how any of these are designed and how they affect behavior.

Here are some intangible attributes you might explore:

Appreciation	*Nostalgia*
Belonging	*Oppression*
Control	*Power*
Encouragement	*Safety*
Empowerment	*Slyness*
Happiness	*Vulnerability*
Innocence	*Wisdom*
Intrigue	*Zip*

Take thirty minutes and, working on your own or with another person, come up with a five-minute experience that a small group could do to elicit the feeling of one of these listed attributes. To accomplish this, you will need to create something life-size that people can experience in their bodies. You can use physical objects, rearrange your furniture, design an interaction people can have, or simply create an experience of your chosen attribute through the positions that other people will be in, relative to others.

For example, you might have people sit on high stools or low chairs and discuss a recent topic in the news to create an embodied feeling of a power differential or inequity. You might design an experience in which one person shares something they need help with, and everyone writes down the guidance they would give as if to a cherished sibling in order to create an embodied experience of support. You could ask people to try to put together a puzzle, where one person can only see the image on top of the box and the other can only touch the pieces to create a feeling of connection and collaboration.

When the experience has occurred, discuss it. What did the participants actually feel compared to what you were aiming for? What provoked those feelings?

Take these insights with you and use them to help you intentionally design for the intangible qualities that you want to shine through in your work.

––––––––

Once you start to realize that everything around you is designed, you will become more curious about how to fine-tune the experiences you create. Embodied prototyping helps you take an abstract or theoretical idea, like "I want my dinner guests to experience nostalgia" or "I hope my customers experience whimsy when they use my product," and put it into the real world so you can learn from others' interaction with it. As with any act of prototyping and testing, it helps to take the perspective of others. You can use this assignment as a deliberate act of inclusion and pluralism, helping you broaden your understanding and consider unique or overlooked perspectives you haven't yet incorporated into your creative process.

I created this assignment as a hook, to get my students thinking about the relationship between bodies and ideas. I wanted to get each

body in the class moving, exploring content in the most active way possible, and interacting with each other. There is value in freeing up the body. I want you to learn with your hands and learn with your feelings.

A student group once decided to embody the concept of "power" and how it is entangled in all of our societal relationships. The students had everyone sit in a circle on stools. Each person had three pieces of paper and wrote down the first three associations that came to mind on the idea of power. The only constraint was that each had to be a noun.

One person read their first word—gavel— while holding a ball of yarn. Then, whoever had written down a word associated with gavel put their hand up. The first person threw the ball of yarn to the second person. The second person read their associated word—judge— and then read their second word—crown. A third person put up their hand and, after receiving the ball of yarn, said queen, and then read their second word—tall. Everyone held the yarn they'd received the whole time. At the end, the whole group was connected. The yarn showed the entanglement that we have with these different things in society, and illustrated just how connected these concepts are.

The students found a really simple yet effective way of making a theoretical concept come to life in the physical world so that other people could engage with the ideas together.

—Zaza Kabayadondo

The Test of Silence

Featuring the work of Scott Doorley, Dave Baggeroer, and Enrique Allen

Getting feedback is essential to advancing whatever you do in both your life and your work. If you can't receive constructive, incisive feedback, you are stuck performing at your current level. You might already be good, but over time you'll face new challenges, contexts, mediums, and roles, which means you need a way to keep advancing your design abilities. By regularly seeking feedback, you'll be able to tackle harder challenges and put forth bolder ideas.

When you're trying to create useful things or experiences meant for other people, what matters is not whether *you* understand how to use your amazing thing, but whether *someone else* gets it when you're not there to explain. If that's your goal, then the more feedback you get in the early stages of your design work, the better. Exposing your work early and often to people with diverse perspectives provides very important insights about the gap you're trying to close between a thing that works for *you* and a thing that could serve the needs of many others.

When it comes to testing ideas, most people routinely get in their own way by jumping in too quickly to clear up any misunderstandings and make sure the work is clear. When people react to your work *after* you've told them the goal, they are reacting to a mixture of the goal and the work itself, obscuring important information about whether the work can be understood without your explaining it. The strong desire to be understood and respected squares off against our much wimpier appetite for seeking critical feedback. Absolutely no one really *wants* to hear that their work isn't landing the way they intended it to. But when it's true, you need to know it as soon as possible. The tussle between being appreciated and being critiqued is not really a fair fight, but this assignment will help you tip the match in favor of you achieving your *real* goal: improving your work.

Giving and getting feedback are separate skills, both worth developing. This assignment specializes in building your capacity to receive feedback. It's most useful when you are working on something that's partially done so that you don't wait until the very end to change course if necessary. You'll need to involve at least one other person, and preferably a few, to react to your work. (Also try out *How to Give Feedback* on page 196 for more practice with the other side of the equation.) »

Prepare yourself to hear comments that will make you sweat or even upset you. If that happens, note it, but don't get caught up in your emotions—try to stay focused on what you are learning about your work.

It's worth repeating: you need to find a way to watch other people interact with your work *without explaining it to them.* Your strategy is to present your work and remain silent. You might say, "I'm working on something, and I'd love your input—I'm going to stay quiet and just watch while you interact with it. I really want to see how people respond without my explaining it."

If it's something digital, like an app, a website, or a financial model you built in a spreadsheet, you can just hand over your device or computer, then observe. If it's something physical, others can interact with it directly. Whatever it is, set it up so they interact with it on their own. Keep your mouth firmly closed (seriously, a roll of duct tape might come in handy) and curb your impulse to jump in and correct someone who is "doing it wrong."

Before you start, ask the person checking out your work to talk out loud about what they are thinking and feeling as they use it. It helps to grab a few more friends to also observe what's happening—then the group should respond to what they just saw.

You might hear things like, "Oh cool, I want to know what this is," "This seems so intuitive and interesting!" or "I can't understand what is going on here."

If you're testing with more than one person, each person should take a turn before you respond in any way. It sounds weird,

but you might come to enjoy observing people having a conversation about your work as if you're not there. Seeing it used by others breathes life into it. Once the pace of feedback slows down, only then may you allow yourself one minute to explain what you made. This usually inspires a second round of feedback.

Record the feedback you've received. Note the positive and the negative, and document new questions and inspiration for your next version.

Here's why it's critical that you don't share your intent or explain your work ahead of time to your testers. Doing so reminds them of how invested you are in the work. It also comes across as a subtle defense mechanism, and your testers' very human tendency to spare your feelings will make the feedback less real and honest.

Somehow, hard feedback has become equated with being mean. A structured approach to critique helps both you and the people you're asking for help to overcome that problem.

We created an elaborate method for critiques in a class on digital design, which this assignment borrows from. Everyone turns in their device with their half-finished work loaded on it. The unlocked device is put on a table that has an overhead camera (video image, no sound). One person sits at the table to explore the work and has five minutes to use the device in front of the whole class, without knowing whose it is, while narrating their experience. The scene is being projected on a screen so everyone can see it.

We don't want the students to know whose work is whose, to further separate the objective thing that's been created from the tender-hearted human who is its creator. Our goal is to help the students realize that their design has to stand alone. When they create something, they won't be there to explain it or share all the reasons behind the millions of choices that go into anything creative.

In today's world we get a lot of false "feedback" that's just about feeling good—but "likes" on social media tell you very little about how to get better and keep learning.

You might have to be brave enough to ask for that yourself.

—Scott Doorley

How to Give Feedback

Featuring the work of Andrea Small, with inspiration from Aaron Irizarry, Karen Cheng, and John Moore Williams

You might think that the hardest thing about feedback is receiving it, but the ability to give good feedback is also quite an art. To provide useful input, adopt the mindset of "benevolent critique." Your words don't help if you leave someone feeling crushed by your statements. But benevolent critique is not just a mindset; this assignment provides practical ways to embody the idea.

On the receiving end, remember that it's not a good critique if you hear only positive things about your work. Don't aim for approval or acknowledgment. As designer and educator Juliette Cezzar says, "Think of a great critique as one in which you get two or three insights, ideas, or suggestions that you are excited about, and that you wouldn't have thought of on your own."

No one is naturally good at giving and getting feedback, but you can get great at both through practice. If you become skilled at giving feedback on creative work, your friends and colleagues will start to seek you out for it. It's a rare and valued ability, and if you set up conditions in which benevolent critique can thrive, it's also one way to help bring more creative approaches to your environment.

For this assignment you'll need two friends or colleagues and something to share that

each of you would like feedback on. Because this is really about practice, that piece of work doesn't have to be something you're too invested in. Don't let the lack of what you think might be a critique-worthy piece of creative work stop you from trying this out. Write a haiku, make a sketch, or bring a draft vacation itinerary that you want input on.

Share the principles for giving and receiving feedback with everyone (see box on page 198), and take a few moments to let your partners digest these before you begin.

———

Each member of your trio will play a specific role: the presenter, the critic, or the observer. You will then rotate these roles so that everyone gets lots of practice in each posture.

You will conduct two feedback sessions, and each session will have a slightly different focus.

Session 1

Focus on separating the person from the work.

The first person takes two minutes to present their work. Then the second person takes two minutes to critique the first person's work. And the third person takes two minutes to share what they noticed about the dynamic between the presenter and the critic.

Rotate the roles so each person is in a new role, and repeat the process.

Rotate the roles one final time and repeat the process so everyone has presented, critiqued, and observed.

Pause to reflect with your trio.

How did that session feel?
How did the different roles feel?
Did you learn anything new about your skills in giving and receiving feedback?
Any other insights?

Session 2

Focus on the goal of the work. What elements of the work are related to its objective? Do those elements meet the objective? Why or why not?

Use the same timing of two minutes per role, and rotate the roles for three rounds as before.

Again, pause to reflect and discuss the questions above with your trio.

———

Giving and receiving feedback is highly influenced by the culture you're in. In different cultures, individuals feel more or less empowered to offer opinions or give greater deference to those perceived as experts. Pay attention to those dynamics in your context, and adapt this assignment in any way you think is most appropriate to your circumstances. »

PRINCIPLES FOR GIVING FEEDBACK

STARRING . . . THE WORK!

YOU'RE NOT EVALUATING THE PERSON WHO MADE THE WORK; YOU'RE REVIEWING THE WORK ITSELF. INSTEAD OF, "THE CHOICE YOU MADE HERE DOESN'T . . ." SAY "THIS ASPECT OF THE WORK DOESN'T . . ."

OPENING ACT: QUESTIONS!

LEARN MORE ABOUT THEIR OBJECTIVES. EXAMPLES THAT HELP FRAME A CONVERSATION ARE "WHERE ARE YOU IN YOUR PROCESS?" OR "WHAT CAN I HELP YOU WITH THE MOST?"

CRITICS RAVE . . . "IT'S A PERFECT BALANCE OF STRENGTHS & WEAKNESSES!"

BALANCE CRITICAL FEEDBACK BY POINTING OUT THE POSITIVES. CRITIQUE ISN'T JUST ABOUT FINDING THE THINGS THAT AREN'T WORKING OR STATING EVERY NUANCED WEAKNESS. IT'S TO ANALYZE A DESIGN OVERALL.

FEATURING . . . SPECIFICS!

THOUGHTFUL OBSERVATIONS AND POINTED SUGGESTIONS FOR IMPROVEMENT ARE MORE HELPFUL THAN SAYING, "I DON'T LOVE IT." (OR "I LOVE IT!") IT'S MORE PRODUCTIVE AND GENERATIVE WHEN CRITICS EXPLAIN WHY THEY DO OR DO NOT ACCEPT THE SOLUTION. STATE WHY IT IS GOOD OR BAD.

AND . . . RESTRAINT!

IT'S UP TO THEM TO COME UP WITH A SOLUTION. IT'S NATURAL TO SEE SOMETHING THAT IS NOT MEETING A SPECIFIC GOAL AND WANT TO FIGURE OUT HOW TO FIX IT, BUT IT'S IMPORTANT TO REMEMBER THAT CRITIQUE IS A FORM OF ANALYSIS. IF YOU START PROBLEM SOLVING, YOU ARE SWITCHING AWAY FROM ANALYSIS. EACH IN ITS OWN TIME.

BUT NO PERSONAL PREFERENCES.

AS AUTHOR SCOTT BERKUN SAYS, YOU MUST SHATTER THE IDEA THAT ANYTHING YOU LIKE IS GOOD, AND ANYTHING YOU DON'T IS BAD. EVEN IF SOMEONE CAME TO YOU BECAUSE THEY WANT YOUR PERSONAL OPINION, BE OBJECTIVE TO HELP THE DESIGNER REACH THEIR GOAL.

FABULOUS APPEARANCE BY TIM GUNN!

ADOPT PROJECT RUNWAY DESIGN MENTOR TIM GUNN'S METHOD OF LEARNING IN THE MOMENT. IF TIM DOESN'T UNDERSTAND WHERE A DESIGN IS GOING, HE OPENLY ADMITS IT ("I'M PUZZLED . . ." OR "I'M INTRIGUED . . ."). ASK SOME QUESTIONS TO UNDERSTAND THE INTENTION: "CAN YOU TELL ME MORE ABOUT YOUR OBJECTIVES?" "WHY DID YOU CHOOSE THIS APPROACH?" "WHAT CONSTRAINTS INFLUENCED YOU?"

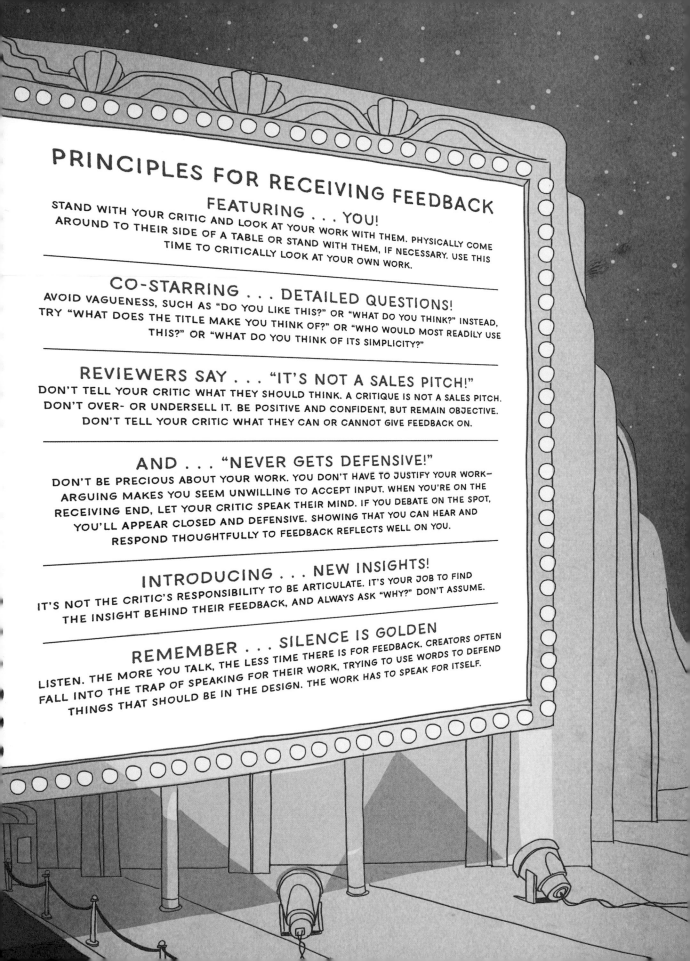

PRINCIPLES FOR RECEIVING FEEDBACK

FEATURING . . . YOU!

STAND WITH YOUR CRITIC AND LOOK AT YOUR WORK WITH THEM. PHYSICALLY COME AROUND TO THEIR SIDE OF A TABLE OR STAND WITH THEM, IF NECESSARY. USE THIS TIME TO CRITICALLY LOOK AT YOUR OWN WORK.

CO-STARRING . . . DETAILED QUESTIONS!

AVOID VAGUENESS, SUCH AS "DO YOU LIKE THIS?" OR "WHAT DO YOU THINK?" INSTEAD, TRY "WHAT DOES THE TITLE MAKE YOU THINK OF?" OR "WHO WOULD MOST READILY USE THIS?" OR "WHAT DO YOU THINK OF ITS SIMPLICITY?"

REVIEWERS SAY . . . "IT'S NOT A SALES PITCH!"

DON'T TELL YOUR CRITIC WHAT THEY SHOULD THINK. A CRITIQUE IS NOT A SALES PITCH. DON'T OVER- OR UNDERSELL IT. BE POSITIVE AND CONFIDENT, BUT REMAIN OBJECTIVE. DON'T TELL YOUR CRITIC WHAT THEY CAN OR CANNOT GIVE FEEDBACK ON.

AND . . . "NEVER GETS DEFENSIVE!"

DON'T BE PRECIOUS ABOUT YOUR WORK. YOU DON'T HAVE TO JUSTIFY YOUR WORK— ARGUING MAKES YOU SEEM UNWILLING TO ACCEPT INPUT. WHEN YOU'RE ON THE RECEIVING END, LET YOUR CRITIC SPEAK THEIR MIND. IF YOU DEBATE ON THE SPOT, YOU'LL APPEAR CLOSED AND DEFENSIVE. SHOWING THAT YOU CAN HEAR AND RESPOND THOUGHTFULLY TO FEEDBACK REFLECTS WELL ON YOU.

INTRODUCING . . . NEW INSIGHTS!

IT'S NOT THE CRITIC'S RESPONSIBILITY TO BE ARTICULATE. IT'S YOUR JOB TO FIND THE INSIGHT BEHIND THEIR FEEDBACK, AND ALWAYS ASK "WHY?" DON'T ASSUME.

REMEMBER . . . SILENCE IS GOLDEN

LISTEN. THE MORE YOU TALK, THE LESS TIME THERE IS FOR FEEDBACK. CREATORS OFTEN FALL INTO THE TRAP OF SPEAKING FOR THEIR WORK, TRYING TO USE WORDS TO DEFEND THINGS THAT SHOULD BE IN THE DESIGN. THE WORK HAS TO SPEAK FOR ITSELF.

58

What? So What? Now What?

Featuring the work of Leticia Britos Cavagnaro, Maureen Carroll, and Frederik G. Pferdt

Reflection is an immensely powerful tool for learning. Going through a challenging experience is often chaotic, so it helps to disentangle what you felt in the moment from what you think about it now. By forcing your brain to review that experience, you build a new layer of interpretation and judgment about what worked and what didn't, which helps you grow. In the same way that players on a pro sports team review recordings of their game-day performance to see where they can improve, you can also develop a reflection practice.

Reflection helps you take ownership of your own progress toward mastery on just about anything. Try this assignment when you're starting out on a challenging project or learning something new in any domain. It's useful for building more learning into a creative project at work, a class at school, or something personal like training for a marathon or perfecting your gardening acumen.

There are many methods for reflection; give yourself a head start by trying out these prompts using the What? So What? Now What? method.

Identify the experience you want to reflect on. Each time you reflect on it, be concrete and specific. You will benefit from these details later.

Decide when you are going to reflect: will it be right afterward? A day later to let it settle? Don't wait too long, or your reflection will be less vivid. If you will be reflecting on a recurring experience (like training runs or moving through different phases of a design project), pick a frequency and set a daily or weekly timer to remind you to complete your reflection. Record your reflections in a notebook or in some digital format you can access later.

Use these prompts to elaborate on your reflection:

What?

Describe the setting, using words or sketches. Capture details from all of your senses (sight, sound, smell, even taste) and include your own body language. Note the body language and verbal responses of others. Describe how you felt. Describe what you were thinking.

What did you observe/notice about yourself?

So What?

Evaluate: What worked well? Provide evidence. What did not work well? Provide evidence.

Infer: How might you explain some of the observations that stood out to you? What connections might you make with other experiences you've had?

In what ways is this relevant to you?

Now What?

What did you learn from your experience? What did you learn that you can apply as you move forward? What new questions did this experience bring up for you? How did this experience validate your beliefs about yourself or others? How did it challenge them?

At the conclusion of your project (or an important milestone), set aside time to go back through and analyze your reflections. What themes do you notice? How did you grow? When did you struggle? What's next?

―――――――

Many people don't think of reflection as a skill or a challenging thing. But introducing this structure to our students has had a noticeable effect on the quality of the reflections and their growth. We have them submit their first reflection with no guidance, and then they compare the quality of their reflection before and after they use the framework. They get to decide what is most valuable from the more structured approach and apply it however they want going forward. Reflection is personal: no one size fits all. You should feel free to use and adapt this model until it works best for you.

―Leticia Britos Cavagnaro

High Fidelity, Low Resolution

Featuring the work of Erik Olesund, Sarah Stein Greenberg, and Carissa Carter, with inspiration from Paul Rothstein

The dominant narrative in our world is that good hard work moves in one direction: forward. But creative work stands apart from other ways of working because it doesn't move in a straight line.

This is a pretty big difference, if you think about it. Physicians are trained to rule out as many options as possible to zero in on what's wrong with you and then start treatment. Machinists building a car start with parts and end with a vehicle.

Predictable linearity is great in many situations; it leads to more reliable outcomes, creates standards that you can hold people accountable to, and lowers costs or increases safety. But if you're working creatively, the answers—even the exact direction—aren't known or predictable, so you need a slightly different tack. There are times when work moves forward and times when it moves sideways—in several directions at once—to help you explore hunches that aren't quite provable yet. This looks and feels weird if you're not used to it. But one of the most productive and essential processes that designers use—and anyone can adopt—is the method of exploring multiple versions of the idea you're pursuing, simultaneously, and using outside feedback to calibrate the way forward. Making this a habit is useful no

matter what kind of work you do. It helps you quickly cover unknown territory and eliminate a lot of bad options. If you pursue just one idea at a time, you are more likely to plod along in that direction rather than consider other possibilities—to avoid "wasting" the effort you've already spent. Help yourself avoid that trap by embracing parallel prototyping and testing.

This assignment takes you through a process of testing your ideas to inform your ultimate direction. Use it when you've developed a bunch of different ideas but aren't yet sure which ones you'd like to pursue further. Before you start, you'll need to bring a few of these concepts to life in a rapid, low-cost way. How you do that depends on the type of project you're working on. Building something physical? You could start by sketching it out, then make a low-resolution model out of foam core boards, hot glue, and so on. Designing a classroom space? Make an interactive life-size model of the area using furniture or cardboard boxes. Working on a new service experience? Set up a role-play to bring someone through the experience, and be sure to include physical props that create the atmosphere or interactions you envision. Many materials and methods could work, but there are a few rules of thumb to follow:

The prototypes themselves aren't valuable, but what you learn from them is. Treat your prototypes as a means to an end and not the end result.

Don't get emotionally attached to what you create—that will hinder your process.

When in doubt, make something. Thinking does not equal doing.

You could create different prototypes of different ideas or multiple prototypes of just one idea. If you're testing just one idea, you could build three different parts of the concept or develop prototypes to highlight three different assumptions. Or you could represent three very different ways people would interact with your idea: a physical version, a digital version, and a service experience.

Once you have several different prototypes, recruit a few other people to test and react to your concepts; then complete the following assignment.

———————

In this assignment, your goal is to increase the quality of the feedback you get by designing the thing you are testing, the interaction that happens during the test, and the environment in which the test occurs. Being intentional with all parts of this experience really pays off. You're going to create a scenario for the test that feels as real (high fidelity) as possible, while keeping your prototypes unfinished enough (low resolution) to make your testers comfortable critiquing them.

Let's say your basic concept is a twenty-minute express dog-grooming service, and you're testing out three assumptions about what makes the service most compelling: should you make it feel *technical, magical,* or *simple*? For all of your tests, the core of your low-resolution prototype stays the same: you will hand your tester a stuffed

animal toy and ask them to pretend to be a dog owner who is coming into your storefront to experience different versions of the same service.

Here are some tools for increasing the fidelity of your test and some ways you might use them, drawing from a framework developed by design educator Paul Rothstein.

Atmosphere

Set the stage. Where are you? Why are you there? What does it feel like in this environment? Make the atmosphere as rich as possible. It's easier than you might think to use music, lighting, or rearranged furniture to dramatically shift what a space feels like. For your dog-grooming experience, you might rearrange the furniture in your living room and tape off different zones that represent the parts of your "storefront," then vary the lighting and music you're playing to emphasize three different moods you want to set for your attributes of *technical, magical,* and *simple.*

Actors

Give each participant a clear role. Are they playing themselves or someone else? (Fidelity is higher when people play themselves or when they share some of the qualities of the type of person you are designing for.) Who are you playing? What motivates each character? In your storefront scenario, ideally you are testing your concept with people who are actual pet owners playing the role of customer, but if that's not possible, you might hand a card to the tester on their way into the scene with a few notes about their motivation to help them get into the mindset of their character. ("Thirty-seven-year-old single man, grew up owning dogs and currently has two; loves tennis and having a clean car.") You yourself might play a key role like that of the groomer, or you could ask someone else to step in so you can observe the whole time.

Artifacts

What objects are in this environment? Who interacts with them? How? Why? Find or create basic props to represent these objects. Deceptively simple artifacts like a name tag, a hat, or a cardboard box that represents a machine can pull your testers right into your make-believe world. A basic costume like an apron for your dog groomer and a pet carrier or stuffed animal for your customer will go a long way. You might also have cardboard boxes of different sizes represent a tub and a cash register.

Activities

What are the actors *doing* in this new world that you're creating? Are they pretending to do something or actually picking up something and using it to accomplish a task? What actions must happen for your concept to work? Give everyone an initial set of directions (and think about how these would vary as you test your three different attributes), then let the scenario run and everyone react. For example, while testing the *technical* version, the groomer who is play-acting the grooming experience might describe all the biological needs of the dogs that receive grooming. In the *magical* version, the groomer might whisk the dog off behind a sparkly curtain.

After you design your test environment and interaction, improvise your way forward to run your test the first time. Start the scene and act it out. When the experience is over, say "cut" to bring everyone back to real life, then debrief with the

person who is testing your prototype. (If your prototype has multiple scenes, debrief after each one.) It might take a few rounds to refine a consistent protocol for testing.

After each test session, capture and summarize what you've learned in the following categories:

What was the tester's body language and actions while using your prototype and experiencing your test?
What memorable quotes did you hear?
What worked?
What didn't work?
Which of your assumptions were confirmed or disproved? How do you know?
What new questions arose?
What new ideas do you have?

Use these insights to improve your current concepts or eliminate a particular direction.

———

The value of testing multiple ideas in parallel will become vividly clear during this process. It is much easier to let go of something that's not working if you have alternatives on hand that you are also interested in pursuing.

Testing is your chance to refine your ideas and make them better, as well as a way to better understand the needs or perspectives of other people you are designing for or with. If people don't shower praise on a particular prototype, it's served you well: you'll often learn more from a failed prototype than from a successful one.

When failure happens, try to understand the reason for it. Was it the idea that failed? Perhaps the concept just wasn't sound. Was it the prototype that failed? The way this concept was manifested in the world may not have been the right form, but the idea could still have merit. Or did the test fail? It could be that your prototype and idea are still good, but you simply didn't execute your test well.

Increasing the fidelity of your test experience helps your participants react to your concept as they might in the real world. This effort makes it more likely that people will have an emotional reaction, not just an intellectual one, which gives you more complete data about how they might respond to the final work and leads to better conversations about what they value or need out of your solution. The play-acting and scenery don't trivialize the work, as many people fear; rather, they have the positive effects of drawing people in and showing that you're so committed, you're willing to do something a little unusual.

I once had a team of students who were trying to design entertainment opportunities for people experiencing long hospital stays. They had an idea for a wall-size screen that would connect patients directly to their homes to help them interact with their loved ones at life scale, as if they were living life more normally. To test a very early version of the idea, they had one person lie down on a low table as if in a hospital bed, while another group wearing lab coats—the "consulting doctors"—came in and held a discussion about the "patient." The students then shared their prototype of the wall screen and how it would work. This use of atmosphere, actors, artifacts, and activities gave the test patient a short moment of vulnerability, which stimulated a real emotional resonance. The feedback they got from this test was more empathetic toward the real patient experience than it might have been otherwise, and it allowed testers to focus more on the desirability of the concept than on its technical feasibility, which is what was most helpful to the students at that time. It turned out the idea was ahead of its time, as we can see from the widespread use of Skype, Zoom, Portal, and many other ways for individuals to stay connected to loved ones.

Early prototyping and testing isn't limited to officially creative projects. In practically any setting, there are moments where creativity is needed, and carrying forward multiple directions in all kinds of work enables you to explore and improve different ideas in parallel.

Productive Struggle

The first time I heard that a feeling of gloom might be a normal part of creative work, I was incredibly depressed about what I was currently producing. It was a project focused on irrigation tools for small-plot farmers in Myanmar, and a week before the final presentation I was having a full-blown crisis of confidence. Compared to the needs of the farmers we were working for, our solution for redesigning and thereby reducing the cost of a water pump seemed inconsequential. A far more experienced designer named Nicole Kahn was mentoring me. Seeing my dejected attitude, she told me bluntly, "I know exactly what you're feeling. I call it the trough of despair, and every designer I know relates to this feeling." She went on to explain that for everything she's ever created, she has had a moment when she fully detests what she has produced. She sees only the flaws and none of its merits. Even though she might have welded something magnificent out of steel, she only sees the slight imperfections in shape or tiny nicks in the metal.

Then something happens. Maybe someone shares a little positive feedback that punctures the cocoon of self-doubt, or Nicole figures out on her own how to improve the work and begins to regard it differently. She regains a sense of pride or accomplishment. Over time, Nicole told me, she has learned to understand the terrible trough for what it is—an important part of her own creative process.

Despite the many pleasures of creativity, one of its toughest aspects is that there is almost always a part of your process that feels terrible. The good news is, you're not the only one who feels this way. The better news: that discomfort serves you.

In the case of my pump project, I did make it out of the trough. My team's initial designs were well received, and our partners in Myanmar at Proximity Designs were excited to get their hands on it. Over the following summer I spent six weeks in Yangon. We tested the concepts with lots of farmers, they told us how to make it much better, and the Proximity engineers and workshop team took it from there. A few months after that, 1,500 more affordable pumps were in service in fields across the region.

What I have come to realize is that the trough of despair isn't just normal, it's essential. The negative feelings you experience in the trough tell you whether the work you're doing is hard or complex enough to deserve your full creative attention. Only challenges that don't have easy answers require you to take the kinds of difficult creative leaps that lead to breakthroughs. Only work that requires you to push yourself to develop new skills—not just deploy the ones you already have—keeps you on the edge of your own learning curve and, therefore, reaching toward your full potential.

Over time, if you're like Nicole, or me, or the many thousands of d.school students, you'll begin to feel that problems and work that don't have this quality are missing something. They're a little . . . boring. You'll notice that you prefer challenges with a good dose of unknown and uncertainty. You'll invite more ambiguity into your work or life. You'll keep pushing yourself to try harder things. You'll find the perilous feeling of not-knowing-yet a little bit intoxicating, and you'll want more. That's when you can tell that you've reframed the queasy feeling of *not knowing* into the far more powerful feeling of *I'm in position for a breakthrough to happen.* And breakthroughs feel amazing.

If you dive deeper into the trough of despair (metaphorically, please), you'll find different names for it. My favorite is "productive struggle." This term comes from research and practice in mathematics education. It turns out that students who effortlessly solve a math problem get fewer right answers when they face similar problems in the future, as compared to students who struggle with the initial problem. The lesson is that your learning is deeper and you retain more of the knowledge when it takes some time and effort to figure out how to do something. I think of this fact whenever I see the proverb "Smooth seas rarely make skilled sailors."

The tension you experience in between the bright possibility of a breakthrough and being off-balance while struggling to get there is embedded in every assignment in this book and most learning experiences we design at the d.school. We like to sit right in that uncomfortable place. We do that by asking our students to work on projects that don't have simple, clear answers. We put them on teams of people with disciplinary and cultural backgrounds unlike their own and teach them how to value and take advantage of the divergent thinking that results. We help them adopt a mindset of discovery. We give them experiences of drawing knowledge not just from expertise and past experience, but also from building, action, and experimentation.

Sounds amazing, right? However, in practice this often feels like, well, a struggle! We're committed to preserving space for our students to expend the effort it takes to find their own way, so we have to understand both what that looks like and how to deal with difficulties when they arise. Jules Sherman, a medical device designer who teaches courses focused on complex needs in maternal and neonatal health care, describes how struggle comes up in her classes at the d.school: "What seems to be the common thread for any challenging assignment we give our students is that when they struggle, they say it's too hard. This often goes something like, 'This is too much work and it's taking up too much of our time.' Or 'We need more time to do a good job.' Although it doesn't sound like it, this is actually a good sign. I know from past experience that complaining means they're struggling. They care about the work, but at first they want it to be simpler than it actually is. My job is to hold a mirror up to them, to help them through the most difficult parts, but not to make it easier."

Jules's experience helps her interpret the discomfort of her students: they're making a routine, fairly pedestrian complaint, and of course they are genuinely very busy, and she asks a lot of them. She's not unsympathetic. She just reads between the lines and sees that what's showing through the cracks of the regular excuses is actually Nicole's trough of despair. It's swirling with fear about not measuring up, that the work isn't good enough, or that because you can't predict exactly how it's going to land, you might not be able to bring it over the finish line.

It's really useful to recognize both when and why you are struggling. The natural instinct to first rail against the external circumstance ("It's too much work; the project is too complicated") just distracts you from turning the lens inward. A more constructive approach is to use your own past experiences as fodder for understanding how you work and learn best. To do this right now, go to page 246 and make a learning journey map to help you investigate and assess your own experiences with productive struggle.

That assignment, and practices like it, are based on an idea called "reflection-on-action." It's a term coined by philosopher Donald Schön to describe the habit that experts in many different fields have of looking back and assessing their past performance to learn from it and improve. If you practice reflection-on-action over time, you will know when you personally experience the most struggle, and you'll be better prepared to think on your feet about how to proceed. For some people, just being able to label a moment as productive struggle can get them unstuck.

Not all struggle is productive, of course. If you're too overwhelmed with difficulty or complexity, your brain and body become flooded with stress and fear. When that happens, you can't perform or learn. Can you learn to tell the difference and, better yet, know how to navigate yourself into the right type of struggle? I think so. To start, it helps to be in the right zone.

When it comes to tackling new challenges, there are many things that you already know how to do. This zone feels easy and familiar. There are also some things that you'll never be able to do, and if you wander into this space, you might feel panic. And then there are lots of things that you can do, as long as you have a bit of guidance. This zone feels hard, and also exciting. It's the feeling of *I'm not sure, but I'd like to try*. Its formal name is the "zone of proximal development," first described by psychologist Lev Vygotsky in the 1920s and '30s. Basically, this zone is the one in which you can do more today than you knew how to do yesterday, as long as what you're doing is something just a *little* beyond your current abilities *and* you've got some help.

You may be familiar with the phrase "in the zone" as it relates to a flow state, where everything you do seems effortless and perfect, and you're not even sure how you're doing it so beautifully. That's great when it happens, but I'm talking about something really different here—the challenging zone that you actively embrace in order to experience struggle. When you are beginning to struggle, you can turn to a set of practices that help you activate the guidance that you need, which is how you can flip the switch from unproductive struggle into struggle that helps you in the long run.

The easiest form of guidance involves seeking help from someone more experienced than you, so you can see how they would handle your uncertainty and ambiguity regarding your specific situation. This sounds obvious, but since the arena of creativity is suffused with the myth of the lone genius who is just naturally gifted in their craft, it's worth saying explicitly: you don't have to suffer alone; you don't have to figure out everything for yourself. Don't let moments when you need help derail your work for fear of exposing your weaknesses. Your chosen experts can be helpful in developing your concrete skills to solve a particular problem, and they also might help you just because they've been through enough cycles to know how to anticipate and deal with the struggle when it occurs. It's this awareness that made the advice I got from Nicole Kahn so valuable. She named the struggle and reminded me that it's normal, which helped me to break out of it. Experienced practitioners understand the rise and fall of creative work, and they have their own strategies and techniques for breaking out of the trough that you can learn from and adopt.

The process seems mysterious until you've had and reflected on enough of your own experiences. You'll find that in creative work, productive struggle happens at certain critical moments—to the point that it's almost predictable. One of those moments is while you are making sense of your observations and findings to figure out what direction your work should take. Another is when you or your team is trying to converge or decide. Even if you're working on your own, reconciling competing perspectives about what to do when you're working on ambiguous problems is just plain hard. No one can tell you you're making the "right" decision. You cannot be certain, and that's rough.

Another moment that commonly provokes struggle is receiving difficult feedback. (To work on this, try out *The Test of Silence* on page 193.) Knowing that these hard times (and others) are universally challenging is one way that working alongside more experienced practitioners can help you, and you'll soon start to notice and be able to anticipate these moments for yourself.

Another form of guidance can include "scaffolding," a concept that is deeply woven into the way that we teach and learn at the d.school. You can see this philosophy in many of the rubrics, protocols, and frameworks we use in teaching creative methods. Katie Krummeck, a designer from the d.school who works with educators around the world, is often the first person to introduce new methods of design within a given school community. In her view, "Often people approach problem-solving by trying to draw from within. When you do that without prompts, frameworks, or new inputs, you're inherently limited to what you already know how to do. With a little bit of creative prompting and external structure, you can summon from within some new perspectives that wouldn't have emerged without that support. Tools and frameworks are liberating: they help people to see more of what can come from within."

You have many opportunities to experiment with scaffolds and frameworks throughout this book. Try *Solutions Tic-Tac-Toe* (page 171) to see how a framework can push you to create multiple, divergent prototypes. *Protobot* (page 144) supports you with concrete prompts that liberate you to focus just on building. *Identify, Acknowledge, Challenge* (page 78) is a scaffolded approach to help you have potentially challenging conversations about bias, exclusion, and your own design work. And the final section, *Putting It All Together* (page 251), is itself a scaffold that helps you explore design challenges of escalating complexity and difficulty.

There may come an important moment when you turn to these frameworks and think *These are too simple.* Or *Where's the scaffold for the exact thing that I need to do?* That is a wonderful moment when it happens. In my life, this sometimes arrives in the form of a student who is frustrated that they can't locate just the right tool or method. Often, this is because the framework they need hasn't been created yet. Embrace this: it's the moment that you outgrow our tools and begin to adapt or make your own.

Other tricks to handling or shaping moments of struggle involve how you use time as an ingredient in your work. *The Final Final* (page 242) will give you one provocative way to think about pacing by actively designing your deadlines. Break up your project by giving yourself regular moments when you have promised to share something with someone else. Stage your own *Units of Energy Critique* sessions (page 224). There's no better way to force yourself to get it done, as long as you choose someone whose opinion you care about.

As you continue to develop new and personal approaches to supporting and stretching your own creative work, remember that although breakthroughs feel great, struggle is how you get there. This tension—that the thing you want (a breakthrough) is something that you actually don't want to come by easily—is simply one of the big ironies, joys, and perhaps even mysteries of creativity. Make the space for yourself to dwell in the tension, in an effortful struggle, to set yourself up to produce more impactful, beautiful, or satisfying work now and in the future. Everything you tackle creatively using the design abilities and mindsets that you're exploring in this book is an opportunity both to make something good right now and to prepare yourself for the next big challenge.

60

I Like, I Wish

Featuring the work of Julian Gorodsky,
with inspiration from George M. Prince and Rolf Faste

This is probably the single most powerful assignment in this book. If practiced regularly, this assignment is the soil in which a culture of openness and excellence can emerge and grow. If you want to make just one change to improve your work, your family, your team, or your organization, consider this.

Once you've completed a project, it's easy to move right on to the next thing without taking a moment to reflect. But debriefing an experience is a powerful developmental tool that helps you make just about anything better. A good debrief propels you into an active approach to learning and improving.

You can append this assignment to almost anything: a meeting, a class, a project, or a family reunion. It helps you create space for constructive feedback, regardless of how skilled the group is at creative work.

This activity demonstrates the value you place on making the work better. If you're leading it, you show this value by listening, not talking. It helps you avoid defensiveness and shows that you're not threatened by the ideas of others—including participants or people who have less decision-making power than you. You express through your actions that you believe everyone's ideas can

make the work better. This has a profound impact on the culture of your group.

———————

At the close of any shared experience, dedicate fifteen to thirty minutes to collect and hear feedback. If you make this a ritual, your group will become accustomed to thinking and sharing in this way, and the check-in can even become a five- to ten-minute quickie.

Organize the participants in a circle if that is possible.

Describe your commitment to improving—your relationships, your work, the class, your team meeting, and so on.

Invite everyone to reflect on the experience they've just had and to offer feedback using a statement that begins with "I like . . ." or "I wish . . ." You might give an example, such as "I liked how our teams were interacting with experts today" or "I wish the pace of activities had allowed for more time to pause and document what we were absorbing." (It's not necessary for people to offer *both* an "I like" and an "I wish.")

Allow anyone to start, and avoid going around in a circle. People process their reactions and are ready to share at different speeds. Some people will be more active; if you're leading, it's your job to understand the right moment to pause and ask folks who have already spoken to hold off until you get to hear from a few new voices.

You may need to gently encourage participants to stick to the format at first. Sure, it's a little awkward, but the framing really helps people stay succinct and constructive. You might find that you need a third category that affords people the opportunity to offer a semi-formed solution, such as "What if?" or "How might we?" Encourage people to snap their fingers if they hear something they want to echo—this helps avoid duplicate comments.

Record the feedback using a method that's visible to everyone. For example, you might have someone type each comment as it's being shared and project it on a screen that everyone can see. People value knowing they've been heard.

If you're the formal leader of the group, you have a hard job throughout, and it's imperative that you take the role seriously. You cannot respond to the feedback except to say thank you. You may ask for clarification, but your job is to hold the space for the feedback to emerge, not to deal with it in the moment. You can, however, participate and offer your own feedback—be sure to stick to the regular format!

When the group has finished, you'll know it (this comes with a little practice).

Later, you can privately review the likes and wishes and decide what you're going to act on. Separate the act of soliciting and receiving feedback from the act of evaluating and selecting what feedback to use. You'll get much better advice.

You can also adapt this assignment into a personal practice you do solo: jotting down a list of personal likes and wishes after a meeting or an experience gives you a habit of viewing everything as both valuable and improvable. You can even solicit likes and wishes anonymously. But the magic »

I LIKE

I WISH

of this assignment comes from creating and holding the space for a group to do this live, together. It is the essence of creative collaboration: making a space for change and iteration to occur is doing the work, not something separate from it.

———————

I Like, I Wish was very important to the way the d.school itself evolved. It works because it's not *I Like, I Hate*! It helps everyone hear positive feedback where it's warranted, and negative feedback as a constructive opportunity for improvement. That balance is very important. Too often organizations hear only one or the other. But things are never that binary: there's always good and bad, and different people see and experience things differently. Using this assignment regularly helps you hold space for those differences to become visible and to coexist in the same space.

During the very first course at the d.school, students would sit through a class period, and at the end be asked to say what they liked and wished about it. It was mind-blowing to the students that they could comment in real time. Their opinions were taken seriously. The teaching team would respond to the feedback and make changes that affected the next class session. It was very exciting, and it helped us move quickly to make things better.

We didn't just use this method with students; we used it with everyone. When I started at the d.school, it was led by a group of established faculty members. Everybody was a founder. There were a lot of sensitivities about collaborating; faculty members were used to teaching alone and being the stars. It was hard for people to put their significant and well-deserved egos aside to work collaboratively. But here we were, teaching students to take risks and share their own creativity. This activity spoke strongly to me as a way to walk the talk in how we were creating a safe atmosphere.

In California, we let it all hang out. But not all cultures are wide open. Some people needed encouragement to say something that may be perceived as critical in front of an authority figure. This means a little more hand-holding or a willingness to demonstrate how you do it. If you want to hear direct feedback, you have to meet people halfway. I Like, I Wish can help with that.

—*Julian Gorodsky*

WHAT IF

What Went Down

Featuring the work of Seamus Yu Harte, with inspiration from Kenn Adams

Sometimes polite people ask you what you're working on or what's keeping you busy. Thinking back to your most recent creative project, you might launch into a detailed description of every person you talked to, each failed prototype you built, that night you stayed up until 4 a.m. trying to get your printer to work, the triumphant first glimmer that the thing was going to turn out brilliantly, the 153 different ways you plan to improve your current solution . . . and so on. (If you're anything like me, this will sound familiar.) When you finally pause to take a breath, you notice that the person is quietly checking their phone for any urgent text messages that may have arrived in the fifteen minutes since you started talking.

Your own creative brain is a fascinating place for *you* to hang out, but other people need a map if you want them to follow.

A creative process is usually opaque to people who are outside of it. But you don't have to let this lead to confusion. Certain elements of your journey are important for others to know because they might help someone realize the very reason that your work is useful or innovative. You can give others the generous gift of insight into your creative process if you take the time to craft clarity out of this complex, nonlinear way of working.

This assignment is a way to put together a good story about a creative project—or any situation in which you learned something valuable—even if the underlying experience has a lot of twists and turns. Use it not just to inform others, but also to distill and share your experience in a succinct, compelling manner.

———

First, establish the entire possible story landscape by thinking back to when you started doing the work and when you stopped. Make a quick list of all the things that occurred, in the sequence in which they happened.

Grab a piece of paper and draw a horizontal line across it. This line represents the average of your experience. Using this average as your anchor, graph the process that unfolded from left to right, showing all the highs and lows you went through. (Another assignment with a similar setup is *Learning Journey Maps* on page 246. That one takes you to a very different place. Try them both!) »

Now isolate the most dramatic moment. You find this moment by seeing where the shape of your graph goes from the highest high to the lowest low, and back up to high again. Focus in by drawing a box around just this portion of your graph. In doing so you're creating a tighter frame—literally and figuratively—for your story. Ignore everything else on the page, and for a moment, explore how to use that segment as the story of your creative journey by articulating what's now in that small box.

Capture four elements by writing them down or voicing them out loud:

Where were you, when was this, and what you were trying to do?

What went wrong?

How did you finally fix it? What did you do?

What is the takeaway?

Elaborate on these elements—and you've got a story to work with.

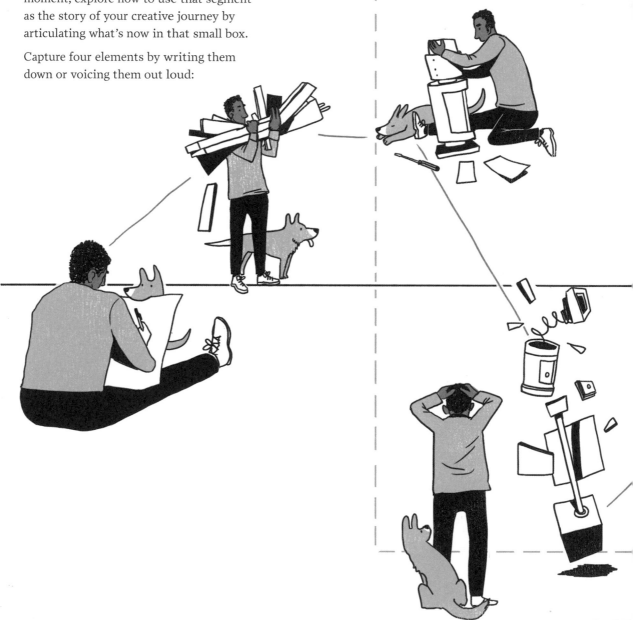

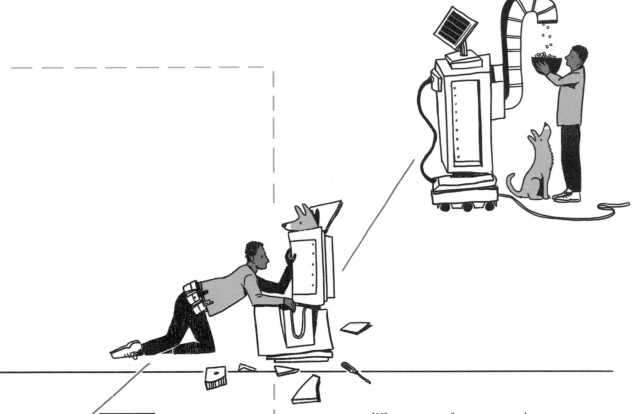

When you share a story that you have built using this assignment, your listener will resonate with it because the underlying structure of a very familiar tale is embedded. The context sets the scene, then an obstacle or problem creates tension. The way you overcome the issue offers relief from the tension in the form of a resolution, which leads to a lesson or idea that helps your audience make sense of what has happened. Meaning is transferred between humans, and culture moves forward.

Of course, there's never just one story for your design work, or any other experience you've had. There are many ways to look at it. If you shift your focused frame to a different part of your map, what story would result? How would people think differently about you and your work?

This assignment is so useful because before you put words to your story and spend time writing or talking it out, you can walk through the entire journey quickly. It is a low-resolution, story-prototyping tool. If you share your story even at this basic level with the person or people you're trying to communicate with, you'll find out what's relevant and what's resonating very quickly.

62 Your Inner Ethicist

Featuring the work of Stuart Coulson

Navigating the present-day world in an ethical manner is confusing. Views collide on social media and immediately repel each other into opposite corners of public debates. Societies around the world are changing rapidly and face tremendous new challenges. And emerging technology is advancing the edge of what's possible daily, whether that's automating work or sending people to Mars. It's complicated to wield your design abilities in the pursuit of creative approaches to global and local needs, so this effort is critically important.

To act and design in an ethically responsible manner, you must put personal effort into understanding ethical tensions and conflicts. If you try to follow any predefined "safe" rules, you will soon find that they fall flat, especially as things change. Ethics is a process of learning, not of compliance. Making time to think about ethics throughout your life helps you interpret and update your behaviors and approaches over time as values, norms, and codes of conduct shift in your society.

Given that people have different points of view, most decisions or actions you take can be viewed as both moral and immoral at the same time. Design and ethics have this in common: there are no single right solutions—just choices that have positives and negatives.

Any kind of design is in some way an intrusive activity. You are always designing for somebody else, and whether that somebody else seems exactly like you or very different, you are extending your worldview and offering it to others through the things you create. Design is a use of power; recognize this, and think carefully about the effect you have on others when you wield it.

In addition to the *what,* consider also the *who.* Get in the habit of asking yourself: *What is it about me and my background that gives me the authority, power, and access to try to address this problem? Will my contributions be valued or seen automatically as better (or worse) because of who I am? How might that affect the creative work that results?*

This assignment is a starting point for recognizing the complexities of ethical considerations in creative work. It's about experiencing how ethical considerations are not necessarily clear-cut and recognizing that not everyone has the same opinion.

You'll need a small group of four to eight people—for example, your design team, your book club, your family. Any group of people who want to thoughtfully examine their place in the world can benefit.

———

To prepare for the assignment, compile a set of short readings that embody different points of view. Op-eds are perfect starting points because they often argue about a broader meaning or reasons why an author thinks something is the right or wrong approach—not just about the mechanics of solving a certain problem. There are so many online publications these days that you won't have trouble sourcing material.

Collect a number of articles that explore different ethical issues that relate to your topic, then narrow it down to a set of four. (You can use this approach on just about any subject: from whether your town should create more bike lanes to whether your state should have voter ID laws or how companies should deal with sexual harassment.)

In advance, you and the rest of the group will read all four articles.

When you meet with your group, bring a mindset of flexibility and curiosity. You are going to stage four ten-minute mini-debates, one for each article you've read. Each will be followed by another five or ten minutes of unstructured discussion. Choose two people to run the debate for each round. They are the debaters for that round, but everyone in your group can respond and reflect during the free discussion. Flip a coin for each pair to see who will argue for or against the point of view expressed in each piece. Then draw the articles out of a pile in random order, so that everyone has an equally fair shot to grapple with material that they naturally agree or disagree with. »

There is no way to "win" these debates: your aim is to thoroughly discuss and hash out differing ethical perspectives. However, at the end of each round and open discussion, every group member should privately vote on which position they prefer. Don't share until the very end.

After you've gone four rounds, tabulate all the votes.

With your group, discuss what you think about the results of the voting. Does your group largely agree or disagree about the issue? What are the implications of alignment or dissent? Did this conversation bring up any ideas for new norms or practices people in your group want to establish?

This assignment originated in a class in which students at the d.school work on design projects in international contexts alongside a partner organization based in each location. Many of the ethical questions that arise involve, first, design work that spans cultures, borders, levels of education, and degrees of affluence and, second, the resulting considerations of who has agency and who is most likely to benefit or be injured because of the work. The ethical issues that make sense to discuss in that context may be similar to or different from yours, but you can draw inspiration from the underlying structure of the assignment and then adapt it to suit your group's needs.

There's a common block that people have about discussing ethics or morals with coworkers or friends. You might feel scared to find out that you're doing something others perceive as wrong, or that you don't all agree on what that means. But these conversations tend to be a real release

valve—*someone* in your group is already worried or wondering about some of these issues, and getting them out in the open can depressurize the topics. It can have the effect of deepening your group's commitment to their work by seriously considering how much their work affects others. No one is equipped with the "right" answers on many topics. Only by creating a process and a practice for yourself to actively engage different points of view can you find your way to the set of behaviors that accord best with your values.

With forty students in each class, we've never had a thirty-to-ten vote during this assignment. It's always split closer to fifty-fifty. It's a surprise to the students that there are people in the same class, within the same educational context, who see things so differently. They are all gray areas, judgment calls, practical calls. My students see that what they think is right is not exactly what everyone else thinks is right.

We have you vote on each article, because outside of school, there's no safety net. You will be in situations large and small in which you have to take a stance, whether that's to confront a practice you think is unethical or to keep modifying and adjusting your own behavior as both you and your context changes. We're trying to help people bridge from ethics in the abstract to ethics as a practice.

—Stuart Coulson

The Futures Wheel

Featuring the work of Lisa Kay Solomon,
with inspiration from Joel Barker

Whenever you make things, you make other things happen as a result. As you apply your creative abilities in different parts of your life, you'll notice that the actions you take and the things or experiences you design have effects. These might be positive or negative and intentional or unintentional.

Design offers you many tools to explore and interpret the world, develop a creative point of view, and experiment your way toward new approaches to meaningful needs and opportunities. Using design well means that you embrace responsibility for both the intended and unintended outcomes of your work, you do your best to think about these implications long before you release your work into the world, and you consider these implications from diverse perspectives. Of course, this would be so much easier if only you could see into the future!

This assignment will help you to SEE INTO THE . . . just kidding. I can't predict what's going to happen, and neither can you.

But you can train yourself to consciously explore the many possible implications that might result from your creative work. *The Futures Wheel* will help you do just

that by embracing the part of design that involves imagining different futures so you can shape the future you most want to see. Use it to flex your thinking in a new way and to see the significance of your design work regardless of whether you're working on something big or small.

This assignment has wide applicability, since it's often helpful to map out the broader context of your work so you can see how it fits into a bigger picture. And there are a few cases when it's especially critical to use this tool. Use it whenever you are building with an emerging technology that is still developing rapidly and therefore still has unknown impacts. Current examples include machine learning, synthetic biology, blockchain, and social media. Another case is when you are designing new policies, rules, or systems, which often have broad, unpredicted effects. Finally, be sure to use this assignment when you are working with a community that has been harmed in the past, either by neglect or by actively designed changes in their environments or lives, and consider how you can involve these folks in the assignment itself. »

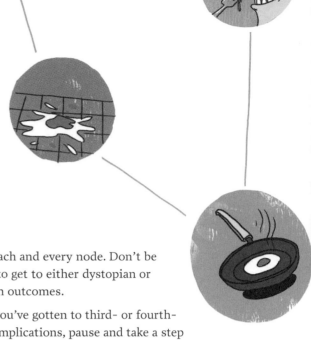

First, pick an observable trend happening now that you think will meaningfully influence your future in the next five to ten years. This could be a really big-picture issue, like advances in autonomous vehicles, robot delivery services, increasing automation, or more health care services being delivered remotely via video call. It might be socioeconomic, like the growing imbalance in wealth distribution or the rise of the gig economy. Or your trend could be local, like efforts to build new playgrounds in your neighborhood or the diminishing presence of small businesses in your town.

Write down your trend in a circle in the center of a large piece of paper (allow space for three or four wide concentric zones to be filled in).

Then draw three lines emanating from the center and write down at least three different implications of your trend. "If we see more driverless vehicles in our town, maybe . . . we'll have fewer accidents . . . we'll need fewer driving teachers . . . we'll need to build special lanes just for autonomous vehicles until the public feels they are safe." You might have more than three—spend as much time as you need to flesh out the space around your center bubble. These are your first-order implications.

Then project out to the next layer by imagining three more implications for each of the first-order nodes. "If we have to build special lanes . . . we'll reduce the amount of road space for other cars . . . we might have to come up with new ways to finance that infrastructure . . . we might wind up encouraging more people to take public transportation . . . some people might get angry at the city and start a protest" and so on.

Keep going. Push yourself to explore both negative and positive consequences from each and every node. Don't be afraid to get to either dystopian or utopian outcomes.

Once you've gotten to third- or fourth-order implications, pause and take a step back. What if a few of these implications became true? What would the world look like? What are the implications you prefer? What could you do or design right now that would help nudge the future in that direction? What unintended negative consequences have you uncovered that you most want to prevent? In response to any of these observations, who could you interview to learn more about this?

Try applying this method to any topic you're currently focusing on. What changes are happening? What new technology are you considering using? What new product or service are you aiming to launch? You'll find endless uses for this flexible mapping approach.

The Futures Wheel is often used by groups of people who are trying to explore the surface area of a trend and its implications in order to make good decisions about how to act or what to create. If you use it on your own, while still valuable, you get just one person's perspective. A diverse group is particularly useful because you'll get much more divergence. One person will see the tremendous potential of a new medical procedure to save lives, and another person will see increases to the cost of care.

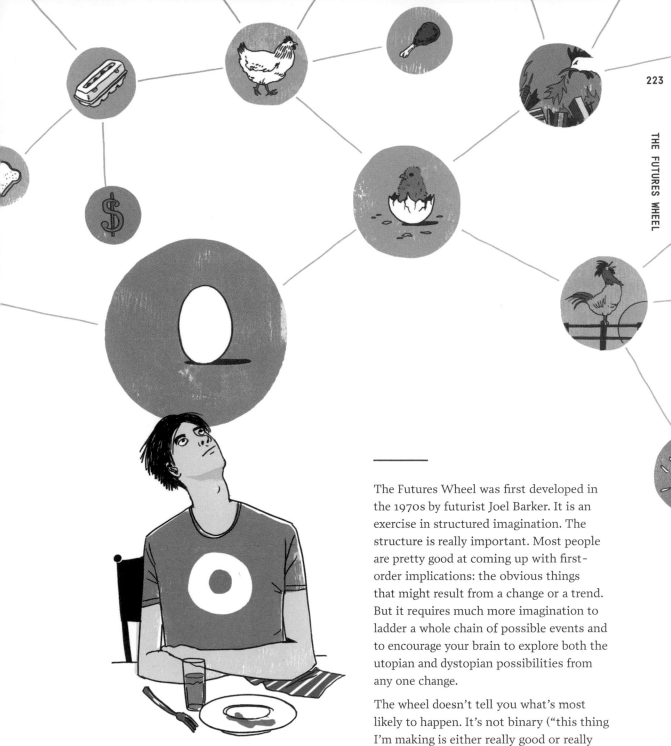

The Futures Wheel was first developed in the 1970s by futurist Joel Barker. It is an exercise in structured imagination. The structure is really important. Most people are pretty good at coming up with first-order implications: the obvious things that might result from a change or a trend. But it requires much more imagination to ladder a whole chain of possible events and to encourage your brain to explore both the utopian and dystopian possibilities from any one change.

The wheel doesn't tell you what's most likely to happen. It's not binary ("this thing I'm making is either really good or really bad"); it allows you to visit and explore the gray areas in between. It quickly takes you from something concrete and observable into the space of imaginative possibilities. Once you're there, you can exercise your values and priorities to design toward the future(s) you most wish to see.

Neither is right or wrong; thinking about both implications together gives you a better sense of the possible futures. Knowing this gives you more power to design things that can help, rather than harm.

64 Units of Energy Critique

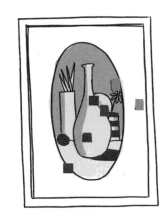

Featuring the work of Jeremy Utley, Perry Klebahn, and Kathryn Segovia

Judgment is a vital yet frequently misused capacity when it comes to creative work. It's often applied too early in a creative process, which cuts off great potential ideas before they can bloom, or too late, which results in subpar or even harmful work getting out into the world.

You are already skilled at a kind of blunt-force judgment; rapidly evaluating a situation or experience for threats or opportunity is hard-wired into your brain to keep you safe. This assignment helps you take advantage of your instinct to judge and channels it into a productive form for creative work called "critique."

How do you make your judgments more deliberate? Most people have strong instincts or feelings about what constitutes "good" when it comes to design, but they don't take time to think about what "good" actually means. When you react to work and judge yourself or others based on hidden criteria that you have not exposed or defined, you're more likely to make idiosyncratic or biased decisions. Part of being deliberate in this case is sharpening your definition of good, which helps you hold yourself and others to a high standard of work.

Engaging in *critique* means you periodically take an active stance of evaluation for the purpose of improving the work. Critique should happen not just once, but at specific moments throughout any creative process. (This also means critique should not happen *all* the time.) Knowing that you have set aside a specific time and approach for critique frees you up to have an exploratory, nonjudgmental mindset at other times. This method is the essential component to working in an iterative way: each time you pause to critique, you start a new cycle and take your work not just to the next part of your process, but also to a higher level.

This assignment is a playful approach to critique. You can use it on your own to reflect and calibrate your work, but since any definition of "good" work needs to be viewed through many different lenses to hold water in our diverse society, your work and the impact you want to achieve are more likely to improve if you critique with a group of people who provide a range of perspectives.

At different stages in your creative process this assignment offers different benefits. If you use it early on when you're still gathering inspiration for your work, it will help you to build a set of design principles

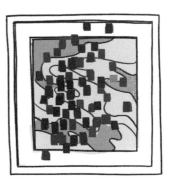

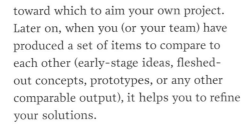

Post images (or the work itself) up on a wall. Identify each with a number on a sticky note.

To set the tone for the critique, say, "Imagine that everyone else here is from Mars, where there's no ownership of individual work, no authorship, no attribution. We're all trying to understand what constitutes spectacular design in order to advance our own work." This playful frame helps you get personal egos out of the way and encourages everyone to view the work objectively, rather than as an extension of self. The make-believe really helps, as does the effect of seeing your own work alongside everyone else's.

Ask everyone to use their internal sense of enthusiasm as an initial indicator of quality for the work being critiqued. You might say any of the following:

When you see a particular direction or problem statement or concept, how enthusiastic do you feel about it?

If you could jump in and help with any of these, which ones would you actually devote your own energy to?

Which one of these do you wish you had come up with? »

toward which to aim your own project. Later on, when you (or your team) have produced a set of items to compare to each other (early-stage ideas, fleshed-out concepts, prototypes, or any other comparable output), it helps you to refine your solutions.

First, everyone in the critique group needs to bring something for feedback. Or you need to have multiple things to share with the group. For example, perhaps everyone produced a statement of direction for a given project or created initial concept sketches showing what they might build into early prototypes and then test. You'll be able to use the variation across a similar set to help the group figure out what "good" looks like.

Ultimately, you're trying to discern which of the projects transfer a sense of purpose and meaning to you. These are not traditional criteria, but they work well to help you cut straight to your instinctive judgment.

Give everyone a sticky note and explain that it represents a unit of energy. Write your initials on yours, along with the number of the work that energizes you the most, and ask everyone else to do the same. After all, you're an independent, autonomous Martian licensed to work on whatever these humans have made! This is very different from how people work most of the time, where you may have to just put your head down and slog through whatever project has been assigned to you. As a side benefit, placing your units of energy with the work that you resonate with most helps you uncover more about what really moves you, which you can later apply to your own work.

To avoid group-think, where a popular choice gains momentum and attracts all the units of energy, ask everyone to post their sticky notes next to their project of choice at the same time. Then step back and observe. You've made a heat map. You can see where the group's collective energy lies: it's right in front of you.

Pause to ask the group to reflect and start a critical discussion. There are usually some clear favorites that get most of the energy. But this isn't voting: the whole point is to ask and understand why people responded favorably to what they selected.

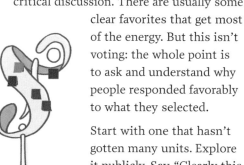

Start with one that hasn't gotten many units. Explore it publicly. Say, "Clearly this one is lacking something. I'm not saying that whoever made it is bad; I'm saying it's a poorly constructed piece of work, and whoever made it—and by the way, we don't need to know, so please don't say it—there are a couple of changes you can make to improve it." This is a point-in-time measurement; it's not an indictment of the designer, but it is a criticism of the particular artifact you're evaluating. This kind of statement makes the critique feel purposeful; you're having a hard conversation now because the information will generate better work. This is the embodiment of the principle "hard on work, soft on people." Be sure to ask the one or two people who did like this work, "Why was this one energizing to you?" Usually there's something they picked up on that turns out to be an interesting design principle or criterion. Maybe that person has a unique lens because of their background. Now you have a chance to discuss a good thing you might have missed without that one person's observation, as well as what the piece is lacking.

For the projects that have gotten more units of energy, find out why that is. Ask someone who liked the work to explain, and then ask if anyone liked it for an entirely different reason. Maybe that work did one thing well, or perhaps it has a range of positives. Another benefit of the structure of this assignment is that since everyone has an equal number of units of energy to deploy, you know that everyone has an opinion you can bring out. You're less likely to develop criteria that are informed only by a few loud voices dominating the conversation.

Use what is and what isn't working about each piece to create a running list of what would make something a great piece of work in this particular context. For example, let's say you're sharing ideas about how to make the airport security process more streamlined. A concept might be critiqued because it would work for only one type of traveler. As a result, your group might decide that one principle of the desired solution is that it needs to handle everyone from families to business people to folks with limited mobility. Or you could define a different principle—that every type of traveler should feel like they have a customized experience—and set about trying to figure out what solutions would make that possible. After each piece of work has been critiqued, look at this running list and refine it. Ultimately, you want to end up with four or five principles that everyone can use to fuel the next round of iterations.

Over the duration of a project, your criteria will evolve and you can keep building on them. At the beginning, you might have been focused on the basics, like:

Does this accomplish a critical function?
Is it clear what this does?
Is this easy to use?

Later on, your group should ask bigger-picture questions:

How will this really help people?
Who might be excluded from using this?
Will this create any negative environmental consequences, like waste?
Are there any other social impacts?

When you design, you're responsible for both the intended and unintended impacts of what you put into the world. Infusing your critique with a broader lens during the later stages of your work helps you make sure that your work is living up to your definition of quality on behalf of both others and yourself.

———

This style of critique is an honest assessment format. In any kind of creative work, you need a way to learn that quality really matters, that there is such a thing as bad work and good work, that those terms are

highly subjective, and that you need lots of input from different people. In addition to building a set of principles, each person walks away with concrete, actionable feedback that informs the next iteration.

This assignment is most effective when you give and get substantive feedback—both positive and negative—to every single thing on the wall. In many environments, people do not get feedback on bad work. It's more common to point out aspirational examples that everyone should aim for. But that's way too abstract. To build this muscle of critique and hone your design abilities, look at the whole set.

Full anonymity with regard to whose work is whose might not be possible in every context—and that's fine. To help with this, make sure the work is shared in a standard format. You're just trying to create a more unified, objective experience. As your group gets better and better at this type of critique, you won't need to work so hard on the anonymity aspect.

When I'm working with a group of executives or students on a design challenge, I repeatedly make the group evaluate the work they are producing, almost in real time. This makes their design projects stronger, and it demonstrates how useful it is to develop a process for public critique and evaluation that is both supportive and rigorous. It's not helpful for your company or school if you can't be honest about poor-quality work, and it's also not useful in the long run if your process shuts down people's creativity. Here's what I've seen: the folks who attract less energy and get more brutal feedback make way more progress and sometimes lap the other people after the next round of iterations.

—*Jeremy Utley*

65 More Brave People

Featuring the work of Zaza Kabayadondo

Like any set of tools or approaches that create change, design can have positive or negative outcomes. You may be aware of the many ways design can be used to improve people's lives, but it has also been used to reinforce or deepen social problems like segregation, technology addiction, and drug dependence.

What does this say about the nature of design as a tool? Does it have its own moral attributes or is it all in how you wield it?

Think of an example when design has made a positive difference in your life or in the world around you.

Think of an example where design has made things worse.

What conclusions can you draw from these examples?

How do they make you feel about your own power to shape interactions, artifacts, or environments that others will experience?

Who are Zaza's "brave people"? What does being both creative and brave mean for you?

It's a good thing that design is implicated in social problems …

It means oppression and exclusion are not part of the natural order of things, they are human-made problems. It means there's a chance we can design our way out of this mess.

The more brave people who think about design as a powerful tool for shaping the world, the better a chance we have.

—Zaza Kabayadondo

Build a Bot

Featuring the work of Ariam Mogos, Laura McBain, Megan Stariha, Carissa Carter, and Karen Ingram

Have you met Alexa? Or "her" frenemy, Siri? Had a helpful customer service chat box pop up unexpectedly in the corner of your computer screen when you were trying to decide what size pants to order online? If so, you've had a conversation with one of the many virtual assistants based on the technology of artificial intelligence (AI).

These AI assistants are attentive and useful, but they are not people. They are computer programs designed to respond to your commands. If they feel "friendly," that's because someone imagined what most people might find to be friendly and designed the interaction that way. Siri or Alexa could just as easily be programmed to say, "Well, dummy, even a second grader knows what the weather is going to be like tomorrow, but since you don't: it's going to rain in the early afternoon. Dress appropriately!" (Mean Siri might not be something you'd want to pay for, though.)

Your conversation with any AI assistant was designed. The name of the assistant, the qualities of its voice, and your perception of its gender affect how you relate to it based on your own life experience. All of those elements are the result of conscious decisions made by the designers of the interaction experience.

One of the key design choices is the dataset of words and sentence fragments that will be used to respond to commands. A big dataset of lots of different responses must be compiled because users might ask it a million different questions. (The computer program that runs the AI assistant gets more accurate at interpreting requests and supplying the right answer by practicing responses and being told whether they're right or wrong. Then it tries again. That's the training process for what's called "machine learning.") If an answer is not in the dataset, the AI assistant can't come up with an entirely new response on its own the way a human brain can, although it can mix things together in new ways.

That means interactions are still governed by the limitations of human designers. Our identities, biases, blind spots, preferences, and predilections all play a role in what we produce, including the design of advanced technology. Unless we're careful and intentional about it, the same stereotypes and inequities that exist in the analog world are easily reinforced or worsened by how they play out in the digital one.

This assignment is a way for you to practice what it's like to design a conversation for an AI assistant, and you don't need to know any kind of computer code to try it out. You can do it on your own, and it's even more fun with a friend. Use it if you're curious about how you're being influenced by the digital helpers in your life or if you want to develop a basic sense for how the emerging field of voice design could help reduce injustice, not amplify it.

———

Build a Bot has two rounds. The first asks you to come up with a creative new name for an AI assistant. The second helps you to design a dataset that an AI assistant might use and to consider different perspectives while you do it. If that sounds confusing, don't worry—you don't need any special expertise to do this assignment.

Round 1: Name a Bot

Come up with a new name for an AI assistant, with the following constraint: your new name can't reinforce any negative stereotypes. For example, say you choose a name you like: let's go with "Jenny" for now.

In your notebook or on a piece of paper, make a list of all the attributes you can think of associated with that name. You might come up with "female," "two syllables," "popular," "Western," "nickname." For each of these attributes, come up with two or three different implications of using that attribute for the name of an AI assistant in terms of what ideals are being reinforced. For example, for "female" you might write, "reinforces the idea that secretaries and assistants are generally women" and "non-threatening." For "Western" you might write, "reinforces the idea that 'everyone' is or should be familiar with English names." For "two syllables" you might wonder who might find the name easy or hard to pronounce. This last implication

is less about stereotypes and more about usability, but if your mind goes in this direction, that's great; you're beginning to consider the implications of your new AI assistant from different people's perspectives. Try this again with a different common name.

Now that you've thought about some of the challenges, can you come up with some new names that don't have any of the negative implications you're trying to avoid? Can you come up with a name that fights stereotypes? This is a tough challenge! Once you have a few different ideas, run your favorite name by a friend—preferably someone with a different background or view on the world—to see if they can spot any stereotypes or negative implications you might have missed. »

Round 2: Design a Dataset

A dataset is a collection of different types of information that are related to each other, organized or structured so that someone can retrieve that information easily. People might look at the different parts of a dataset to try to understand the big picture of what's in front of them. For example, a dataset about your health might include information about your height, weight, blood pressure, pulse rate, and the results of your last ear and eye exams. Other potentially relevant information might be left out, like your stress level or your home life. Why might this be left out? It could be that the person who designed the tools for recording and structuring the dataset decided that certain information wasn't important. It could be that they didn't know how to record that information. It also could be that they've never been stressed at home, and it never occurred to them that it would be important to capture.

These choices have implications—the type of treatment you might receive for a particular ailment will differ depending on what kind of information about you has been deemed important to collect and store. And those choices reflect the specific perspectives and life experiences of the person or people who made them.

In this round you will practice being one of those designers, and you'll see how varying your perspective affects what you think is relevant to include in a dataset.

First, imagine that someone is going to ask your newly named AI assistant the question, "Hey _____, what's a tree?"

You'd like the answer to include some words and an image.

For inspiration, look at the trees depicted here.

You can imagine that your assistant might respond:

"Trees are big plants with roots, trunks, stems, branches, and leaves or foliage. You can find them in parks, neighborhoods, forests, and many other places. Trees can be used for lumber, furniture, firewood, and paper."

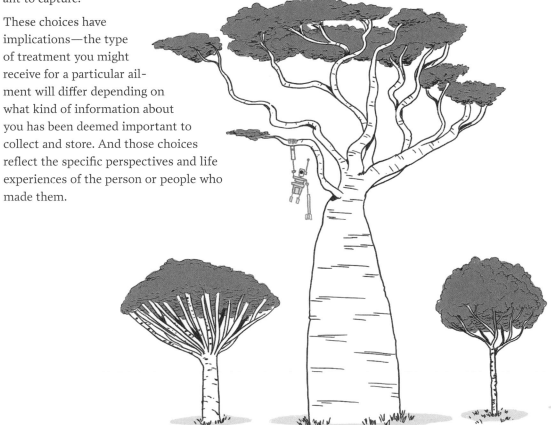

That's a good answer, but it's not the only possible answer. Come up with three other datasets from three totally different perspectives. For each of your different perspectives, draw a picture of a tree, and write out a sentence or two like the example above. Imagine whose perspective on a tree might be the most interesting to envision: An ant? A bear? A bird? An arborist? A biologist? A person who practices *shinrin-yoku* (Japanese for "forest bathing")? For each perspective you adopt, include information that would answer these prompts:

"A tree looks like _____, it can be found _____, and it's used for _____."

Now you've created three different datasets, all of which could be used to respond to the same question: "What is a tree?" How would you decide which perspective is the right one to offer someone who asks your AI assistant this question?

———

For every question you ask an AI assistant, a dataset is being used to supply the answer. Every dataset reflects the identity, values, and biases of the people who defined what went in and what stayed out. Many datasets reflect a "dominant narrative"—the primary view of something that seems accepted by most people. But often there's a missing step—questioning what "accepted by most people" really means. Is it really "most people"? Or is it "most of the people in charge"?

These questions pose conundrums for people designing these datasets and defining the parameters for how AI-based tools respond to commands and requests. For example, if you search for images of "CEOs" online, you will find pictures of mostly White men. Very few women and very few Black, Indigenous, or people of color show up in the results. That's because the dataset available for that search is drawn from published images of actual CEOs, and in the United States, most prominent CEOs likely to be photographed for publicity are White men. Their photos are highly represented in any large dataset. So on the one hand, the search result you get is largely accurate in that it reflects our society's status quo. On the other hand, the search result reinforces the stereotype that White men are more suited to be CEOs, so in terms of who is "suited" for the position, it is largely inaccurate. And there are long-term implications. These search results mean that women and people of color see fewer people like them as CEOs. Being repeatedly exposed to

this subtle (or not so subtle) reinforcement of a stereotype has a predictive effect on what kinds of career paths people choose and whether or not others accept them in roles that haven't traditionally been open to them. The way this particular dataset works can help ensure that future CEOs are either more or less diverse than at present.

What should the designer of this dataset do? Change the search results to represent a more balanced view of CEOs? Work to diversify the dataset? Leave it alone? The answer you choose depends on your values, your identity, and your perspective. It's important for all of us to examine how these influence how we design experiences with technology and the unintended consequences they may have for people with different lived experiences.

AI assistants are goldmines! They can be gateways to so much information. Emerging technologies have the potential to make great contributions to society, and at the same time, I believe there is an urgent need to address the embedded bias, dominant narratives, and the replication of real-world structural inequities they perpetrate.

I want everyone to be knowledgeable about the ethical implications of emerging technologies and have the agency to design, reflect, and participate in decision-making processes. My goal with this assignment is to provoke you to ask informed questions about emerging technologies and to interrogate and reflect on how our identities are embedded in our design work. I hope it helps you to start asking questions like "Who decides where all the datasets that power my technology come from? Whose perspective do these datasets represent? What influence can this have on the world?"

—*Ariam Mogos*

67 Designing Tools for Teams

Featuring the work of Nicole Kahn

If you are seen as a highly creative person, you may someday face what feels like a punishment: someone will ask you to lead a *team of other people* in order to produce something creative. It's often assumed that possessing a strong personal creative practice will just naturally spill over into a broader group by osmosis or magic, but individual creative work and group work have very different qualities.

When you lead a team, you pay attention to many dynamics at once: the progress and quality of the work itself, the needs of the team members for both autonomy and direction, interpersonal dynamics, and the interests of other people who want or need your work to succeed. A lot of these forces feel like invisible pressures, and if you don't have training or guidance, it's hard to know what to do.

But the same creative principles you use regularly in design can help you create new group norms, rituals, or tools that support your team and improve its work. Team and leadership challenges are great canvases for creative approaches, though they're not often viewed that way. In fact, you can use your design abilities to make invisible behaviors,

tensions, or challenges more visible, and therefore something you can address.

This assignment will help you practice a designer's approach to leadership. You'll start to see that the process of building a team culture and advancing your leadership style is something you can prototype and experiment with; it's yet another area in your life where your creativity can be useful.

For this assignment you'll need to figure out how to get access to a team that comes together for the purpose of working together but that you're not regularly a part of. (You want to have a little distance.) Although this is a bit unusual, there are lots of ways to access a working team. The subject of the work doesn't matter—it could be anything from a formal work team that you connect to through a leadership program at your job or the human resources or training department at your company to a book club, a project-based class at a school that you're able to sit in on, or a new parents' group. You could also find a willing group by shadowing a mentor who works on a team or even by setting up an exchange: a team you're on helps another team through this assignment, and then vice versa. When proposing this assignment to a group, you can share that you're trying to bring more creativity to your own leadership approaches, or any other description that fits your context.

———————

To begin the assignment, spend an hour or so observing your chosen team in a meeting and taking detailed notes. Notice behaviors, individual roles, the feeling in the room, how people interact, and how people seem to feel about the work that's being accomplished.

If the meeting is being held online through videoconferencing with a distributed team, it's even easier to fade into the background. After introducing yourself and your purpose, you can just turn off your video, and even change your screen name to "team designer" or something else that feels right.

After the meeting, think about what you saw. Be deliberate about this, and spend some time assessing what stood out and why. Write down a few areas where the team could benefit from a new practice. For example, maybe you observed the team struggling to make a decision. Perhaps there were frequent interruptions, and that led to frustration. Whatever you observed, name those opportunities.

To address the opportunities, come up with some prototypes that others can experience. For example, what kind of tool could help the indecisive team celebrate a decision and move forward? What if it were a physical object? What about a saying? Or what kind of ritual could provoke a really dominant team member to ask more questions and leave more space for others? Come up with a bunch of ideas, and then decide which ones you want to build and test.

Try out your new tool ideas with one of your own teams first to see what people

think of them. The tools don't have to work perfectly. In most cases they will function as provocations, helping a team gain greater self-awareness and willingness to experiment with different levers to improve how people feel and the way the work gets done.

The assignment could end here, or you can take it a little further. If you return to the team you observed for a second visit, introduce the tool and see what happens when they try it out.

———————

Both leadership and creativity are abilities that some people erroneously believe to be inherent, immutable qualities: either you have them or you don't. But if you treat team leadership as a design opportunity, you can bring intention to your approach, experiment to learn more, and keep refining your methods.

I originally designed this assignment for a group of new design students. I noticed that later on in their program, when they had to lead an interdisciplinary team, they were just getting trampled by other students who had more leadership experience but didn't know much about design. The quality of the work was really suffering.

I had the first-year students observe the teams that second-year students were leading. It was doubly powerful because they kind of worshipped those older students but also saw what a struggle it was to lead. They didn't want to end up leading dysfunctional teams in their second year, so they were motivated to try a lot of bold prototypes and really learn. And as a result of their conviction, their ideas were really helpful to the current teams.

The reason this work was impactful—and even surprising—is because it showed the new students that with a little bit of knowledge and an hour or two of design work, they could

apply design to their own leadership, something they saw as abstract. Design is all about taking messy, complex problems and finding specific, concrete ways to make changes, and this is no different. The students could see that leadership and running a team can be designed, and that teams don't just work one way, but many ways.

That's really what I want you to take away: you can develop fluency in different leadership styles that you can adapt depending on what is going on. If you gain this skill now, then in the future you will be able to design your way out of a bad dynamic if you ever find yourself in one.

—Nicole Kahn

68 This Assignment Is a Surprise

Featuring the work of Perry Klebahn and Jeremy Utley

Most of us want to be seen as the type of person who fulfills a promise. As a result, we behave differently when we think there is someone watching to see whether our actions measure up to our intentions. You can take advantage of this when you decide you want to do something you find challenging, whether it's taking up jogging, finding a more satisfying job, or learning a new language. You are more likely to complete the action if you make your commitment public by sharing it with others. Doing this puts you under social pressure, which complements your internal motivation and helps it along. It's quite difficult to change your behavior or break out of old habits, and it helps to understand how to intentionally create the conditions under which you are most likely to succeed.

This assignment invokes a little social pressure (and a little time pressure) to help you kick a specific habit: the fear that you are not yet "ready." You might be used to thinking that you're ready to do something only after you've made the perfect plan, passed the test, gotten the degree, or received affirmation from an expert. And if you're in a field like medicine, I can see the argument for receiving a formal credential before you start, you know, surgery-ing. But with creative work, by waiting for external validation as your primary cue that it's time to advance you risk diminishing the part of preparation that is internal, like your willingness to try some things before you know you'll be totally successful and, in doing so, to stretch a little further than you might think you're capable of. This assignment gives you a stretch experience. Tackle it when you are feeling almost—but not totally—ready to take a leap forward in your skills and confidence.

There is just one extremely important pre-requisite: You must have completed one or more of the other assignments in this book before you read on. In fact, make a list of your five favorite assignments here:

1.

2.

3.

4.

5.

Five Chairs (page 136), *Tell Your Granddad* (page 181), *ABC Sketching* (page 92), *What's in Your Fridge?* (page 68), *Dérive* (page 34), or *Talkers & Listeners* (page 48) are also great candidates for what's about to happen. Next, *before you read on,* put down this book and assemble a small group of people who are generally interested in the topics in this book or invested in you as a friend or colleague and have an hour to spend together.

(Are you thinking about peeking ahead before you've completed the homework? Obviously, I can't stop you; I'm completely powerless here. You are the boss of this book! I will explain more about the source of this assignment and why it's so helpful to wait in just a bit. So I hope you do . . . wait.) »

Okay, you've assembled your small group. And, surprise! You're going to lead one assignment with them, right now.

You may feel slightly underprepared— that's normal. Embrace the role of leader and guide, and make sure you model the behaviors you want to see in your group by actively participating. Think of it this way: if you're taking people on a hiking trip, you don't just drop them off and tell them where to go. You're out there in front of the group, taking every step along with them, even though some of the terrain is unknown. That's the type of leadership that will help you in this assignment.

From your list of five, choose the assignment you want to lead your group through. Pick one that pushed you to try something new or got you to do something that felt unfamiliar and challenging.

Give yourself ten minutes to prepare how you will take others through the experience, but don't overthink it. Improvise materials if you need any.

Get started.

Once you've completed the activity, lead a debrief with your group. Ask them for feedback. (If you'd like a ready-made structure, try out *I Like, I Wish* on page 212.)

Where did folks get stuck? What did they learn the most about? What was fun and what was hard? How did reactions and experiences vary across the group?

Take some time afterward to reflect on what you learned: as a leader, as a "let's just try this out"-er, and about the essence of the skills you explored in the assignment you led. (*What? So What? Now What?* on page 200 is an excellent tool to support your personal reflection for this final part.) Ask yourself: *What did leading this activity teach me about how I might do my work in the future? How can I connect the tactics I just used to my future work?*

Finally, congratulate yourself! You are an amazing example of someone who learns by doing.

―――――――

You have probably heard of the educational model called "see one, do one, teach one," but it's rarely put into practice. It takes guts to try to bring others along when you are still exploring a subject or skill, but it's a tremendously effective way for you to cement what you've learned and to understand it from different perspectives. The key is to focus less on the outcomes or being perfect in your "instruction" or leadership, and more on what you yourself learn about the underlying practice by being forced to explain it to others. Doing this assignment is a way to help you take a big leap forward and move from student to practitioner, or thinker to doer, even while you are still in learning mode.

This is an assignment that we use routinely at the d.school. When experts from education, business, or any other field attend a workshop or class to learn about design, there comes a time at the end of the day when things start to wind down. The participants feel really jazzed to try out the new tools in their own professional or home contexts. The faculty congratulates the participants for their hard work and accomplishments, and the participants start thinking about how they will adapt what they have learned to suit their own needs. The feeling in the room is like a sigh of relaxation, of moving from action to more passive contemplation when you think you've put the hardest work you have to do behind you.

Then, all of a sudden, the instructors surprise the participants with the news that the two hundred or so strangers milling about in a different part of the building are actually there to take a two-hour mini-course . . . from them! The moment the participants realize that the instructors are completely serious is always intense: a combination of confusion and disbelief ripples audibly throughout the room.

It takes people to a place that they never thought a learning experience would go. The surprise element is essential. With just a few minutes to prepare for the session they are about to lead, the unexpected reveal gives them only a sliver of time to worry and instead helps them spring into action.

After a few minutes to set up a space, the participants lead small teams of complete strangers through a simple exercise, like "redesign the dining out experience" or "how might we make waiting in line at a market more interesting?" It is very structured, which isolates the core of what we are trying to get them to take in: how much you learn by doing, rather than planning.

When the participants debrief their experience, they are amazed at their own ability. Some things always go wrong or are messy, but the experience gives them real fodder to work with. They grasp with certainty what they need to get better at doing and how much they have already learned. They gain a lot of confidence through their first experience of leading in this way.

And while it feels risky, the instructors know that the activity is so well scaffolded that the two hundred mini-course participants will still gain value from the experience. It feels like the stakes are high to the people stepping into the lead role for the first time, but it is carefully designed so that everyone benefits.

You can take these principles and extrapolate them to other settings in your life. When you are nervous to try something new or feel that you are not yet ready, can you create a way to take a very small risk and gain some more experience before you actually have to perform? It really increases the chances that you will have the confidence to do something when the stakes are high when you know you've already done it. The imperfect experience of actually having done something is a hundred times more valuable than the most perfect, untested plan.

The Final Final

Featuring the work of Carissa Carter and Ashish Goel

Sometimes, even with great intentions, you produce creative work that is not the best you can do. It's easy to attribute the miss to something about yourself: a deficit of skill, a lack of practice, or some other internal flaw. Honest personal reflection is always healthy, but you should also think about the conditions you've established *around* your work. Like, for example, how you use *time* as an ingredient.

Pacing your work is critical to any project. Your pace should allow for extra time for whatever feedback is necessary to make the final product that much better. For many people, there's a rush of activity as the final deadline gets closer: urgency spurs focus and commitment.

But despite that big adrenaline-fueled push at the end, you may emerge after a final presentation at school or work feeling, *Now that I've already brought my thing to fruition, I know what I could have done better.* You realize that with one more iteration, your work could reach its full potential.

This assignment is so simple that it shouldn't work. But somehow it does. I don't fully understand why, but it's a reminder that language really matters.

Try this out regardless of whether you're a procrastinator or a steady-pacer. You just need to be someone who wants to take your work to the next level.

————

Think about your next big deadline coming up. It should be something important to you in any realm in your life. It might be a project for work or school, but it could also be your first time cooking the turkey for your family's Thanksgiving meal.

Make a final deadline and a specific moment in time during which you will present your "project." This date should be a few days or a week *before* the "final, final" event. Invite an audience whose feedback matters to you. It doesn't have to be big or formal, but you need an external accountability mechanism. Set up a presentation in your living room and ask your best friend to sit through it, or get out the fancy silverware. This will help you take your final deadline seriously.

After you present your "final" work, you will really know how to make your thing all it can be. You'll see what you're capable of, you'll know how to reach for it, and you'll still have time to get there.

One year I tried an experiment with my students to help them take their output to an entirely new place. Instead of just accepting that post-class sensation of unrealized potential, I headed it off with a second "final" deadline. I was completely transparent with the students: it wasn't a surprise or a trick. Everyone knew the day that the Final was due, and then the day that the Final Final was due.

It was important to get the word final *on there. When you see the word* final, *you think, "That's when my thing needs to be as good as it can be." They know they have to bring their best work. Framing it as a "rough draft" just isn't taken as seriously.*

When they submitted their Final, we did a real critique of that work. Then I said,

"Next week is the Final Final: the exhibition or the showcase. You have time to make something completely different." I didn't know what would happen, but an incredible number of students pivoted. The step-change improvement from Final to Final Final was the most amazing shift in the quality of work.

It's after the Final critique that most students realize what they are capable of. I'm making space for them to take the work to that level. Now I do this every year.

My challenge to everyone is to find a way to build in a Final Final to your own creative timeline. You'll be amazed by how much more extraordinary your work can be.

—Carissa Carter

70 Personal Project

Featuring the work of Bernie Roth,
with commentary from Terry Winograd

You're born into a life with all sorts of constraints on it. These might be your geography, your family situation, or your access to resources. That's a design problem. Design means taking action, not just creating an artifact or thinking about new approaches or ideas.

For more than forty years Bernie Roth taught this seminal assignment in design classes at Stanford, starting long before the d.school existed. It will help you instill a bias toward action in your own life and to confront and then move past constraints that you perceive as obstacles. This is an unusual assignment in that there is no set process, and there's very little structure. You cannot get a grade for it, even if you were one of Bernie's students. It doesn't give you detailed instruction, and how could it? It's your personal project. You can take what you know about design already and develop a new level of personal responsibility about how you apply those approaches.

This assignment is useful when you are dissatisfied with some element of your life. Instead of directing your design abilities toward creating a solution for someone else, it helps you remove some barrier in your life to make you freer, more able to accomplish your goals, or simply happier.

————

The setup is minimal; you just need a confidante. They could be a mentor, a parent or close sibling, a trusted colleague or friend. Consider them your "Bernie." Tell them their role is to keep you accountable.

For your project, decide either to solve a problem that you want to be rid of, or to do something that you have always wanted to do. Ask yourself these three questions:

How long will I spend on this project?
What would be a satisfactory conclusion of having done the project?
What would that mean to me?

In the past, people have used this assignment to tackle things they were never sure they could do but always wanted to. Sometimes it's been very personal, like building a relationship with an estranged family member and inviting them to an important life event like a graduation or wedding. Or ambitious: one person wrote a book and got it published. Several people have learned the languages of their parents.

And of course, people jump out of planes, go hang-gliding, or do stand-up comedy in public. You have a lot of latitude to pick something that matters to you.

Once you pick a project, talk to your Bernie about what you want to do. Make a contract privately with them. You're still responsible for the project, but they can remind you from time to time that you made this contract.

Halfway through the time you have allotted, meet with your Bernie again. You might decide you've chosen the wrong project and want to morph it into something else. If you are stuck and don't know where to go, they might send you to some people they know, or they may share resources.

Think about a simple process model as you do this: Express your idea. Test your methods. Cycle (go back and do it again).

———————

This assignment reflects a belief that you don't need to be stuck with some of the stuff in your life that isn't working for you. You have the license to make changes. It's your project, and you have to own it.

My original intent with this assignment was that students would do things independently. It has been wildly successful, and it has also changed me in a way. For me, being a designer is the same as being a person. It means being a person in society. Everyone is a designer one way or another, believe it or not. It's just being in life. It's the whole idea of not waiting for tomorrow to get stuff done. To just get up and do stuff.

—Bernie Roth

For decades this assignment has made people realize that the main pathology of academia is detachment. It's as if the researcher or student is not a part of what she is studying. Through this approach Bernie is saying, "Understand how you are a part of it: you are designing your own life. It's not what a design firm does about products; it's about how you build design into your life to shape it."

—Terry Winograd

71 Learning Journey Maps

Featuring the work of Sarah Stein Greenberg

Action, then reflection. It's the peanut butter and jelly of creative work: one without the other just doesn't make sense.

When you do, make, or learn something, it's easy to fall into the habit of just moving on to the next thing right away. Endings are satisfying! But at the d.school, you haven't really finished something unless you've reflected on it.

This assignment is a go-to for how to think critically about whatever you've just gone through, especially when you know you learned something new along the way and you want to reinforce it. It's also particularly useful because learning isn't always easy—and in fact, it shouldn't be. Using a learning journey map helps you chart your own experience over time and identify the moments when you soared effortlessly and when you ran into challenges. It will help you take something that's usually internal and invisible—your own learning—and bring it outside yourself, where you can examine it more objectively and make some important discoveries.

Use this assignment to get closure and insight at the end of anything or everything.

On a large piece of paper, draw a vertical line on the left-hand side of the page. That line represents a scale, from very negative at the bottom to very positive at the top (see pages 248–249).

Draw a horizontal line at the bellybutton of the first line to bisect it, and extend that line all the way to the right-hand edge of the paper. The second line represents the length of time of the experience you're going to map. It could be a day, a few months, or even years.

Add some evenly spaced milestones along the horizontal line that help you divide up all that space, like hours, weeks, or months. Decide how granular to get based on the length of experience you're mapping.

In a notebook, make a list of all the things you remember from the experience, big and small. It might help to think about what happened on the very first day or at the first moment (or even right beforehand). What was it like walking in the door or getting started at the beginning? Then ask yourself what happened next. And after that? Don't worry about whether the things that come up are typically associated with what or how you learn; just jog your memory about everything that happened.

Draw a new line on your map that shows the ups and downs of your learning journey, from negative events at the bottom to more positive ones at the top, using points in time from your list. Use a solid line, or a specific bright color, like blue. Chart the ups and downs: when were you learning a lot? When did you stall out? Sometimes it helps to start with either your highest high or your lowest low—to anchor your map in a scale that is relevant to your experience. On the same map add a second line, using either a different color, like orange, or a distinct style, like dashes. This one will show your emotional journey. When did you feel elated or excited? When were you frustrated or nervous?

For both lines, label the highs and lows. Recall and capture in detail what occurred at those moments. These are critical inflection points: they show moments of change that either happened to you or you made happen.

Step back and observe. What is this map telling you about your experience overall? What caused the highest highs or the lowest lows? What conditions or actions (yours or other people's) led to the turnarounds at the inflection points?

The final step is to look at where your lines diverge or converge. What was happening during the overlaps or the gaps? Try to make sense of this. If you can, share your map with someone else, especially someone who has been through the same experience and also made a map. You'll gain insight from seeing where your journeys were similar or different. Ask yourself how your learning experience is related to your emotional experience and how you could take

advantage of these insights the next time you tackle something creatively ambitious that involves your learning along the way.

––––––––––

This kind of map can give you many useful insights into what helps you learn or perform well and what holds you back. Then you are better able to seek out or create those conditions in the future. »

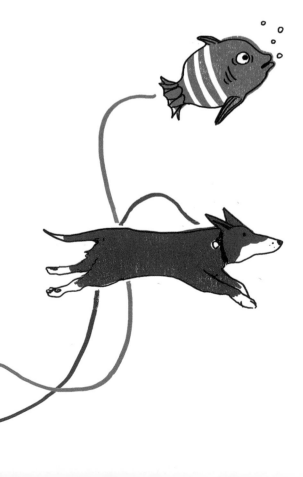

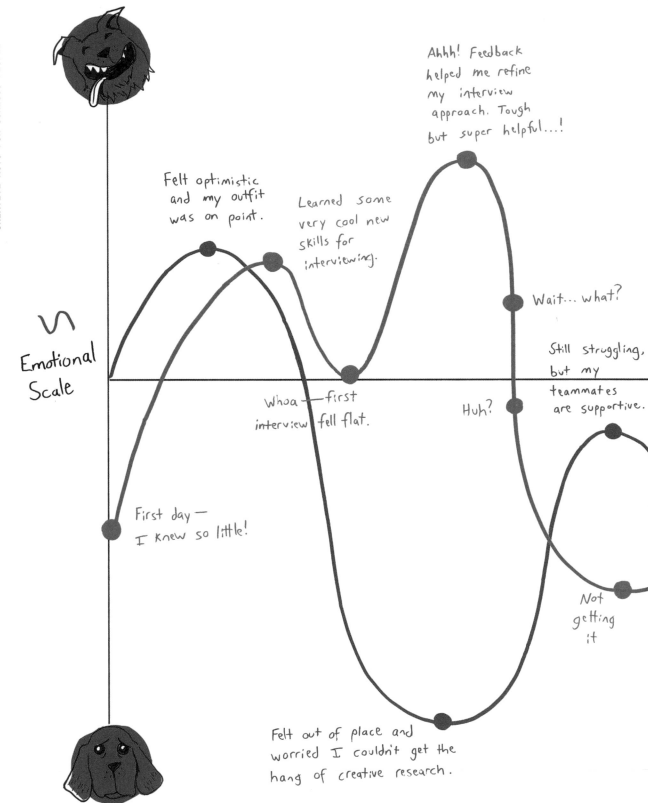

Ahhh! Feedback
helped me refine
my interview
approach. Tough
but super helpful...!

Felt optimistic
and my outfit
was on point.

Learned some
very cool new
skills for
interviewing.

Wait... what?

Emotional
Scale

Still struggling,
but my
teammates
are supportive.

Whoa — first
interview fell flat.

Huh?

First day —
I knew so little!

Not
getting
it

Felt out of place and
worried I couldn't get the
hang of creative research.

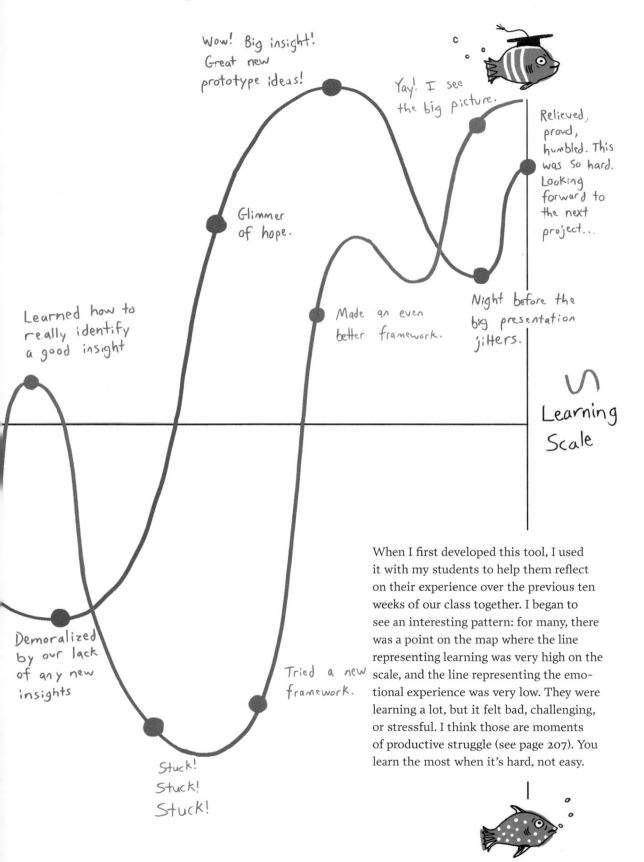

Wow! Big insight! Great new prototype ideas!

Yay! I see the big picture.

Relieved, proud, humbled. This was so hard. Looking forward to the next project...

Glimmer of hope.

Learned how to really identify a good insight

Made an even better framework.

Night before the big presentation jitters.

Learning Scale

Demoralized by our lack of any new insights

Tried a new framework.

Stuck! Stuck! Stuck!

When I first developed this tool, I used it with my students to help them reflect on their experience over the previous ten weeks of our class together. I began to see an interesting pattern: for many, there was a point on the map where the line representing learning was very high on the scale, and the line representing the emotional experience was very low. They were learning a lot, but it felt bad, challenging, or stressful. I think those are moments of productive struggle (see page 207). You learn the most when it's hard, not easy.

Putting It All Together

This wouldn't be a d.school book if I didn't give you some integrated, real-world projects to work on. We believe that you don't have to wait until you have a degree or a stamp of approval from someone else to start applying your creative skills in service of others. These final assignments will help you do that. This section encourages you to try projects of increasing complexity in order to take your design skills to a new level.

My first formal design experience occurred when I walked into the d.school the first week there was a d.school to walk into. It was early January 2006, and I was a graduate student at Stanford. Within minutes, I was told to take out my wallet—not to pay for books or materials, but to exchange it with another student's wallet. And with that, we had begun the very first assignment in the d.school's inaugural class.

What soon came to be known as The Wallet Project was a brilliant little sixty-minute distillation of the essence of design. In about an hour we all had a chance to create something for our partners inspired by their habits, wants, concerns, or frustrations with their current method of carrying money or whatever else was in their wallet. It turns out people use wallets for many different things. Going on a "tour" of someone else's wallet is a little like visiting their childhood bedroom the first time you meet them. It's an awkward start, but then you get into a great discussion about their baby pictures or third-grade sports trophies.

As an instructor, I later ran The Wallet Project many times. Each time I did it, people produced a wide range of ideas. A few made a literal wallet for their partner, but with better organization or different aesthetics or a chain to keep the wallet from getting lost. However, most followed their partner down an unexpected path—into nostalgia or connection—and ended up designing a way for a wallet to remind the carrier of family or an important life event. Or a personal confession about scarcity sparked the design of a routine for sticking to a budget. What seemed simple on the surface could yield a conversation of surprising depth and intimacy, which in turn led people straight to the most powerful part of design: an opportunity to reframe the problem.

If you first discover design during this assignment or a similar one, the opportunity it delivers in the moment is priceless: a cathartic experience of breakthrough. You start the project with only your own projections about what is useful in a wallet, and an hour later you are suddenly aware of how much broader and more interesting the design space around "wallet" can be. You glimpse the potency of starting your design work with an open mind and a deliberate practice of investigating the needs of others, and you sense that the ways in which you could apply your creativity and inventiveness are so much vaster than if you frame and execute creative projects only using your own mind.

The Wallet Project introduced people with no background in design to the fundamentals without losing anyone to abstract theory along the way. Most of the assignment was tightly scripted: you got a range of outcomes only because participants were each interviewing a real person and following that person's individual story. The Wallet Project was just like a kid using a balance bike to start learning to ride a regular bicycle: it's hard to learn to pedal, balance, and steer simultaneously. Balance bikes have no pedals and are so low to the ground that it's nearly impossible to fall, even when moving. To go forward, you just walk or run, kick off, lift up your feet, and glide. They isolate the part of riding a bike that is the hardest: the act of balancing in motion. It's encouraging to finish your first ride without falling and scraping your knees; it sets you on your way. In a similar way, The Wallet Project—and many starter projects like it— helped you get your balance by taking you through the arc of a process. Creative work is hard and risky. Everyone deserves a start that builds up a little confidence.

Having completed The Wallet Project, people almost always remarked on how different their partner's needs and interests were from their own; how the rushed pace of the assignment quieted their internal censor and forced them to share unfinished work, which in turn garnered more constructive feedback. And how delivering a sketch or prototype before the end of the assignment pushed them to deepen their idea just by making it.

Now essentially retired and replaced by newer introductory projects, The Wallet Project's underlying structure embodied several important principles that permeate teaching and learning at the d.school. It helped people learn by doing. It allowed them to practice lots of different parts of design work and to string them together to produce a creative solution. It started beginners off in an easy way and set the stage for work that became increasingly complex, open-ended, and ambiguous.

In a d.school class, we generally operate in two distinct modes: breaking down a complex process or practice into small pieces to get better at one element, or putting all the pieces back together to see how to integrate them. For instance, if you want to expand your culinary repertoire, you might take time to learn how to prepare Brussels sprouts in several different ways: steam them whole, roast them in halves, and cut them into ribbons to sauté in butter with a dusting of paprika. It is useful to go deep into sprout territory to get really good at this somewhat tricky vegetable, but you also need to know which foods Brussels sprouts taste nice with so you can serve them as part of a meal. You can't be a great cook if you *only* know how to deal with Brussels sprouts.

Most of the assignments in this book help you isolate and develop a specific muscle or ability. *Tether* (page 168) is about noticing through patience. *Blind Contour Bookend* (page 30) is about locating and dealing with your inner critic. *Solutions Tic-Tac-Toe* (page 171) is about building on and extending your original idea so you can build and test it in multiple ways and increase the odds of its success. *Tell Your Granddad* (page 181), *What Went Down* (page 215), and *A Day in the Life* (page 156) are three very different approaches to learning how to cook Brussels sprouts—that is, if sprouts prep were the same thing as storytelling.

But design is ultimately an integrative way of working. It borrows from different fields and melds them together. It invokes many modes of learning and doing, and it requires you to move back and forth between action and reflection. So in addition to working out individual muscles as in assignments #1 through #71, you need to also learn how to synchronize flexing your muscles together.

In fact, unlike courses of study that make you first focus on all the different small pieces or theory before allowing you to build up to the "real" thing, d.school learning experiences almost always start with a short, integrated project, and then study separate parts of the approach after you have some hands-on experience to reflect back on.

While exploring these final assignments, you will also see how we use constraints to formulate *projects* that increase the odds of getting to powerful, creative outcomes. Students at the d.school don't often get to see the tremendous work that goes into framing and scoping the projects we ask them to tackle. That happens behind the scenes and usually before a class starts. We seek out the right project partners with legitimacy in the community, research opportunities where design might be useful, and find open-ended problems where human needs or behaviors play a significant role (as opposed to purely technical or business problems). And we must constrain the challenge to be appropriate to the project's time frame and the students' skill levels.

Seeing how we do this can help you adapt our projects to your own context or start a project from scratch when you spot an interesting need or opportunity. You'll gain the fluency to frame and scope your own challenges and apply your creative skills more independently. To get good at this, you need to understand where to create tight constraints and where to leave room for discovery and novel ideas to emerge.

———

The best way to get a feel for how these projects work is to see a few and try a few. I've repurposed some projects that d.school students have tackled over the years to fit on these pages. The sequence ahead follows our principle of starting simple and slowly escalating the complexity. You can start with a lot of support to feel some early success in *The Haircut* (page 254) or its cousin *The Ramen Project* (page 255).

When you're ready to level up, tackle intermediate projects like *Family Evening Experience* (page 258) and *Thirty-Million-Word Gap* (page 259). These two assignments will help you understand scoping and framing. They reveal places where the balance bike was supporting you, but also its limitations. You'll begin to intuitively recognize the types of decisions that affect the work you're doing, and you'll gain confidence in making those choices.

To explore even more complex projects, look to the final set: *Organ Donation Experience* (page 262), *Stanford Service Corps* (page 264), and *Post-Disaster Finance* (page 266). These reflect the greater challenges—and satisfying rewards—of taking on design work that involves partnerships, systems, and multiple stakeholders, as well as your ethical responsibilities when working with people who are vulnerable or in crisis.

But before you go there, start with *The Haircut.* It lets you try out your skills and experience the range of feelings that come with doing design: moments of both struggle and satisfaction. The sensation of using these new skills will get you excited to continue.

Now, lift your feet off the ground and take your creative abilities for a spin.

72 The Haircut

Featuring the work of Ashish Goel, Taylor Cone, Adam Selzer, Katie Krummeck, and Eugene Korsunskiy

Beehives, bobs, bowls, comb-overs, locs, pompadours, pixies, weaves, mohawks . . . throughout history, new hairstyles have emerged. For some, haircutting is an act of personal expression—even rebellion. Haircuts can be more meaningful and more personal than you might think. For others, haircutting is a mundane act to keep the mop atop their heads under control. Think about the range of products and services that surround the hairstyling industry: barbershops to salons, dry shampoos to boar bristle brushes. The US haircare industry totals more than $85 billion annually— globally, the industry is much, much larger.

Your challenge is to conceive of a product or service to reimagine the haircut experience for another person. The worksheet that begins on page 280 will guide you step by step through a design process. Is this the only way to do design, or even to work on this topic? Definitely not. But it's a great place to start.

The Haircut brief doesn't tell you exactly what to do. That's deliberate: in design you have to make choices about where to focus. But the worksheet does provide a strong scaffold to support you. More on that soon.

If you want a similar experience with a different topic, The *Ramen Project* is an alternative to *The Haircut*. Use exactly the same method as the one given in the worksheet starting on page 280.

If you want to double up on using the scaffold, do both topics and get two full cycles under your belt. Using a similar approach with two different themes gives you more experience with the techniques and sequence and a chance to compare the two yourself. This helps build more rigor into your practice. If you do this, notice whether some of the tools or techniques work better in one project or the other. Ask yourself whether you felt more or less energized around one topic. Why was that? Cultivate this level of awareness in a project where you closely follow a recipe, and you'll begin to move from novice cook to proficient chef . . . able to improvise when something doesn't go as planned and ultimately take on a wider range of challenges.

73 The Ramen Project

Featuring the work of Alex Ko, Scott Doorley, George Kembel, and Alex Kazaks

Instant ramen: it's a meal for some people, for others a hot snack. Some people eat it every week, and some people only ate it in college. It's study food, emergency food, camping food, and bulk food with a longer shelf life than your shampoo. There are so many ways to prepare ramen. Some people eat it raw and crunchy, some follow the directions precisely, and for some, it's a blank canvas for whatever is in the fridge.

Your challenge is to design a better ramen experience. Use the same structure as the one given for *The Haircut*.

Ramen is a million different things to millions of people in the United States and around the world, so you should be able to design a million different ways to make it better.

At the end of every project in this section, don't forget to debrief the experience. Use *I Like, I Wish* (page 212) or *I Used to Think . . . & Now I Think* (page 272) to unpack your own personal experience and identify what learnings you took away from these final projects.

As you progress, reflect on the scoping and framing of a project. You must always balance time and resources while leaving room for creativity, and it's not obvious how to do that well. Shaping a design challenge while preserving the right amount of room to explore is a quintessential Goldilocks challenge. Even the most experienced d.school instructors say it's one of those things you know you got right only in retrospect. Fortunately, as you get better at scoping, you gain the ability to adapt any challenge or opportunity to your own context and skill level or to that of the people you're leading through a project.

Scoping is all about finding the right amount of work to bite off, while still leaving enough room for you to discover a really valuable opportunity for design. *The Haircut* and *The Ramen Project* are intentionally designed as starter projects. There's just the right amount of room to maneuver as a beginner. A more broadly scoped version of these projects might start you out on "grooming" and "convenience food," which are enormous spaces that don't point you in a terribly interesting direction. You'd have to find some way to tighten the scope yourself, through secondary research or preliminary interviews.

A project with a scope that's restricted would ask you to focus on just one aspect of these experiences, like "redesign the barber's chair" or "improve ramen packaging." Those are *very* targeted and don't leave room for much exploration. If you started with these constraints you might realize that the group you're interested in designing for doesn't use a barber chair, or there might be nothing functionally wrong with ramen packaging, but there you are, locked into that specific direction. There's only a little room for design to play a role, so you'd probably need to add a new angle to make the project more interesting or relevant, like making a chair that costs much less than existing alternatives or figuring out how to design ramen packaging in an ecologically sustainable way.

The way that *The Haircut* and *The Ramen Project* are designed gives you the experience of doing some framing yourself as you launch the project—not by constraining the solution space (say, "packaging"), but by choosing a specific type of person to design for. Choosing that group is excellent practice to hone your skills on a core aspect of human-centered design: being intentional about which humans you are designing for. The inspiration you gain from focusing on a specific group at the beginning leads you to powerful insights.

If you find yourself in a design challenge with limited scope for a solution, ask yourself whether you're sure there's a need for the thing you're designing. That's why you want to start with a human framing, rather than leading with a finite solution space. You want to give yourself a chance to uncover the right question, not just the right solution.

The Haircut and *The Ramen Project* work as starter projects for a few more reasons. For one thing, getting a haircut or eating instant ramen are nearly ubiquitous. You have no trouble finding people to design for and interview in just about any part of the world, and it's possible to speak directly to them and observe them in action. This is a big consideration in scoping a design challenge: are you able to connect directly with the people you are designing for or with? If not, it's hard to take their perspective, to build an empathetic understanding of their needs, to get feedback on your ideas throughout your work, or to substantively collaborate and codesign. How you will engage with other people in the work is the most crucial question to answer before you begin the project.

Despite the accessibility of these topics, there's a surprising degree of depth, too. It turns out people have deep feelings and preferences about both hairstyles and noodles! These topics can take you as deep as you're willing to go: you might end up having a truly unique ramen experience in someone's home or being invited to observe someone else's culture around hair maintenance that helps you see life through their eyes in a powerful way.

The variety of perspectives ensures you have an opportunity to challenge your own point of view and to be surprised by the extent of someone's unmet needs around your chosen topic. This is how you know you are valuable and relevant as a designer: you are creatively addressing a problem that really matters to someone. When you find those opportunities, they feel as if they have been just waiting for you to find them, like a calling.

Finally, both topics can be experienced at a small scale, which ensures you can rapidly prototype new experiences or products without worrying first about the technical feasibility of your concept or changing a big system.

But remember that balance bike? It guided your process for these starter projects by imposing significant constraints. After you do one or two of these projects, you'll begin to see how they limit you. Most obviously, they are organized in a linear way. They assume that you have all the insight you need from each step and that you always move forward. In any longer, more nuanced project, you often revisit different methods and modes, to deepen insight, confirm hunches, test ideas, or shift direction altogether. There's no precise road map for this; you decide how to improvise your process along the way. This variation is what makes design work so incredibly interesting—and challenging. Usually with these short beginner projects, after you select who you're interested in understanding and designing for (and figure out how and where to engage with them), you don't have to make a lot of choices about your process.

Once you work your way through *The Haircut, The Ramen Project,* or both, it's time to add pedals and test your balance a little further from the ground. The two assignments that follow them are great opportunities to try some solo rides. They will take time to execute, and they require you to interact and engage with real places and people. (Need a warm-up? Revisit *How to Talk to Strangers* on page 32.) They are enormously flexible and with very little adaptation can be used just about anywhere. Both of them center around the needs of children, but in very different ways.

Most notably: there is no singular, prescribed process for tackling these project assignments. You get to design your own approach. Take this as its own mini-assignment—at the d.school, we call this "designing your design work." Sketch out your plan of attack, share it with others, get some feedback, and don't be afraid to iterate throughout.

74 Family Evening Experience

Featuring the work of Erica Estrada-Liou

Evenings are a fantastic time for families to connect and spend quality time together. Family dinner, bedtime stories, bath time, and other rituals give kids a sense of love and security, which are paramount for healthy child development.

But for many parents, such an ideal evening is far from reality. Working parents come home exhausted or spend evenings apart due to shift schedules. Everybody wants something different for dinner. Kids are tired and cranky. Some parents don't see the importance of this time; others might not have personal experiences to draw from. Glowing screens are a lure for everyone. Whatever the reasons, this can be a very difficult part of the day.

Your challenge is to redesign the evening experience for families. What do parents and kids wish for? What behaviors are most productive for the kids? What tools, experiences, services, products, or other solutions might help families?

Because this is a meaningful and emotional time for many, it is a rich problem space. Start by understanding the family evening experience. See if you can observe this moment firsthand in other people's families. Pretend to be an outside observer in your own household; what do you notice? Seek out teachers or experts in child development.

Your solution can be a product, a service, an experience, or . . . you name it.

75 Thirty-Million-Word Gap

Featuring the work of Ashish Goel,
Alissa Murphy, and Erik Olesund

For decades, educators, researchers, and policymakers have puzzled over achievement gaps: the disparities in academic performance between children from low- and high-income families that show up on standardized tests, in grade-point averages, and via a host of other measures.

These disparities are clear even before children enter kindergarten. Disadvantaged children in the United States enter their first year of school significantly less prepared than their peers in terms of early skills, behavior, and health. Less than 50 percent of poor children are ready for school at age five versus 75 percent of kids from families with moderate and high incomes.

One key aspect of the readiness gap is that disadvantaged children hear fewer than a third of the words that children in higher-income families do, a detriment that has many implications in the long run. In fact, by age four, children in lower-income families have been exposed to thirty million fewer words during conversations and interactions with their caretakers than those from high-income families. Research shows that merely exposing children to more words is not enough; the quality of the communication and language is significant too.

Your challenge is to design a new way to address the thirty-million-word gap.

As you will discover when you dig into this topic, many groups and individuals are already working on addressing this issue. There are policy approaches, informational approaches, research-inspired approaches, and so on. You should take a human-centered approach. Look at this problem from the lens of the people experiencing it, and it might give you a new frame on the problem that's missing in the existing research.

This project is inspired by the work of Sesame Workshop, the educational not-for-profit organization behind *Sesame Street*. During this project, you might imagine that you're tackling this problem from different points of view: how would you advance your ideas if you were working directly with Sesame Workshop? Your local children's museum or zoo? What if you had a seat on the school board? The ability of an organization to implement any given solution is one important aspect to consider as you narrow in on the solutions you're shaping. Taking this into account can stretch your thinking toward types of solutions you wouldn't have considered otherwise.

Both the *Family Evening Experience* and the *Thirty-Million-Word Gap* are far more open-ended than *The Haircut* or *The Ramen Project*. Kids are involved in both, though neither project specifies that kids have to be the people you design for.

In the *Family Evening Experience*, all of your focus is on just one part of the day, and there are some preliminary assumptions about the kinds of challenges you might observe. However, it's up to you to figure out what type of families you want to work with, and within the loose frame of evening time, there's no limit to what you might uncover and the direction in which your design work might go.

The key to success in this project is for you to take a strong hand in scoping the "who" from the outset. Create some constraints, like "urban professional families" or "families with many children," that will make the project more interesting or fruitful for you. Then your intuition for what is an interesting problem to design around will really get a workout. Find patterns that spark your interest or feel like a genuine area of need. This will help you figure out what to ultimately design.

The *Thirty-Million-Word Gap* has an entirely different starting point. It's describing a known, complex problem that unfolds over time. You have to figure out how and where to observe it in action and then decide from a long series of experiences, contexts, and people where to place your efforts in order to design a meaningful solution. It's clear from the outset that you're primarily concerned with the experience of lower-income families and children, but the problem space is enormous.

Success in this case requires combining tactics: do some research and talk to a few experts so you understand how others frame and have tried to address the problem, then use *Experts/Assumptions* (page 146) to surface new ways of thinking about it. Look for places where you think a human-centered perspective will be most illuminating. You'll almost certainly have to reframe your project along the way: your ultimate mission is to reduce or eliminate the thirty-million-word gap, and your project framing will become more specific and pointed as you discover what people who experience this problem really need and what you can bring to the table.

Because this topic is framed around the needs of lower-income children, you'll also need to think through the various issues that might come up that relate to your own identity. If you're from a lower-income background yourself, you might have great insights and strong connections with others who have experienced this challenge themselves. The experience that people have of sharing their stories with you might be different from sharing them with someone from a higher-income background. You also might have some preconceived solution ideas that you need to consciously stow away so that you can approach the challenge with fresh eyes. If you are from an affluent background, this is a topic on which to ask yourself questions about what you might gain from doing it and how that compares to what people with less power or privilege might gain from the work you produce. For everyone working in this space, identify the ethical approaches that you want to adhere to, including how you will assess the impact that might happen (intended and unintended) from your work.

You can look at scoping the problem as analogous to turning two knobs that determine whether your focus will be narrow or broad. One knob is for selecting a type of person to design for, and the other is for naming the problem space. If both controls are turned up all the way (wide open), you'll be drowning in options and indecision. Where do you start? Which problem are you focused on? If they're closed down all the way, there's no room for discovery. By finding the workable setting on the controls you can manipulate the degree of ambiguity in any piece of work you take on.

When you leave the constraint loose, you will generally learn the most—about both how to strengthen your own design abilities and the nature of the problem or opportunity—because you must make decisions *during* your work (rather than beforehand while scoping) to home in on your ultimate focus. This requires that you spend time pursuing directions that you don't ultimately settle on. Along the way, you learn a lot about the breadth of design opportunities you *could* pursue and how to calibrate what makes one direction better than another. This takes considerable effort—and hones your judgment over time.

For example, if the team that ultimately founded Noora Health had been given a tighter, more prescriptive set of constraints on who they were designing for, they most likely would have ended up creating a solution with the clinician or the patient as the intended user. Conventional wisdom says that's how you improve health care outcomes. Maybe this would have been helpful. But because the *who* was not narrowly prescribed, the team had room to discover the previously overlooked but very important needs of the hospital patients' families. As you'll recall, this meant the team learned a lot about directions they didn't ultimately go in, and it also created a challenging phase for the members when they had to figure out which of these needs were the most compelling. It was a great learning experience, and a great outcome.

You might be focused more on one than the other (learning versus outcome). If you're focused primarily on learning and developing your skills and you're less attached to reaching a specific outcome within a certain time frame, then you can practice gaining empathy and insight for a broader range of people, place fewer constraints and structure at the outset regarding who you are designing for, and tighten up the solution space. Or you can leave more room to push yourself on the complexity, form, and medium in which your solution might take shape, in which case you should place fewer constraints on the nature of the problem.

Once you've worked through one or both of these projects, you will start to understand the ingredients for an excellent design project.

The four assignments coming up are more advanced. They will help you explore challenges that are complicated by their historical context or involve multiple systems or stakeholders and touch on some of the ethical issues that arise when you lean into more sensitive topics. Tackling them well may require you to partner with other people and/or local organizations in your community, which are great ways to develop relationships that lead to your work being implemented.

These assignments are each tailored for a particular context. I've preserved the specificity here so you can see how important it is to know something about the situation and issues these challenges present. They will spark ideas for you about how to modify them and make them relevant in your life and work. You can use any of them as inspiration and a starting point to create and scope design challenges more closely tied to the specific opportunities and problems that you will encounter, whatever those may be.

76 Organ Donation Experience

Featuring the work of Taylor Cone, Ashish Goel, and Adam Selzer

One of the most agonizing spots in medicine is the transplant list. When I've referred patients for organ transplant—heart, liver, kidney—it is the start of an anguished wait. The clock ticks for my patient as we watch her clinical status decline, all the while harboring that excruciating hope that someone will die soon enough to make an organ available. In the case of kidney donation, which can come from a live donor, it is the desperate hope that someone will decide to make this enormous personal sacrifice. Some of my patients have died waiting, which is, sadly, not an unusual outcome. It is estimated that eighteen patients on the waiting list in America die every day.

—*Danielle Ofri, MD*

In many countries, organ donation depends on opt-in altruism. The system anticipates that people will sign up as organ donors because they feel morally compelled to do so, but this mechanism consistently fails to produce sufficient numbers of organs to satisfy the demand for those in need.

According to the US federal government, while 90 percent of adults are in favor of organ donation, only 60 percent are signed up to donate.

A common way people express consent for organ donation in the United States is on their driver's license. Some experts fear that as ride-sharing and other alternative forms of transportation take hold and diminish the number of people with drivers' licenses, the percentage of registered donors may fall further.

Most people don't spend a lot of time thinking about this problem. But if you or someone close to you has had any personal experience with the transplant system, you know just how crucial it is. In fact, one donor can save the lives of eight other people.

Your challenge is to design a product, service, or experience that improves the organ donation experience in the area where you live, with the aim of increasing organ » donor registration rates. You might choose to narrow your scope to the actual sign-up experience, what happens after you have signed up, the actual donation act itself, the role played by family or friends, or something completely different.

For this challenge, start by learning more about the topic through secondary research. But in addition to finding out everything you can about the regulatory, infrastructural, and medical roadblocks that might be particularly relevant in your own city, don't forget to look at this as a human problem too.

Why do people donate organs? What ethical and religious considerations come into play? Do some exploring to help you pick an interesting and inspiring group to focus on. Could it be college students, YouTube stars, people from South Asia, athletes, or teenagers? Could you involve people in need of an organ transplant?

Unless you are planning to start a new company or organization, be on the lookout for an implementation partner. You will need to build relationships so by the time you have a solution that can be tested or piloted, you have a means to do so with others.

This topic is extremely challenging, which is part of its appeal. It is a great example of a mystery of human behavior, which means that design is exceptionally relevant in finding solutions. Any time you spot an inconsistency between what people say and what they do—in this case, being in favor of organ donation without fully embracing the role of organ donor—you know that design can help.

This issue is broad and complicated. You will have to tap experts and do some research (books, articles, podcasts, and so on) to understand the policy context and health systems in place in your area that feed into this problem. It's a meaningful opportunity to weave together many skills to succeed. This is a great project for trying out a systems-design tool like *Stakeholder Mapping* (page 149) or the *Hundred-Foot Journey Map* (page 138).

Next up is a site-specific project. Each year a number of d.school students work in teams on design challenges with different members of Stanford's campus community who provide varying types of services: groundskeepers, the police department, maintenance workers, cafeteria workers, fire inspectors, and many others. The work of these employees has usually been quite invisible to students, so the experience is both eye-opening for them and an opportunity to bring their design skills to bear to benefit a group that is usually playing the service role. Here is one example of that type of project—then read on for ideas about how to adapt it for your own context.

77 Stanford Service Corps

Featuring the work of Nell Turner Garcia and Joan Dorsey, with inspiration from Jim Patell and Erica Estrada-Liou

The transportation department at Stanford University has the massive task of managing the many different ways people come in and out of campus. From bicycles, cars, and the shuttle from the train station to hundreds of daily charter and tour buses, this department orchestrates all of it!

One aspect of this department's work includes getting students around campus when they have mobility challenges. These could be permanent, in the case of a life-long wheelchair user, or temporary, like a broken leg. This program existed for years before it was placed under the management of Stanford Transportation.

Your challenge is to work with staff in this department to gain insight into how the program is functioning and how it might be expanded to include anyone who might want help getting across campus (think Stanford's own internal ride share service). From coordinating online requests to ensuring that no student is left without a ride, there is a lot to consider.

A Stanford Service Corps project is one of many that have been crafted for d.school students as their first experience of working directly with a partner. In these partnerships, the department provides a wish list of challenges to the students to get them started. These often center around a change that has happened (like relocating a program into a new department) or one that is desired. Change in organizations is a great catalyst for design, because there is less investment in how things have always been done. Nonetheless, working with partners changes the designer's role in challenging and productive ways. For example, stakeholders in the department have different views about how things should happen. Power and hierarchy come into play. There may be feasibility constraints to the solutions.

How could you adapt the Service Corps approach to your own context to identify some meaningful areas for design work? Think about what groups provide service in your community but are rarely designed for. Can you use this as a way to extend your skills while being of genuine help to others? What kinds of partnership and support will be necessary to make it a successful experience for everyone?

78 Post-Disaster Finance

Featuring the work of Seamus Yu Harte, Bruce Cahan, Eli Woolery, and Emily Callaghan

In 2018, 2019, and 2020, wildfires in Northern and Southern California destroyed and uprooted many towns, neighborhoods, businesses, and lives. Unfortunately, natural disaster scenarios are becoming more frequent and severe all over the world due to climate change.

Once disaster responders have made their contribution, affected communities, banks, insurance companies, and government agencies are challenged to fund the rebuilding. The survivors, who are trying to rebuild more resilient communities, struggle with confusing, disorganized, or even conflicting timelines and a lack of transparency concerning insurance claims, building plans and permits, and bank loans. There seem to be no incentives for the different parties to coordinate; add to this the difficulties presented by pre-disaster inequality in household wealth, financial literacy, and other situational challenges. In some places whole neighborhoods may never be rebuilt.

Bankers are among the most systemically important decision makers to fund this rebuilding. Can you find a way to bring design and empathy to a bank's post-disaster loan approval process?

Your challenge is to reimagine post-disaster finance.

For this challenge, you will need to interview bankers, bank regulators, and borrowers to visually map the post-disaster loan approval process from multiple perspectives, with the goal of revealing better design opportunities. Given the complexity of this space, maps of many kinds (journey maps, stakeholder maps) will be key to approaching this topic and making sense of it. Once you've identified an opportunity you wish to pursue, design a way to bring new solutions and ideas to life in this challenging, overlooked design space. Or use this as an exercise to speculate about a radically different future scenario for this system, and bring that future to life through storytelling, visualization, or other media.

If you take on or adapt this project, you'll find that it is challenging in part because the people you are designing for and with are experiencing some degree of shock or trauma. Your responsibility as a human is to show up empathetically and to never put the needs of your project ahead of a participant's safety (physical or emotional). You may want to collaborate with someone who has experience as a counselor or therapist—at minimum, to give you advance feedback on your interviewing approach.

You'll have to prepare differently for this type of work. To develop greater empathy for the people who have experienced the fires, think about an analogous experience you might go through as in *Immersion for Insight* (page 38). Try out *Empathy in Motion* (page 66) to change the power relationship between you and those you are designing for. Or, if you come to the project with deeply held assumptions about either the people affected by the disaster or those who work for the banks, the assignment *Identify, Acknowledge, Challenge* (page 78) will help you surface your own stereotypes or biases so you can minimize the chance that they begin to leak into your creative work.

Make sure to be transparent about the nature of your work. Do you expect your solutions to directly benefit the people you're engaging along the way, or will they be aimed at helping others in the same situation in the future? Are you working directly with a financial services partner to implement the solutions, or will you be searching for a way to use the concepts during the project?

If you live in a place with challenges related to a different type of natural or human-caused disaster, think about how you might adapt the framework of this assignment to suit those needs.

———————

Once you've worked through some or all of the projects in this section, you will understand much more about how initial project framing and scoping shape your design work.

To make all this insight stick, try to *Scope Your Own Challenge* on page 270. It's nearly the last assignment in this book, but it might be the very first thing you do on your way to owning your own design work. You'll feel the wind in your hair as you ride off toward your many future creative adventures.

79 Taking Responsibility

Featuring the work of Liz Ogbu

Liz Ogbu uses her two-client lens to set her ethical compass and balance her focus. As an architect and designer, she takes responsibility for discovering where these distinct sets of needs overlap and intersect. But that doesn't mean all parties have an equal starting point. Often the people who have to live with the result of design work aren't in the room. Beyond just a commitment to ensuring that outcomes don't harm one while benefiting the other, Liz prioritizes delivering benefit to those who have experienced harm in the past.

Liz's approach reflects the reality that differences in power—who has more and who has less—is part of the context for design. When you use your creative abilities, you bring a special kind of power to the table: the ability to shape people's experiences and perhaps even affect their lives. You might not have the most power in a given situation, but you probably don't have the least. How do *you* navigate this terrain?

Think about your last creative project and reflect on these questions:

Who did you feel responsible to, and what did you feel responsible for?

Did any tensions arise? What kind?

How did you navigate those competing needs?

What did you learn from this? Would you do anything different in the future?

I always have two clients in any project.

I'm responsible to the people who pay me to design and the people who have to live with my designs.

—*Liz Ogbu*

80

Scope Your Own Challenge

Featuring the work of Thomas Both

This is an invitation to dream. What do you really want to work on?

The penultimate assignment in this book is for you to scope and frame your own project. Do this whenever you have a challenge you want to tackle and you want to make sure you're leaving room to be creative.

This assignment will help you frame an open-ended design project: a challenge that doesn't dictate the solution or the form of the solution. Be thoughtful about not constraining yourself too much. Most people stick a solution right into the challenge statement the first time they try this. You might have a tiny budget, a short time frame, or a difficult-to-please partner you're designing for, but err on the side of inviting varied possibilities.

This is the art of scoping. You need to create an actionable direction but also leave room for exploration. The goal is not to eliminate ambiguity but to invite a desired amount into your creative process. Ambiguity is necessary to allow for new discovery.

Inevitably, scoping will happen. It will happen either prior to your project or during the project. It may be more

efficient to narrow the scope prior (save time by preventing wide investigation), but it may be more effective to narrow the scope during the project (allow a human-centered process to lead you to the most meaningful and fruitful opportunity).

Just as you shouldn't jump to a solution, avoid presuming people's needs before you talk to them. Allow room to discover the specific issues to take on. How will you know that true discovery has happened? You'll end up with an insight that you could not have thought of before you engaged with the challenge.

THE CHALLENGE

REDESIGN THE

EXPERIENCE

Finally, don't forget to scope for excitement. Take on a challenge with enough depth that talking to people and observing contexts are likely to surface compelling new information. Do work you find meaningful and engaging.

———————

Use this simple framework to help scope your challenge. Adjust each blank to alter the framing.

Redesign the _____ experience
for _____
while considering _____.

This framework helps you be explicit about designing for people and their experience, rather than focus on the "thing" you are creating. Use it verbatim to the extent that it serves you; if you find that the format is too rigid and is holding you back, tweak the wording or sequence of the blanks.

Notice that what you put in each blank can drastically change the challenge scope (both the topic and how broad or narrow). So lay out the playing field in a specific way, but leave yourself room for discovery.

Use these questions as a checklist to evaluate your draft challenge:

Is your project a human, subjective challenge in which understanding people is key to the project success?

Is your project geared toward discovery (not perfecting something that already exists)?

Does your framing already embed a solution? (If so, get it out of there!)

Does your framing presume you know what people's needs are already? (If so, what's left to discover?)

Do you actually care about this challenge? (If not, why are you doing it?)

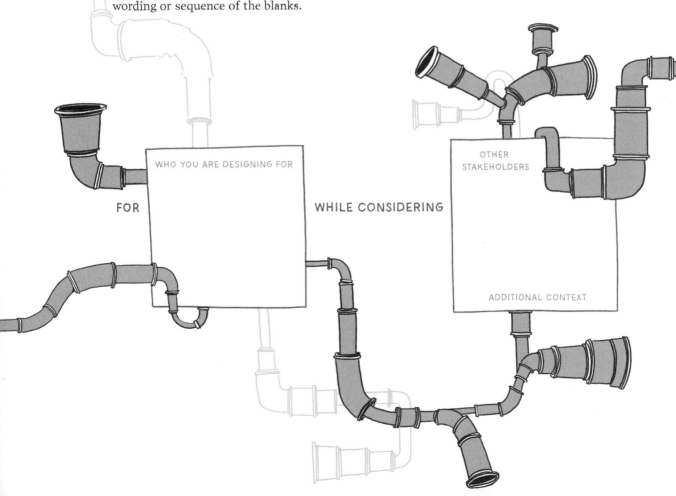

WHO YOU ARE DESIGNING FOR

OTHER STAKEHOLDERS

FOR

WHILE CONSIDERING

ADDITIONAL CONTEXT

81

I Used to Think . . . & Now I Think

Featuring the work of Megan Stariha and Mark Grundberg, with inspiration from Richard F. Elmore

Taking a few minutes to observe and document changes in your own thinking over time helps you make sense of what you're learning and how you're growing.

This assignment was inspired by a book of the same name in which experts on education reform described how their minds had changed toward the topic (or occasionally, how their convictions deepened) through their long experience in the field.

It's rare these days to hear experts—or anyone—say that they have changed their minds. Change happens gradually, particularly about ideas, behaviors, or conceptions of self. It can be hard to notice change while it's happening. But if you're excited to adopt the creative behaviors and mindsets expressed through the assignments in this book—or if you're in the midst of any other kind of learning experience or transition in your life—using this assignment

to note incremental changes will help you consolidate and reinforce those new abilities and ultimately firm up the direction in which you wish to move.

————

First, do any other assignment in this book.

Then take a piece of paper and divide it into two columns.

At the top of one column, write "I Used to Think . . ." and on the other "And Now I Think . . ."

On the "Used to . . ." side, list your previous ideas or preconceptions about the assignment activity or topic, and on the "And Now I . . ." side write your thoughts on the same subject after completing it.

Although every assignment in this book is designed for a specific purpose, there's no guarantee that what you take away is what was intended. You may have multiple interpretations based on your own life and prior experiences. One goal of *this* assignment is to free you from my assumptions about the value of any particular learning experience and to prompt you to articulate the impact in your own words.

You can also adapt this framework to any other learning experience, on your own or with a group. Use it with colleagues after you've all attended a conference together or completed a team retreat. Use it with friends or family to process a political shift or an emotional event. Ultimately, you may find this phrase creeping into your everyday vocabulary as a shorthand to describe how you are developing and changing as a person and as a creative thinker and doer.

Creative Acts:
Behind the Scenes

My father is an extremely handy person: a professional photographer; an extraordinary baker, sewer, carpenter, gardener; and a more than proficient plumber and electrician. I grew up seeing him endlessly tinker and create. He taught himself these skills by reading, trial and error, talking to experts, and mostly by making things. He wrote a dissertation documenting the positive effect on children of having a parent who builds things, and I can proudly say that I'm living (and lucky) proof. Now retired, he volunteers at the largest tool library in Portland, Oregon, repairing broken tools and returning them to circulation so that others can borrow and use them. On many topics, learning from my dad has been the most important apprenticeship of my life, as well as the longest.

As I saw by watching him at his workbench in our Philadelphia basement, in carpentry (and all kinds of creative work) you need tools beyond just the ones you can get at a hardware store. This includes what's called a jig, which holds what you're working on in place and helps you guide a more well-known tool like a saw or a drill to modify the wood in just the right way. In many cases it's not something you can buy; you have to make the jig yourself to support the exact outcomes you're aiming for, by defining the contours of a unique shape, or stopping yourself from going too far with a cut. For doing complex work well, jigs are important, even essential.

Each assignment in this book is the equivalent of a different "learning jig"—a special tool that someone created to help you learn and make things, ideas, stories, connections, maps, and skills of your own. They hold your focus on a particular area and guide you to make use of your natural abilities in new ways.

From the start, I knew that this was going to be a book not just of design methods, but of deliberately designed learning experiences. These experiences were crafted— often in precise increments of time and detail—by the hundreds of designers, educators, academics, and topical or industry experts who have dedicated their time and expertise while offering classes at the d.school over the past fifteen years. It's an extraordinary group, and the making of each of these assignments is itself a highly creative act! They spring up in response to a need to teach a skill or approach in a more personal, collaborative, or experiential way, and they evolve through student feedback, iteration, and interpretation by the many other instructors who adopt and adapt them.

Everyone deserves to have great teachers in their life. By tackling the assignments in this book, you get to try out apprenticing yourself to one or more of the contributors whose work is featured here: a small version of what it's like to learn from them directly. There are many different perspectives and ideas that intersect and overlap at the d.school. You may resonate immediately with some, and I hope others provoke you to think, act, and make in ways you haven't yet considered or mastered. No single approach is universal. These assignments—much like the different disciplinary voices at the d.school—are in a lively conversation with each other.

Contributors

The labor and love of many people shaped the contents of this book. This list of contributors includes everyone whose work is featured in at least one of the assignments. In some cases they originated the entire concept; in others they are responsible for finding, adapting, and sharing the concepts within the d.school context. This list also includes all those who contributed insights and ideas through an interview, and each person who took the time to critique and improve the assignments and essays. Each and every person here helped shape this resource in some way.

Adam Royalty

Adam Selzer

Akshay Kothari

Aleta Hayes

Alex Kazaks

Alex Ko

Alex Lofton

Alissa Murphy

Andrea Small

Anja Svetina Nabergoj

Ariam Mogos

Ariel Raz

Ashish Goel

Barry Svigals

Ben Knelman

Bernie Roth

Bill Burnett

Bill Guttentag

Bob Sutton

Bruce Cahan

Carissa Carter

Caroline O'Connor

Charlotte Burgess-Auburn

Chris Rudd

Claire Jencks

Dan Klein

Dave Baggeroer

Dave Evans

David Clifford

David Janka

David M. Kelley

Dennis Boyle

Devon Young

Durell Coleman

Edith Elliot

Eli Woolery

Emilie Wagner

Emily Callaghan

Enrique Allen

Erica Estrada-Liou

Erik Olesund

Eugene Korsunskiy

Frederik G. Pferdt

George Kembel

Gina Jiang

Glenn Fajardo

Grace Hawthorne

Hannah Jones

Henry Lee

Jen Walcott Goldstein

Jeremy Utley

Jessica Brown

Jessica Munro

Jessie Liu

Jill Vialet

Jim Patell

Joan Dorsey

John Cassidy

Jules Sherman

Julian Gorodsky

Justin Ferrell

Kareem Collie

Karen Ingram

Karin Forssell

Kathryn Segovia

Katie Krummeck

Katy Ashe

Kelly Schmutte

Kerry O'Connor

Kyle Williams

Larry Choiceman

Laura McBain

Lena Selzer

Leticia Britos Cavagnaro

Lia Siebert

Libby Johnson

Lisa Kay Solomon

Lisa Rowland

Liz Ogbu

Louie Montoya

Manish Patel

Mark Grundberg

Matt Rothe

Maureen Carroll

McKinley McQuaide

Meenu Singh

Megan Stariha

Melissa Pelochino

Michael Barry

Michael Brennan

Michelle Jia

Molly Wilson

Nell Turner Garcia

Nicole Kahn

Nihir Shah

Patricia Ryan Madson

Perry Klebahn

Peter Worth

Rachelle Doorley

Rich Crandall

Richard Cox Braden

sam seidel

Scott Cannon

Scott Doorley

Scott Witthoft

Seamus Yu Harte

Shahed Alam

Shelley Goldman

Stephanie Szabó

Stuart Coulson

Susie Wise

Tania Anaissie

Taylor Cone

Terry Winograd

Thomas Both

Tina Seelig

Tom Maiorana

Yusuke Miyashita

Zaza Kabayadondo

Collecting and Assembling the Raw Material

To build a collection that spans fifteen years and involves so many different voices required someone capable of shouldering a tremendous research project: interviewing, distilling, and documenting every nuance of each activity. I found that partner in Amalia Rothschild-Keita, who interviewed a wide range of d.school faculty, students, and alumni and logged every insight with meticulous care. A design researcher, Amalia found many important patterns that helped build the foundation of this book. Without the direct, detailed, and formidable way she approached her role, I'm not sure how this book could have come to be.

From there began the difficult process of deciding which of the hundreds of possible assignments to include. I aimed for topics and experiences that would help readers acquire or refine a wide range of skills and explore rich emotional territory.

In addition to offering the original content, the main contributors of each assignment spent time reviewing and providing feedback on my translation from the brilliant way they teach something live to the new format that resides in the pages of this book. The ideas are stronger, the assignments more elegant, and the learning you can take from it more potent because of their generosity. Many people reviewed the essays and gave me useful, encouraging, and humbling feedback, which helped greatly: Bernie Roth, Carissa Carter, Gordon Cruikshank, Jennifer Brown, Laura McBain, Leticia Britos Cavagnaro, sam seidel, Thomas Both, and Tom Maiorana. Bob Sutton and Debbe Stern provided crucial support at just the right moment to help me arrive at the book's title.

Carissa Carter originated the term "citizen creator" and is a beacon at the d.school for an active and rigorous discussion of design's intended and unintended consequences. Several long conversations with Chris Adkins from the University of Notre Dame deepened my understanding of the science of empathy and influenced key concepts around the amoral nature of empathy shared in *Widening Your Lens*. Leticia Britos Cavagnaro and sam seidel's teaching collaboration toward "learning how to learn" built the foundations of *The Feeling of Learning*. Thomas Both's heroic efforts to make the mysterious art of framing and scoping more accessible form the spine that organizes *Putting It All Together*.

Presenting and explaining the assignments without relying on the energy present in an in-person classroom setting was a creative challenge in itself. Mike Hirshon's captivating illustrations bring the assignments to life even more vividly than I dreamed: they show the emotional qualities of these experiences with texture, humor, and humanity. They are full of visual jokes and detail, and you will notice new things about them even after many viewings. Working with Mike was instantly fun and expansive: he is a consummate prototyper. He would offer three, four, or sometimes six different ways to visualize something, and together we'd choose which ones to polish and refine. Seeing the ideas in the assignments refracted through his visual genius make them even more irresistible.

Acknowledgments

This collection reflects the work of the d.school community, and that community has a home because of the efforts of the people who conceived of and led the d.school in its early years, especially the vision and entrepreneurial approach of David M. Kelley and George Kembel. Jim Plummer's kindness and vision as the Dean of the School of Engineering at Stanford made space for this unusual experiment to begin. Along with all the founding faculty, I owe a great personal debt to Jim Patell, whose approach to teaching is one of deep devotion to his students, mixed with a modicum of irascibility and considerable amounts of duct tape. Bernie Roth, who shepherds the d.school's culture and academics, is our exemplar for living a life with infinite curiosity, love, and the boundless possibility of "and."

A special thank you to some of the d.school's faculty contributors and advisors at Stanford: Drew Endy, James Landay, Jay Hamilton, Jen Dionne, Jennifer Widom, Jeremy Weinstein, John Dabiri, Kate Maher, Fiorenza Micheli, John Mitchell, Michele Elam, Nicole Ardoin, Persis Drell, Rob Reich, Tina Selig, Sarah Soule, Sheri Sheppard, and Tom Kenny.

My editor, Julie Bennett, was a constant champion for the needs and interests of the readers. She helped me untangle my most esoteric and convoluted ideas and find a way to wrangle a decade and a half of elaborately crafted in-person learning experiences into a completely new format. Along with the rest of the incredible team at Ten Speed Press—particularly Annie Marino and Kelly Booth—I owe her a huge debt of gratitude.

Thank you to the d.school's literary agents, Christy Fletcher and Eric Lupfer, for being among the very first people to share the vision of our big publishing dream, for their impeccable guidance that helped launch this work, for helping us decide not to make that trip to New York, and for shepherding us through many key decisions and turning points.

Scott Doorley is the standard-bearer for what "finished" work looks like at the d.school. He is that rare human whose mind spans the farthest reaches of a spectrum between the tiniest, most concrete detail and the biggest, most abstract concept. He can spend hours laboring over an invisible, particle-sized component that, once it's right, makes everything else fall into place, and the next moment inspire a group with a perspective-altering metaphor. His leadership as the d.school's Creative Director is one of a kind. Our physical space, our curriculum, our visual idiom, and our values and capabilities as an educational organization would not be what they are without Scott, much of which shines through in the collection of assignments and ideas in this book. Of course, no one is perfect all the time. My very first collaboration with Scott was in 2006 on a student design project on coffee for which we were randomly assigned to the same group. We struggled to find a coherent focus, and it was a complete failure. Scott, I like to think we've improved as a team since then.

Charlotte Burgess-Auburn deserves enormous credit for the book you're holding right now. It's hard to find the right words to express how essential Charlotte has been to this effort and to so many endeavors at the d.school throughout our history. Charlotte has the special gift of being the "how should we get this started?" person on any team. To any challenge she brings her wealth of knowledge about nearly everything (costume design, where to buy rolls of fire-retardant paper, the proper technique for screen printing t-shirts, how the fog in San Francisco works, which software will soothe our temperamental vinyl cutter, how we can hang 100 kites inside from the ceiling beams . . .) and a thousand other things that you didn't realize you'd eventually need someone on hand for. Her curiosity is endless, and her brain is magically acquisitive. And everything she does comes with a huge round of laughter, humor, and friendship. Charlotte, making this book was like singing a two-year duet about our creative partnership, and I'm so grateful.

Many people have deeply affected how I think about learning; some were also among the most generous and creative teachers in my life, especially Carol Corson, John Harkins, Will Terry, Meg Goldner Rabinowitz, Bill Koons, Dick Wade, and Paul Dawson.

Two other educators in my life set my standards for dedication, ingenuity, fairness, and believing in each student as an individual learner, capable of great things if their needs are met: my brother and my mom. A middle-school math teacher for much of her career, my mom used a pioneering method that required her students to write reflective journal entries after each class. Yes, she had them writing about learning math. She had a reputation for being a tough teacher, but what her students didn't see was how she poured herself into understanding each and every one of them. She painstakingly reviewed their entries, spending hours every month with student journals spread out all over the dining room table to glean insights about where each kid was thriving or struggling. She was uniquely attuned to their needs and could always show up with just the framing they needed to master a new concept. Clearly this landed for my brother, who has continued our family's tradition of involvement in Quaker educational environments and is now an innovative teacher building new models of interdisciplinary, student-driven, inquiry-based learning. I'm so proud and lucky to be one part of this family of learning-oriented educators.

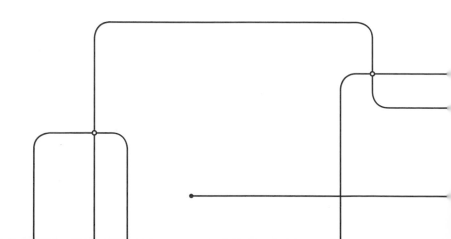

The Haircut: A Design Challenge

Featuring the work of Ashish Goel, Taylor Cone, Adam Selzer, Katie Krummeck, and Eugene Korsunskiy

Beehives, bobs, bowls, comb-overs, locs, pompadours, pixies, weaves, mohawks . . . throughout history, new hairstyles have emerged. For some, haircutting is an act of personal expression—even rebellion. Haircuts can be more meaningful and more personal than you might think. For others, haircutting is a mundane act to keep the mop atop their heads under control. Think about the range of products and services that surround the hairstyling industry: barbershops to salons, dry shampoos to boar bristle brushes. The US haircare industry totals more than $85 billion annually—globally, the industry is much, much larger.

Your challenge is to conceive of a product or service to reimagine the haircut experience for another person. This worksheet will guide you through a design process. Is this the only way to do design, or even to work on this topic? Definitely not. But it's a great place to start.

Use the following steps to guide you, and document and share your work. Write directly on these pages, if you wish, or copy these instructions into a notebook. Adopt the mantra: "If you didn't document it, it didn't happen." Pay close attention to how you work, not just what you produce. Capture your design process as well as your findings. Imagine that you have to share your work with someone else who needs to learn from you once you're done; they'll benefit from seeing how your ideas unfolded and developed.

We give students one week to complete this project and expect that they will spend between ten and fifteen hours on it. You could use less (or more) time, but regardless, set yourself a time limit and stick to that constraint. This assignment isn't about doing every step perfectly, it's about becoming familiar with how these different approaches work together.

At the end of the project, evaluate your work. Grade yourself based on the richness of your documentation, the extent of your design process (who you talked to, the depth of the needs uncovered, the range of ideas you considered), and the degree of innovation in the solution you chose.

1 Plan and Start Your Research

Identify

Your first job is to identify a distinct group of people to design for. The more well defined the group, the more targeted and potentially innovative your solutions will be. Some examples: busy dads, people who live in nursing homes, competitive athletes, aspiring actors, or recent immigrants. You might even consider those who may have an extreme perspective on haircuts, such as people whose livelihood depends on hair or people who haven't had a haircut in years. The most important thing is to remember that you aren't trying to talk to "everyone" about what they experience "in general." Specificity is your friend. If you make something that truly satisfies a need of what you think is just a small group, you often find that a broader segment also responds positively to your solution.

Observe

Spend at least ninety minutes at a hair salon or barber shop (be sure to ask the staff if it's okay for you to sit and observe). Pay attention to people's interactions with each other, with different objects, and with their environment. What patterns do you notice? What surprises you? Draw, snap photos, and write notes about what you see.

Interview

Find at least two people in your target group to interview in depth about their haircut experience. Spend at least one hour talking to each one. For an interview of this duration, you'll probably have to arrange it ahead of time. Explore their feelings and attitudes about getting a haircut. What do they expect of the experience? What do they love and hate about it? Why?

Your goal is to mostly listen and learn as much as possible. Practice moving the conversation along with questions that add color, advance to new topics of interest, and help your interviewees reflect out loud about their own experiences and perspectives.

Document Everything

Choose a notebook that you like to carry with you. Everyone has their own preferences: ruled or unruled, hard cover or soft, big or small. Throughout this project take extensive notes on your thinking, decisions, people you meet, interviews you have, and things you observe.

Refer

Draw on assignments from throughout this book while you tackle this challenge. While researching you'll find *Interview Essentials* (page 56), *Reflections & Revelations* (page 94), and *Tether* (page 168) particularly helpful. While generating ideas, try *ABC Sketching* (page 92) and *Bisociation* (page 102). Use *Protobot* (page 144), *The Solution Already Exists* (page 114), and *Solutions Tic-Tac-Toe* (page 171) when building and refining your ideas. Refresh your approach to testing your concepts with *The Test of Silence* (page 193) and *High Fidelity, Low Resolution* (page 202). Question your biases at any time with *Identify, Acknowledge, Challenge* (page 78).

Want to include alternative approaches to this challenge? Try *Practicing Metaphors* (page 81) to consider what haircuts mean to people through different lenses, *Experts/Assumptions* (page 146) to challenge convention, or *Map the Design Space* (page 106) to envision the haircut ecosystem.

2 Begin to Make Sense of What You've Learned

After your interviews and observation time, review your raw notes, and write down any new reactions or reflections you have while doing so. Capture some highlights using sketches and words below: what was most surprising, compelling, confusing, or emotional? Print out any photos you've taken. Paste them in and annotate. Use this space to capture key tidbits you think might be relevant, even if you're not sure yet. Feel free to clip or staple in additional pages from your notebook.

3 Develop New Insights

Based on what you transferred from your notebook, circle the most interesting photos, quotes, and observations. What really intrigues you? What's most unexpected or exciting?

Use these nuggets to identify at least five insights from your research. Insights come from your inferences and conclusions about the information collected during your empathy work. The best insights are surprising. They should be statements that relate to the people you interviewed, needs you have uncovered, or new ways you are viewing the haircut experience. In other words, what stands out from your research?

Write Five Insights Here:

1.

2.

3.

4.

5.

Gut Check

Could you have made any of these statements before starting the project? If so, dig deeper into your notes and pull out less obvious insights.

4 Define Your Point of View

It's time to formulate a specific direction for your project. Look over the insights you wrote and the notes you circled. Ask yourself why these are important. Use them to generate more clarity. You are about to narrow your focus. While narrowing, you may feel sad to leave behind someone you met or some of your intriguing insights. But focus is a key part of this process; it's equally important to be clear about who you're *not* serving or the needs you're *not* addressing as it is to specify those that you are.

Who Are You Designing For?

You first thought about this when you identified who to talk to. Now, based on what you've learned, you'll narrow and refine your audience. Describe who you are designing for in very, very, very specific terms. Do not worry about whether this is a unique person or a big demographic category. The more specific you are, the more clarity you have, which often translates into more creative and unusual solutions. Specifics might include age, gender, experience level, emotional outlook, ethnicity or race, attitude toward haircuts, certain life experiences, unique hobbies, and situation ("lives far from family" or "preparing for an important job interview").

What Do They Need?

List at least twenty of this person's needs in the form of a verb. (A girl doesn't need a ladder, she needs to reach.)

1.

2.

3.

4.

5.

6.

7.

8.

9.

10.

11.

12.

13.

14.

15.

16.

17.

18.

19.

20.

Try This Format

Use this template to draft at least three point-of-view statements:

A HARRIED FATHER OF THREE RUSHING THROUGH
A BUSY DAY OF ERRANDS
_____ needs to
person or group

ENTERTAIN HIS PLAYFUL KIDS   AT THIS STAGE OF HIS LIFE, EVEN A
WHILE GETTING HIS HAIR CUT   MOMENT FOR PERSONAL CARE ISN'T
                                               A SOLO OUTING
_____ because _____ .
          need   insight

_____ needs to
                 person or group

_____ because _____ .
       need   insight

_____ needs to
                 person or group

_____ because _____ .
       need   insight

_____ needs to
                 person or group

_____ because _____ .
       need   insight

Evaluate

Take a step back and think about where you started this project. Defining a point of view is often the moment when you reframe a challenge as it was given. A lot of opportunity for creativity and innovation comes from framing a problem in a unique or non-obvious way.

A good point-of-view statement compels you to care about the person you're describing and feel motivated to help solve their problem. It doesn't include a solution, but it does establish some helpful constraints so you can move forward. How do yours measure up? Circle the one you plan to use.

If your current problem statement is leading you in different direction than when you started, that's great. It's likely that you have taken advantage of something that you learned that you couldn't have known when you began.

5 Generate Ideas

Your goal now is to generate a large and diverse set of solution ideas in response to your point of view. Explore different types of ideas: physical, digital, services, experiences, and so on.

Make Specific Jumping-Off Points

Start by breaking up your favorite point-of-view statement into actionable questions. For instance, the sample haircut point of view from the previous step could become many smaller, more specific questions:

HOW MIGHT WE MAKE WAITING AT THE BARBERSHOP THE MOST EXCITING, KID-FRIENDLY EXPERIENCE?

HOW MIGHT THE EXPERIENCE INVOLVE KIDS?

HOW MIGHT THIS EXPERIENCE SPECIFICALLY SERVE MEN WITH KIDS, RATHER THAN OTHER PARENTS?

Next, Come Up with Concepts

Create dozens of solutions for a few different *How Might We?* questions. Come up with at least fifty ideas. Be visual. Don't stop at writing a list; make rough sketches of some of your ideas in your notebook and annotate them.

First, Come Up with at Least Ten *How Might We?* Questions:

1.

2.

3.

4.

5.

6.

7.

8.

9.

10.

Finally, Select and Refine

At this stage don't constrain yourself based on what's realistic or what you think you know how to make—it's too early for that type of filter. Choose interesting ideas you'd like to explore, not conventional ideas you think are likely to work.

Choose five very different ideas to retain diversity and flesh them out by thinking through a few of the details. In your notebook, make a five-minute sketch for each one and number them. Show these sketches to a friend to get quick feedback and help you select a few to prototype. Capture their reactions and your new directions on this page to document this milestone.

6 Prototype

Put your ideas into a tangible form so other people can interact with, experience, and test them out. Given the topic, your ideas could be products, services, experiences, or even technologies. Continue to suspend your disbelief about feasibility or viability. In this project, you're working on how to develop a concept that delights someone or meets a need.

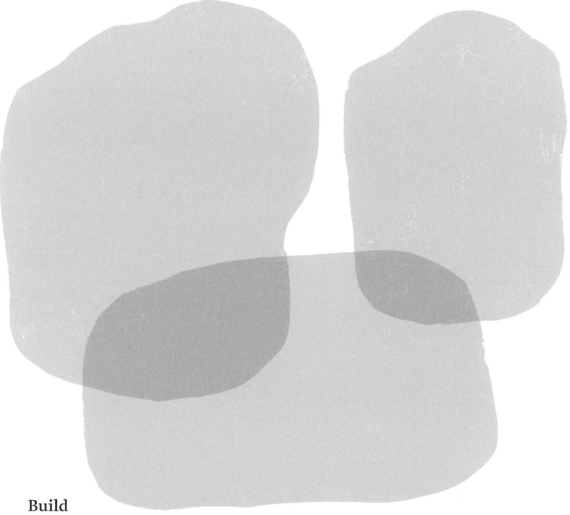

Build

Based on your favorite ideas so far and the feedback from your friend, make at least five five-minute prototypes out of paper, tape, discarded packaging, recyclables, craft supplies, and anything else you can find. Then make at least one of these into a more highly resolved twenty-minute prototype.

Photograph each prototype and tape, staple, or otherwise affix the pics here. Annotate.

Test

Go back to the people with whom you spoke (or others like them). Let them experience your prototypes and get feedback. Test your prototypes with at least three people.

Put your prototypes in their hands (or put them into the prototype). Find or create the context and scenario that will produce the most genuine feedback. When you test, remember that you're not selling your idea. Spend most of your time watching and listening, rather than pitching or explaining.

Take pictures of people interacting with your prototypes, and jot down their feedback next to the photos you paste here. Briefly write down what worked and what didn't and at least one new idea you now have for refining this concept going forward. As always, if you need more room, use your notebook.

7 Finish Your Concept

It's time to combine all that you've learned and refine your solution based on what you discovered from testing your prototypes.

Iterate

Create a final prototype. Take a picture of it and paste it here.

Describe your solution and write down its benefits in a sentence or two. How does it address the needs that inspired it?

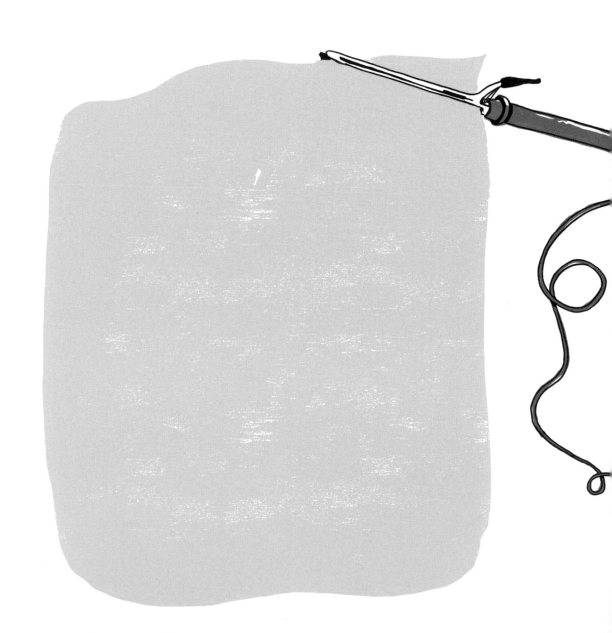

 Reflect

You're nearly done! But before you finish, take stock of what you learned. This is perhaps the most important step, so allow yourself at least thirty minutes to think and write here.

What was your favorite part of this assignment? Why?

When did you stumble or get stuck? Why do you think that was?

What would you do differently next time?

Index

The following photographs are used with permission: page 47 courtesy of AP Photo/Rodrigo Abd, page 82 (top and center) courtesy of Adobe Stock, page 82 (bottom) courtesy of Adobe Stock/Markus Mainka, and page 99 courtesy of Charlotte Burgess-Auburn.

Library of Congress Control Number: 2021936405

Trade Paperback ISBN: 978-1-9848-5816-0
eBook ISBN: 978-1-9848-5817-7

Printed in China

Acquiring editor: Hannah Rahill | Project editor: Julie Bennett
Designer: Annie Marino | Art director: Kelly Booth
Production designers: Mari Gill and Faith Hague
Production and prepress color manager: Jane Chinn
Copyeditor: Kristi Hein | Proofreader: Lisa D. Brousseau | Indexer: Ken DellaPenta
Publicists: Jana Branson and David Hawk | Marketers: Windy Dorresteyn and Daniel Wikey
d.school creative team: Charlotte Burgess-Auburn, Scott Doorley, and Nariman (Nadia) Gathers
Research: Amalia Rothschild-Keita

10 9 8 7 6 5 4 3 2

First Edition